UNDERSTANDING WAR

UNDERSTANDING

WAR

History and Theory
of Combat

Col. T.N. Dupuy
U. S. Army, Ret.

A Giniger Book

Paragon House Publishers
New York

I dedicate this book to Dr. Donald S. Marshall, an objective, dispassionate scholar, and a friend of great compassion, who has led the American institutional search for a theory of combat, and whose help and encouragement have been invaluable to me.

Published in the United States by

Paragon House Publishers
90 Fifth Avenue
New York, New York 10011

for
The K. S. Giniger Company, Inc.
1133 Broadway
New York, New York 10010

Library of Congress Cataloging-in-Publication Data

Dupuy, Trevor Nevitt, 1916–
   Understanding War.

   Includes index.
   1. War. 2. Combat. 3. Military history, Modern.
I. Title.
U21.2.D85   1987   355'.02   86-25151
ISBN 0-913729-57-4

Contents

FOREWORD   XV

PREFACE   XVII

INTRODUCTION   XXI

CHAPTER 1.   **THE TIMELESS VERITIES
              OF COMBAT**   1

CHAPTER 2.   **THE SEARCH FOR A
              THEORY OF COMBAT**   9

The Origins of the Search   9
Napoleon   10
Clausewitz and Jomini   11
Other Theorists since Napoleon   14
J.F.C. Fuller   16
Frederick W. Lanchester   18

CHAPTER 3.   **CLAUSEWITZ'S THEORY OF COMBAT**   **21**

Perceptions and Interpretations   21
Clausewitz's Approach   22
Clausewitz's Philosophy of War   23
Clausewitz and Combat Theory   24
The Law of Numbers   28

CHAPTER 4.   **THE THREE-TO-ONE THEORY OF COMBAT**   **31**

President Lincoln, Military Strategist
    and Theorist   31
The Three-to-One Rule of Thumb   34
Historical Examples of the Rule   35

CHAPTER 5.   **THE SOVIET APPROACH TO A THEORY OF COMBAT**   **39**

Soviet Military Capability   39
Soviet Use of Military History   42
The Soviet View of Military History   43
Soviet Application of Historical
    Studies   46
Correlation of Forces and Means   48

CHAPTER 6.   **TOWARD AN AMERICAN THEORY OF COMBAT**   **51**

The Application of Science to War   51
Problems with Combat Models   52
The Military Conflict Institute   53
Practical Value of a Theory of
    Combat   56
Human Behavior and Battle
    Outcomes   58
The Process of Theory Development   58

CHAPTER 7. **ELEMENTS OF A THEORY OF COMBAT** **63**

Setting the Stage 63
Definition of Military Combat 63
The Hierarchy of Combat 64
The Conceptual Components of
  Combat 66
The Scope of the Theory 71
Combat Theory and Nuclear War 74
Applicability to Air and Naval
  Warfare 78
Definition of a Theory of Combat 79

CHAPTER 8. **THE QJM COMBAT POWER FORMULA** **81**

The Clausewitz Connection 81
Substituting Force Strength for
  Numbers 82
Defining Force Effects Variables 86
Substituting Relative Combat
  Effectiveness for Troop Quality 87
Summary: The QJM and the
  Clausewitz Law 89

CHAPTER 9. **ILLUSTRATION: 1940 FLANDERS CAMPAIGN** **91**

Significance of the 1940 Flanders
  Campaign 91
Allied Force Strength 93
German Force Strength 94
Variable Factors 95
Quality of Troops 96
Overall Comparison 96
The Historical Comparison 99
The Hypothetical Comparison 100

CHAPTER 10. **RELATIVE COMBAT EFFECTIVENESS** **105**

Relative Combat Effectiveness and
    Force Quality 105
Combat Outcome Diagram 107
German Excellence in Two World
    Wars 109
The Performance of the U.S. 88th
    Infantry Division 114
Why was the 88th Good? 117
Relative Combat Effectiveness in the
    Arab-Israeli Wars 121

CHAPTER 11. **DIMINISHING RETURNS IN COMBAT** **125**

Economy of Force and Relative
    Combat Effectiveness 125
Economy of Force and Diminishing
    Returns 126
Reanalyzing the Data 127
Diminishing Returns in World War II 130
Diminishing Returns in the
    Arab-Israeli Wars 133
Diminishing Returns and Economy of
    Force 139
Diminishing Returns for Attacker
    and Defender 144
Friction and Challenge 146
Diminishing Returns and the QJM 146

CHAPTER 12. **ADVANCE RATES IN COMBAT** **149**

Movement and Advance Rates 149
Historical Advance Rates 150

Advance Rates versus Force Ratios 154
The Need for an Advance Rate
   Methodology 156
Combat Advance Rate Verities 158
Advance Rates in the QJM 164

CHAPTER 13. **ATTRITION IN COMBAT** **165**

"Fighting's for Killing" 165
Historical Trends in Attrition 166
Combat Attrition Verities 174
Significance of the Attrition Verities 180
Attrition in the QJM 181

CHAPTER 14. **FRICTION IN COMBAT** **183**

Clausewitz's Concept 183
Measuring Friction in Combat 184
Deployment Geometry versus
   Casualty Rates 184
Explanation of Friction 189
Friction in a Single Battle 191
The Hierarchical Relationships of
   Models 195

CHAPTER 15. **TECHNOLOGY AND HU-
MAN BEHAVIOR IN COMBAT** **199**

Relating Capabilities and Effects—
   Some Dubious Assumptions 199
Historical Eras and Innovations in
   Weapons 200
Ancillary Technical Developments 204
Technological Change and the World
   Wars 207
Technological Change since 1945 208
The Target Rich Environment 211
The Interaction of Military
   Technology and Military Men 212

Assimilation of Weapons 212
Relative Importance of Technology
and Troops 213
Congruence of Weapons, Tactics, and
Doctrine 216
Behavior, Technology, and History 218

CHAPTER 16. **A NEW SQUARE LAW** 221

The Lanchester Equations and
History 221
Combat Effectiveness and Battle
Outcomes 222
A Rare Instance of Things Being
Equal 223
The Lethality-Casualty Relationship 225
The New Square Law Equations 230
Interpretation of the New Square
Law 232
Implications of the New Square Law 233

CHAPTER 17. **APPLICATION: THE
BEKAA VALLEY, JUNE 1982** 237

Practical Analytic Application 237
The 1982 War in Lebanon 237
The Bekaa Valley Operation 239
Modified QJM Analysis 242
Analysis of Advance Rates 247
Analysis of Casualty Rates 248
Implications of the QJM Analysis 249

CHAPTER 18. **APPLICATION:
SUPPRESSION** 251

The Urgency of the Problem 251
Suppression and Neutralization 252

An Elusive Topic 253
An After-Dinner Speech 253
Some Answers from History 255
Human Behavior, Combat Outcomes,
 and Suppression 256

CHAPTER 19. **APPLICATION: FORCE
 MULTIPLIERS** **259**

"Fight Outnumbered and Win" 259
Analysis of Breakthrough Operations 260
The QJM and Historical Force
 Multipliers 266
Force Multipliers and Future
 Battlefields 272

CHAPTER 20. **THE QJM AS A THEORY
 OF COMBAT** **279**

Clausewitz's Amanuensis 279
The QJM as a Model: A Summary 280
The QJM as a Theory 282
Testing the Theory 283
Implications 285

NOTES **287**

APPENDIX A. **SUMMARY OF DATA FOR
 93 WORLD WAR II ENGAGE-
 MENTS** **293**

APPENDIX B. **SUMMARY OF DATA
 FOR 52 ENGAGEMENTS, 1967
 AND 1973 ARAB-ISRAELI
 WARS** **297**

BIBLIOGRAPHY 299

INDEX 306

Foreword

DECADES AGO, Trevor Dupuy and his late father, Ernest, dedicated themselves to the idea that history can teach us the things we need to know about wars of the future. In an enormous sustained effort with their small private research group they produced study after study, book after book, developing a crusade that in its later years (helped by the arrival of the computer) turned toward quantification of battle data for analysis. Trevor has carried this struggle forward with his Quantified Judgment Model (QJM), a mathematical formulation that serves as the basis for war gaming—or for predicting the outcome of battles.

In this book Trevor Dupuy recounts his discovery that comments by Clausewitz on his "Law of Numbers" tend to confirm the equations of QJM. He cites the chapter of *On War* titled "Superiority of Numbers" and also the Clausewitzian term "friction" in support of his own basic formulas, and in his concluding pages adds, "I consider myself not only Clausewitz's disciple but his amanuensis."

Dupuy is convinced that the well-known equations of Frederick W. Lanchester, which establish parameters for force-on-force encounters but which Lanchester himself admitted were vulnerable to distortion by "a hundred and one extraneous issues," can be corrected or "normalized" through the use of quantifiers in Dupuy's QJM. Dupuy also points out, accurately, that Soviet military experts since World War II have given great emphasis to quantification as an aid to battle analysis.

These are strong claims, and Dupuy sets forth resolutely to prove his point and to justify, after his many books, articles, studies, and war games, his complete faith in the formulas of QJM as the best way to relate historical cause and effect in war. As was true of his earlier work, this book will produce controversy. The key question is, how much will battle prediction lend itself to mathematical analysis, and how much will always be dependent on subjective judgment? Can the computer help provide the solution to the complexity of battle analysis?

I am sure that *Understanding War* will be challenged as a concept and in the mathematical details of its formulas, but I salute Trevor Dupuy for his latest and most thorough attempt to cast some light on a subject of great moment: the ability of the scientific mind to fathom and analyze the clash of arms on the battlefield.

John R. Galvin
General, U.S. Army

Preface

THIS BOOK HAS been long in the writing. In fact, I began working on it, after a fashion, soon after the publication of the first edition of *Numbers, Predictions and War*. My original intention was to produce a revised edition of that book, partly to eliminate its embarrassing plethora of typographical and computational errors, partly to update it to reflect new developments in, or applications of, the Quantified Judgment Model (QJM), and partly to record some of my frustrations in my efforts to get the American military Operations Research (OR) community to give serious attention to the QJM.

For several reasons, however, I came to the conclusion that an entirely new book was needed, which would show how the evolving QJM could and should be related to past and current efforts to develop a scientific theory of combat. I decided, therefore, to deal with the errors in *Numbers* by the publication of a revised and only slightly updated version of that book. As to the incredible story of my wanderings in the wonderland of the military OR community, that has been postponed until I have time to develop my voluminous notes into another book.

Thus, this book is single-mindedly devoted to Understanding War, in the context of the significance of military history in fostering such an understanding through its contribution to a theory of combat.

I have received help and encouragement from many people in

the preparation of this book. So many people have offered suggestions or comments that I hesitate to try to list all of them. I fear that the temporary forgetfulness of advancing age may at this writing cause me to overlook someone who made a significant contribution. Nevertheless, I feel I have an obligation to acknowledge such assistance, and I shall do so to the best of my ability.

In particular, I must acknowledge my considerable debt to my colleague, Colonel John Brinkerhoff, USA, Ret., who has painstakingly reviewed two draft manuscripts of this book, and who has offered many suggestions on organization, content, and style. I have accepted most of his suggestions on organization, more than half of his ideas on content, and quite a few of his thoughts on style. Without question, his contributions have greatly improved the book, and I am most appreciative.

Hardly less significant have been the suggestions of Dr. Janice Fain, Mr. Robert McQuie, and Captain Wayne Hughes, USN, Ret. All of them have reviewed the manuscript, and offered comments, criticisms and suggestions, which have undoubtedly served to improve the book greatly. Maj. Gen. Edward Atkeson, USA, Ret., contributed significantly to my presentation of the Soviet approach to a theory of combat, in Chapter 5.

Mr. L. James Binder, Editor of *Army* Magazine, was kind enough to give permission for me to adapt for this book portions of some of my articles in his magazine.

Others who have provided encouragement, as well as extremely helpful comments as a result of their reviews of draft manuscripts, include: Brigadier General Adrian Freiherr von Oer, German Army, Retired; Major General Mukhtar Hallouda, Egyptian Army, Retired; Dr. Joseph P. Fearey; Mr. Michael Flint; Colonel William Bell, U.S. Army, Retired; Dr. Donald S. Marshall; Mr. Herbert Weiss; Colonel Anthony Pokorny, U.S.A., Retired; Dr. James G. Taylor; and Mr. Lawrence Low. Colleagues on the staff of the Historical Evaluation and Research Organization and Data Memory Systems, Inc., who have made both direct and indirect contributions include: Mr. C. Curtiss Johnson, Mr. Brian Bader, Mr. Arnold C. Dupuy, and Lt. Col. Peter Clark, U.S. Air Force, Retired.

It is customary in concluding such acknowledgments for the author to suggest that the merits of the book are due to the contributions of his friends and colleagues, but that the faults are all of his. As I reject this pleasant, polite, but dishonest formula, I am reminded of the response by Marshal Joffre to an interviewer's question after World War I. Joffre responded along the following lines:

"Who was really responsible for the victory of the Marne? Who am I to say? But I know who would have been responsible if we had lost the battle!"

This is my book. If it is good, I have received much help, for which I am grateful. But, good or bad, it is my book.

T. N. Dupuy
Fairfax, VA

Introduction

The Laboratory of the Soldier. Students of military art and military science have long sought fundamental laws or theories that would explain the interactions of military forces in combat and the outcomes of battles. This search has been prompted in part by similarities and patterns among military operations in all times and cultures—patterns so clear and so consistent that they cannot be ignored. The thoughtful student or observer is impelled to ask if consistent patterns in the relationships of men, weapons, environment, and battle outcome are not manifestations of some basic laws of combat behavior that would explain why battles are lost and won, and also to ask why some military leaders of genius have been successful under circumstances very much like those in which lesser men have failed.

There is only one place to go to seek these patterns and to get answers to the questions about the operation of basic laws of combat behavior and the reasons why great commanders have been great and successful: the records and annals of military experience; in other words, military history.

Even in this age of rapid technological progress in which new and untried weapons are available for war, the history of previous combat remains a relevant and important consideration. History provides a base from which the anticipated effect of the new technology can be judged. History also provides insights into the performance of human beings in war, and, despite new technology, combat remains a very human undertaking. The personification of the application of new technology to military affairs, Admiral Hyman Rickover, has written: "A page of history is worth a book of logic."[1]

Military history is essential to the development of military science because—unlike most other sciences—military science is unable to test its theories and hypotheses in laboratory experiments. Military versions of experiments, such as field exercises, maneuvers, and tests, can never reproduce the essential ingredient of war, which is *fear* in a lethal environment. Such experiments are useful, but only to a limited degree.

The science of war, like the science of astronomy, is an observational science. Just as the astronomer uses the heavens as his laboratory, the true laboratory of the soldier has always been military history. No one understood this better than Napoleon who wrote:

> Read and re-read the campaigns of Alexander, Hannibal, Caesar, Gustavus, Turenne, Eugene, and Frederick. Make them your models. This is the only way to become a great general and to master the secrets of the art of war. With your own genius enlightened by this study, you will reject all maxims opposed to those of these great commanders.[2]

J.F.C. Fuller looked at the other side of the coin: "Unless history can teach us how to look at the future, the history of war is but a bloody romance."[3] So he wrote in 1925, in one of several instances in which he tried to impress upon military men that there was little professional benefit to be derived from merely reading military history, no matter how fascinating such reading might be. Fuller also wrote:

> We must first remember that man remains man and that his heart does not change. Secondly, we must remember that the means of war do change and that the intelligence of man must keep pace with these changes. We must keep minds subtle and active, and never let ourselves be hypnotized by traditions; we must criticize ourselves, and criticize our criticisms; we must experiment and explore.[4]

Fuller understood well the value of military historical analysis as a basis for the formulation of military history. No one has made better use of such analysis.

The Use of Military History. There are two basic ways to use military history. One is to read descriptive military history to obtain a general appreciation for past wars and famous leaders. The other is to use information and data from military history as the basis for historical analysis.

Descriptive history involves written narratives, chronologies, and personal accounts of battles, wars, leaders, and soldiers. From these writings are produced books, monographs, and articles designed to tell the reader what happened. This kind of military history is good, and it is beneficial for the professional education and enjoyment of its readers. Often readers can profit from an understanding of the characters and accomplishments of great generals. Traditionally, there has been a great appreciation within the military services and the defense community for this kind of military history.

Military history analysis involves more than the mere telling of the story; it evaluates what the story means. Military history analysis seeks to bring to bear on present problems relevant lessons of the past. Just as the astronomers must make and record many observations in order to formulate hypotheses regarding relationships among heavenly bodies, so the military analyst must develop combat hypotheses by mean of patterns discerned from studying large quantities of combat data. The approach is to use the data as the basis for an objective and scientific comprehensive analysis, seeking patterns, trends, and relationships to provide the basis for the hypotheses. Alternative hypotheses are then tested against the data. As more data is available for study, confidence in the validity of the hypotheses increases.

Military history analysis is based on descriptive military history, but goes beyond it. The descriptive military historian is a recorder of events and an observer of the processes of combat and policy formulation. The military historical analyst seeks to influence events by participating in the formulation of policy, doctrine, and plans. Both contribute to the value of military history, which—as Fuller told us—is to improve the waging of future warfare by pointing out the lessons of past warfare.

The Abuse of Military History. It is possible to abuse military history by citing it to support preconceived ideas. No one would plead guilty to serving up distorted military history, but it does happen. Sometimes the historical facts are incorrect or misinterpreted; other times the historical facts are correct but the application is faulty. Let us examine two (among many) instances of distorted military history from recent articles in military journals.

Many readers will be aware of current US Army doctrine that assures our troops they can "fight outnumbered and win" if only they will use the right "combat multipliers." This assurance—which is really a kind of exhortation—is often supported by reference to military history. Let me cite two typical examples.

In an article published in a military periodical not long ago, the author cited several instances of outnumbered fighters who won. Among his examples were two I noted particularly: Wellington's victory over Napoleon at Waterloo; and the American recovery and victory over the German onslaught at the Battle of the Bulge in 1944.

There is just one problem with both of these examples. The victorious side, far from being smaller, actually outnumbered the losing side by margins approaching two-to-one in both instances.[5] In each instance it can also be shown that the losing side was, in relative terms, considerably more combat effective than the winners, but was nevertheless overwhelmed by superior numbers. The important point, however, is that—through ignorance or indifference—military history was grossly misused in the citation of these two examples.

In another article, exhorting US troops to "fight outnumbered and win," the author tried to demonstrate that relative numerical strength is unimportant to combat outcomes. He related that in most of Creasy's *The Fifteen Decisive Battles of the World* the numerically inferior force won. His argument has a serious flaw. In at least ten—probably twelve—of the fifteen battles the numerically *superior* force won.

The historical examples cited by these two authors actually demonstrate the opposite of what they were trying to prove. Without any real knowledge of the topics, they made erroneous assertions that, if true, would have supported their arguments, but obviously they made no serious effort to check their facts. This sort of thing can give military history a bad name!

It is relatively easy to demonstrate the fallacies inherent in such distortions or misrepresentations. Unfortunately, however, they are rarely corrected. When they are, it is often too late to undo the damage created in unsuspecting minds that rarely see or pay attention to the factual correction. But it is even more difficult to deal with the selective use of historical examples that are factually correct but used improperly to reach erroneous conclusions.

An example is an assertion made in a report a few years ago that history demonstrates that, because numerically inferior forces are so often successful, it is impossible to predict the winner or loser of a battle on the basis of numerical superiority. There is some merit to the assertion, at least to the extent that a casual reader, reviewing from memory a few of the best known battles of history, could even conclude that the numerically inferior force usually wins. That was the case, for instance, in the battles of Arbela, Agincourt, Leuthen, Austerlitz, Chancellorsville, and the Chinese Farm, to name a few.

Yet, it is also true that the numerically outnumbered, but winning, side in each of those battles had a clear-cut combat power superiority. This is because the winning side in each case had the benefit of one or more of the following multiplying factors: defensive posture; or surprise; or superior combat effectiveness. It is also true that, even without considering these multiplying factors, the numerically superior side has won perhaps 60 percent of the recorded battles of history. Moreover, if just the defensive posture multiplier is considered, the numerically superior side has won about 80 percent of the battles of history.

Thus a correct historical fact, true of a minority of cases, has been used to support an essentially erroneous argument. Not only is the cause of truth poorly served, so also is the national interest poorly served, since important policy decisions could be based on such erroneous arguments.

The Value of Military History. Some argue that history is too inconsistent to be useful as a basis for the formulation of reliable hypotheses, theories, or laws regarding what has happened in the past, and thus has no validity for predictions about what will happen on future battlefields. I hope that anyone who perserveres in reading this book to its conclusion will recognize that this argument is fallacious. The patterns of history are clear. While there is some influence of chance on the battlefield, it generally affects both sides equally, and military combat is as close to being deterministic as it is possible for any human activity to be.

When the results of a battle appear to have deviated from an identified pattern, an analysis will almost always reveal that this deviation was due to the operation of another pattern upon the circumstances of the battle.

The reader may rightly infer that it is most dangerous to draw conclusions from a single historical instance, particularly from one that has been selected to prove a point. This does not mean, however, that there is anything wrong or improper about citing a single historical example—particularly one that is dramatic or well-known—to demonstrate a conclusion or hypothesis supported by a preponderance of historical facts.

The value of military history is that, when analyzed objectively and scientifically, it permits us to project forward the trends of real past experiences. This is the only way the relevant lessons of actual combat can be brought to bear on the important national defense issues of today.

Chapter 1

The Timeless Verities of Combat

ALTHOUGH NO ONE can possibly know now what the next war will really be like, there can be no question that the emotional, conceptual and intellectual aspects of combat through the ages are basically the same in war after war. Weapons and the characteristics of armies have changed, and with them the tactics employed on the battlefield, but the fundamental features of combat remain the same. It is obviously important that we should understand why this is so.

Over the past twenty-five years I have, I believe, identified thirteen unchanging operational features or concepts, which I call "The Timeless Verities of Combat." These timeless verities do not constitute a theory of combat, and they are not a substitute for the Principles of War, with which they have something in common. Rather, as I see them, they describe certain fundamental and important aspects of warfare which, despite constant changes in the implements of war, are almost unchanging because of war's human component. If I am right, any theory of combat must be consistent with these timeless verities.

1. *Offensive action is essential to positive combat results.* This is like saying, "A team can't score in football unless it has the ball." Although subsequent verities stress the strength, value, and importance of defense, this should not obscure the essentiality of offensive action to ultimate combat success. Even in instances where a defensive strat-

egy might conceivably assure a favorable war outcome—as was the case of the British against Napoleon, and as the Confederacy attempted in the American Civil War—selective employment of offensive tactics and operations is required if the strategic defender is to have any chance of final victory.

2. *Defensive strength is greater than offensive strength.* Clausewitz said that "Defense is the stronger form of combat." It is possible to demonstrate by the qualitative comparison of many battles that Clausewitz is right, and that posture has a multiplier effect on the combat power of a defending military force that takes advantage of terrain and fortifications, whether hasty and rudimentary or intricate and carefully prepared. There are many well-known examples of an attacker's need for a preponderance of strength in order to carry the day against a well-placed and fortified defender. One has only to recall Thermopylae, the Alamo, Fredericksburg, Petersburg, Verdun, and Tobruk to realize the advantage enjoyed by a defender with smaller forces well-placed and well-protected.

3. *Defensive posture is necessary when successful offense is impossible.* Even though offensive action is essential to ultimate combat success, a combat commander opposed by a more powerful enemy has no choice but to assume a defensive posture. Since defensive posture automatically increases the combat power of his force, the defending commander at least partially redresses the imbalance of forces. At a minimum he is able to slow down the advance of the attacking enemy, and he might even beat him. In this way, through negative combat results, the defender may ultimately hope to wear down the attacker to the extent that his initial relative weakness is transformed into relative superiority, thus offering the possibility of eventually assuming the offensive and achieving positive combat results. The Franklin and Nashville Campaign of our Civil War, and the El Alamein Campaign of World War II are examples.

Sometimes the commander of a numerically superior offensive force may reduce the strength of portions of his force in order to achieve decisive superiority for maximum impact on the enemy at some other critical point on the battlefield, with the result that those reduced-strength components are locally outnumbered. A contingent thus reduced in strength may therefore be required to assume a defensive posture, even though the overall operational posture of the marginally superior force is offensive, and the strengthened contingent of the same force is attacking with the advantage of superior combat power. A classic example was the role of Davout at Auerstadt when Napolean was crushing the Prussians at Jena. Another is the role played by "Stonewall" Jackson's corps at the Second Battle of Bull Run.

4. *Flank or rear attack is more likely to succeed than frontal attack.* Among the many reasons for this are the following: there is greater opportunity for surprise by the attacker; the defender cannot be strong everywhere at once, and the front is the easiest focus for defensive effort; and the morale of the defender tends to be shaken when the danger of encirclement is evident. Again, historical examples are numerous, beginning with Hannibal's tactical plans and brilliant executions of the Battles of Lake Trasimene and Cannae. Any impression that the concept of envelopment or of a "strategy of indirect approach" has arisen either from the introduction of modern weapons of war, or from the ruminations of recent writers on military affairs, is a grave misperception of history and underestimates earlier military thinkers.

"Seek the flanks" has been a military adage since antiquity, but its significance was enhanced tremendously when the conoidal bullet of the breech-loading, rifled musket revolutionized warfare in the mid-nineteenth century. This led Moltke to his 1867 observation that the increased deadliness of firepower demanded that the strategic offensive be coupled with tactical defensive, an idea that depended upon strategic envelopment for its accomplishment. This was a basic element of Moltke's strategy in the 1870 campaign in France. Its tactical manifestations took place at Metz and Sedan; both instances in which the Germans took up defensive positions across the French line of communications to Paris, and the French commanders, forced to attack, were defeated.

5. *Initiative permits application of preponderant combat power.* The importance of seizing and maintaining the initiative has not declined in our times, nor will it in the

future. This has been the secret of success of all of the great captains of history. It was as true of MacArthur as it was of Alexander the Great, Grant or Napoleon. Some modern Soviet theorists have suggested that this is even more important now in an era of high technology than formerly. They may be right. This has certainly been a major factor in the Israeli victories over the Arabs in all of their wars.

6. *Defenders' chances of success are directly proportional to fortification strength.* To some modern military thinkers this is a truism needing no explanation or justification. Others have asserted that prepared defenses are attractive traps to be avoided at all costs. Such assertions, however, either ignore or misread historical examples. History is so fickle that it is dangerous for historians to use such words as "always" or "never." Nevertheless I offer a bold counter-assertion: never in history has a defense been weakened by the availability of fortifications; defensive works *always* enhance combat strength. At the very least, fortifications will delay an attacker and add to his casualties; at best, fortifications will enable the defender to defeat the attacker.

Anyone who suggests that breakthroughs of defensive positions in recent history demonstrate the bankruptcy of defensive posture and/or fortifications is seriously deceiving himself and is misinterpreting modern history.

One can cite as historical examples the overcoming of the Maginot Line, the Mannerheim Line, the Siegfried Line, and the Bar Lev Line, and from these examples conclude that these fortifications failed. Such a conclusion is absolutely wrong. It is true that all of these fortifications were overcome, but only because a powerful enemy was willing to make a massive and costly effort. (Of course, the Maginot Line was not attacked frontally in 1940; the Germans were so impressed by its defensive strength that they bypassed it, and were threatening its rear when France surrendered.) All of these fortifications afforded time for the defenders to make new dispositions, to bring up reserves, or to mobilize. All were intended to obstruct, to permit the defenders to punish the attackers and, above all to delay; all were successful in these respects. The Bar Lev Line, furthermore, saved Israel from disastrous defeat, and became the base for a successful offensive.

7. *An attacker willing to pay the price can always penetrate the strongest defenses.* No matter how alert the defender, no matter how skillful his dispositions to avoid or mitigate the effects of surprise or the effects of flank or rear attack, a skillful attacker can always achieve at least a temporary advantage for some time at a place he has selected. This is one reason why Napoleon always endeavored to seize and retain the initiative. In the great battles of 1864 and 1865 in Virginia, Lee was always able to exploit his defensive advantage to the utmost. But Grant equally was always able to achieve a temporary superiority when and where he wished. This did not always result in a Union victory —given Lee's defensive skill—but invariably it forced Lee to retreat until he could again impose a temporary stalemate with the assistance of powerful field fortifications. A modern example can be found in the Soviet offensive relieving Leningrad in 1943. Another was the Allied breakout from the Normandy beachhead in July and August of 1944.

8. *Successful defense requires depth and reserves.* It has been asserted that outnumbered military forces cannot afford to withhold valuable firepower from ongoing defensive operations and keep it idle in reserve posture. History demonstrates that this is specious logic, and that linear defense is disastrously vulnerable. Napoleon's crossing of the Po in his first campaign in 1796 is perhaps the classic demonstration of the fallacy of linear (or cordon) defense.

The defender may have all of his firepower committed to the anticipated operational area, but the attacker's advantage in having the initiative can always render much of that defensive firepower useless. Anyone who suggests that modern technology will facilitate the shifting of engaged firepower in battle overlooks three considerations: (a) the attacker can inhibit or prevent such movement by both direct and indirect means, (b) a defender engaged in a fruitless firefight against limited attacks by numerically inferior attackers is neither physically nor psychologically attuned to making lateral movements even if the enemy does not prevent or inhibit it, and (c) withdrawal of forces from the line (even if possible) provides an alert attacker with an opportunity for shifting the thrust of his offensive to the newly created gap in the defenses.

Napoleon recognized that hard-fought combat is usually won by the side committing the last reserves. Marengo, Borodino, and Ligny are typical examples of Napoleonic victories that demonstrated the importance of having resources available to tip the scales. His two greatest defeats, Leipzig and Waterloo, were suffered because his enemies still had reserves after his were all committed. The importance of committing the last reserves was demonstrated with particular poignancy at Antietam in the American Civil War. In World War II there is no better example than that of Kursk.

9. *Superior Combat Power Always Wins.* Military history demonstrates that whenever an outnumbered force was successful, its combat power was greater than that of the loser. All other things being equal, God has always been on the side of the heaviest battalions, and always will be.

In recent years two or three surveys of modern historical experience have led to the finding that relative strength is not a conclusive factor in battle outcome. As we have seen, a superficial analysis of historical combat could support this conclusion. There are a number of examples of battles won by the side with inferior numbers. In many battles, outnumbered attackers were successful.

These examples are not meaningful, however, until the comparison includes the circumstances of the battles and the opposing forces. If one takes into consideration surprise (when present), relative combat effectiveness of the opponents, terrain features, and the advantage of defensive posture, the result may be different. When all of the circumstances are quantified and applied to the numbers of troops and weapons, the side with the greater combat power on the battlefield is always seen to prevail.

10. *Surprise substantially enhances combat power.* Achieving surprise in combat has always been important. It is perhaps more important today than ever. Quantitative analysis of historical combat shows that surprise has increased the combat power of military forces in those engagements in which it was achieved. Surprise has proven to be the greatest of all combat multipliers. It may be the most important of the Principles of War; it is at least as important as Mass and Maneuver.

11. *Firepower kills, disrupts, suppresses, and causes dispersion.* It is doubtful if any of the people who are today writing on the effect of technology on warfare would consciously disagree with this statement. Yet, many of them tend to ignore the impact of firepower on dispersion, and as a consequence they have come to believe that the more lethal the firepower, the more deaths, disruption, and suppression it will cause. In fact, as weapons have become more lethal intrinsically, their casualty-causing capability has either declined or remained about the same because of greater dispersion of targets. Personnel and tank loss rates of the 1973 Arab-Israeli War, for example, were quite similar to those of intensive battles of World War II and the casualty rates in both of these wars were less than in World War I.

12. *Combat activities are always slower, less productive, and less efficient than anticipated.* This is the phenomenon that Clausewitz called "friction in war." Friction is largely due to the disruptive, suppressive, and dispersal effects of firepower upon an aggregation of people. This pace of actual combat operations will be much slower than the progress of field tests and training exercises, even highly realistic ones. Tests and exercises are not truly realistic portrayals of combat, because they lack the element of fear in a lethal environment, present only in real combat. Allowances must be made in planning and execution for the effects of friction, including mistakes, breakdowns, and confusion.

13. *Combat is too complex to be described in a single, simple aphorism.* This has been amply demonstrated by the preceding paragraphs. All writers on military affairs (including this one) need periodically to remind themselves of this. In military analysis it is often necessary to focus on some particular aspect of combat. However, the results of such closely focused analyses must then be evaluated in the context of the brutal, multifarious, overlapping realities of war.

Technology has changed war dramatically in the past century and a half. Yet, the thirteen timeless verities of combat have been as applicable and as true in the most recent wars of these fifteen decades as they were in Napoleon's day and as they were in the days of Alexander, Hannibal, Julius Caesar, Genghis Khan, Gustavus, and Frederick.

The reason for this is that, despite the many changes, the essential nature of war has not changed. Wars are fought by men, and there has been no discernible difference in the fundamental nature of man over the past five thousand years of recorded history. Because the nature of man has not changed, neither has his basic objective when he turns to war: the employment of lethal instruments to force his will upon other men with opposing points of view.

Even if we cannot predict when or how future war will occur, or what its course will be, or how its individual battles will turn out, or how it will be affected by new technology or military materiel, the timeless verities will be applicable.

Chapter 2

The Search For a
Theory of Combat

The Origins of the Search

FROM THE EARLIEST records of civilization, it is evident that
thoughtful men have struggled to find some order and predicta-
bility in the great, bloody confusion of war. Using their practical
experience with past conflicts—the only possible laboratory
—and using whatever other information was available, they have
sought general rules about the nature of war that could help them
prevail in future conflicts.

The oldest surviving military treatise was written in China,
about 500 B.C. It was *The Art of War*, by a military theoretician
named Sun Tze (pronounced Soon Dzuh), who displayed a profound and sophisticated understanding of the philosophy of conflict and combat. Practically nothing is known about Sun Tze,
although apparently he was a leading military figure of his time
in China.

Over the next 2,300 years there were other thoughtful writers
on military affairs, who tried to formulate a theoretical approach
to warfare. There was, for instance, Sextus Julius Frontinus, who
wrote in the first century A.D. a book called *On Military Affairs,*
and another on *Strategems*. About two centuries later another
Roman, Flavius Vegetius Renatus, wrote a book also entitled *On
Military Affairs,* more generally known as *Military Institutions
of the Romans*, a favorite reference work of the rare military

scholar of Medieval Europe. There were several theoretical works on war by Byzantines: Mauricius's *Strategikon*, *The Tactica* of Leo the Wise, and others. In the century before Napoleon there were such writings as *Reveries on the Art of War* by Count Maurice of Saxe, and *Instructions to his Generals* by Frederick the Great of Prussia.

Napoleon

One man, more than any other, was responsible for stimulating the search for a theory, or science, or collection of laws on war or combat. This was Napoleon Bonaparte, who seems to have more or less formulated such a theory in his own mind. While Napoleon gave hints about this in his meager theoretical writings and in some of his correspondence, he demonstrated on the battlefield that there *must* be a theory of war. Unfortunately, he never laid out his theory in a coherent, unified form. He never committed his ideas on military theory to paper in clear scientific terms —even though he obviously thought that way. But he did leave an extensive collection of empirical—as opposed to conceptual or theoretical—maxims. From these, and from analyses of his performance, others have distilled the principal elements of his theoretical ideas. In his correspondence and recorded statements, as in his *Maxims,* Napoleon made it clear that his concepts and thinking on war had been derived basically from the study of the campaigns of earlier great generals.

It is impossible to overemphasize the gigantic impact of Napoleon on warfare, the art of war, and military theory. It is difficult —and not very useful—to make comparisons between great men of different eras. It is probably safe to say that both Alexander and Genghis Khan were the equals of Napoleon in intellect and in the relationship of intellect to military skills and virtues. Hannibal and Julius Caesar are also certainly worthy of comparison, as are Gustavus Adolphus and Frederick the Great.

Of these illustrious predecessors of Napoleon, only Frederick was near enough a contemporary to warrant a close comparison. Yet it almost immediately becomes obvious that the two were not comparable. It would have been impossible for Frederick to match Napoleon in strategic and theoretical initiative. Frederick by birth and by circumstances was dedicated to general maintenance of the *status quo,* aside from limited territorial adjustments in central Europe favorable to Prussia. Napoleon was presented by circumstances with open-ended opportunities for the employment of military force. He had the intellect, ability, will, and—above all—genius, to seize opportunities at least equally available to a number of other excellent French generals produced by the wars of the French Revolution. In the process he transformed war as has no other man before or since.

As we have noted, Napoleon never articulated his theory or theories of war, except for occasional passages in his letters—for instance the letter of 27 August 1808, written to try to teach his brother Joseph how to rule Spain, in which he implied that "the moral is to the physical as three is to one"—and the uneven litany of concepts to be found in his *Maxims*. It was necessary for his younger contemporaries, Jomini and Clausewitz, to attempt to give these concepts the theoretical substance they deserved.

Clausewitz and Jomini

Carl von Clausewitz was born at Burg, Prussia in 1780. Twenty-three years later young Captain von Clausewitz was studying at the Prussian War Academy under Colonel Gerhardt von Scharnhorst, who was vainly trying to awaken the Prussian Army to the realities of Napoleonic warfare. Clausewitz served in the disastrous Jena Campaign of 1806, where Scharnhorst's grim forebodings were fulfilled. After the war King Frederick William III permitted Scharnhorst to plan and initiate the reforms he had urged before Jena. Clausewitz, who had been a prisoner of war in France for a year, joined Scharnhorst, August Niehardt von Gneisenau, and a handful of other intellectual officers to become one of the famous Reformers of the Prussian Army during the years 1807–1811.[1]

In 1811, when Napoleon was pressuring Prussia to join France in war against Russia, Clausewitz resigned, and joined the Russian Army. Early in 1813, after Napoleon's defeat in Russia, Clausewitz played a major role in persuading the principal Prussian field commander (General Hans D. L. von Yorck) to shift sides in the war. After the 1813 campaign, Clausewitz rejoined the Prussian Army and served as a corps chief of staff in the campaigns of 1814 and 1815. During much of the 1820s he was the Commandant of the War Academy, and there he wrote most of

On War. In 1831, when another European war seemed imminent, he became chief of staff of an army, under Gneisenau; both he and Gneisenau died of cholera during an epidemic.

Antoine Henri Jomini was a year older than Clausewitz, having been born in Switzerland in 1779. He was an officer in Napoleon's army when Clausewitz was serving in the opposing Prussian Army. Like Clausewitz, in 1813 Jomini resigned from his own army to join that of Russia, but by that time Clausewitz (though still wearing a Russian uniform) was back with Prussian forces. It is doubtful if the two men met during the short period when they were both in the service of the Czar, or later. During the 1820s each was very familiar with the writings of the other and—as somewhat jealous rivals—each was critical of the other's work.

Jomini tried to explain Napoleon's ideas on theory, and he understood what Napoleon had in mind as clearly as anyone has. In his many writings, however, Jomini was never able either to capture the philosophical aspects of Napoleon's thinking on war satisfactorily, or to distill the essence of the theory. The result was a somewhat mixed bag of discussion, rules, aphorisms, and maxims.

Clausewitz *was* able to capture Napoleon's philosophy and to add to it some ideas of his own, but he found himself as baffled by the problems of distilling a theory out of this philosophy as Jomini had been. Like the Bible in theology, Clausewitz can be quoted to support both sides of almost any argument in military affairs, or as a source for almost any sound or unsound concept that one might desire to document. Such quotations are usually out of context, or the seeming contradictions result from the fact that he never had a chance to edit a final version of his master work.

Clausewitz is often quoted erroneously as ridiculing the idea that there could or should be any fixed set of principles of war. Although some of his words out of context could be so interpreted, he devotes several chapters of *On War* to a discussion of a theory of war, and he affirmed that there are principles. He lists —though not in sequential fashion—eight of the nine principles we usually accept. But, he admitted implicitly that the formulation of the theory would require an effort beyond that of *On War* or possibly beyond the limits of what could be accomplished in terms of the scientific method of his time. He did decry attempts to produce precise and mathematical rules for combat to be followed by generals on the battlefield. Yet, as I shall demonstrate in a subsequent chapter, Clausewitz did think mathematically and quantitatively, and from this thinking he gave us the rudiments of the most substantial theory of combat so far produced.

Much has been made of the differences between Jomini and Clausewitz, but these differences were not great, and were essentially philosophical rather than interpretive or practical. Both were stimulated to their prolific writings on war by the example of Napoleon, and both drew essentially the same conclusions from their respective studies of that example. Both were convinced that Napoleon demonstrated that there is—or should be—a theory of war, and that such a theory was based upon fundamental principles. They generally agreed on what those principles were: such things we now call Mass, Maneuver, Objective, and Surprise.

There were two principal differences. The first was in their approaches. Jomini was more doctrinaire, Clausewitz more philosophical. Jomini tried to derive a framework of rules for battlefield success in war from his identification of principles used by Napoleon. Clausewitz, equally impressed by the principles, did not believe it was possible for these principles to provide more than general guidance for a subsequent commander, who should adapt his understanding of the principles to his own "genius." There are many hints in the text of *On War* that Clausewitz believed that it might some day be possible to formulate a more comprehensive, more scientific body of theory in the form of laws and principles than he believed was possible in the 1830s. In his time, however, he was convinced that such a formulation was impossible, and thus he was very critical of Jomini's efforts to draw up rules for generalship.

The second difference was intellectual. Jomini was unquestionably a man of great analytical ability, highly intelligent, even brilliant. Clausewitz was an intellectual giant worthy of comparison not only with a Napoleon and a Scharnhorst, but also with his contemporary philosophers Kant and Hegel. Jomini studied, and understood very well, the warfare of his time. Clausewitz recognized the relationship of the warfare of his time with the behavioral, social, and political natures of man. Jomini identified the trees of war. Clausewitz not only knew the trees; he saw the forest.

Other Theorists Since Napoleon

I have identified twelve theorists since Napoleon who have, in my opinion, greatly influenced the shaping the course of the search for military theory. Two of these, Clausewitz and Jomini, have been discussed. Later in this chapter I shall devote some attention to two great British theorists, J.F.C. Fuller and Frederick W. Lanchester. In this section, I shall merely summarize the significant contributions to military thought and theory by eight other military men of the nineteenth and twentieth centuries. There is not likely to be complete agreement among military scholars as to which names should be included in such a list.[2] It would, however, be difficult to ignore the contributions made by any of these men.

Denis Hart Mahan was essentially a follower of Napoleon through Jomini. He was the first great American military theorist. He compiled his own version of maxims and rules he thought relevant to military theory in America, but he never tried (so far as is evident from available writings) to produce a theory.[3]

Helmuth von Moltke was both an eminent historian and an eminent military thinker. He was also a superb organizer and director of combat. However, he did little to advance military theory *per se,* other than in unrelated though perceptive comments such as that addressing the need to combine the tactical defensive with the strategic offensive. He was essentially a manifestation of the capabilities of an institution of genius; any number of his Prussian contemporaries could have done as well had they been in his place.[4]

Charles J. J. J. Ardant du Picq was perhaps the most perceptive writer on the subject of moral forces (behavioral considerations) in war. (Note that the first name of this French soldier was Charles, and his unhyphenated last name was Ardant du Picq.) His book, *Battle Studies,* is one of the best of a handful of truly great military classics. He was killed in battle in the Franco-Prussian War before his work could be incorporated into any kind of theoretical context, which was unfortunate for France, as I shall show presently.

Alfred Thayer Mahan was an American military theorist in the style of Jomini, of his own father (Denis Hart Mahan), and of Moltke. His focus was on naval warfare and theory. A profound and gifted thinker on military and naval affairs he well understood the relevance of military history to the contemporary military problems of his time. He dominates the roster of naval theorists much as Clausewitz stands out over other theorists of land warfare. He recognized and analytically employed principles, but never attempted a scientific, analytical approach to military theory.

Count Alfred von Schlieffen was the successor (once removed) to Moltke as Chief of the German General Staff. He was another thoughtful, profound thinker on war, who never attempted to distill a theory of combat from his obviously encyclopedic knowledge of military history and the warfare of his own time. The so-called Schlieffen Plan has become a matter of controversy that has inhibited serious study of his military genius by writers or readers of the English language.[5] As a soldier and a general he was probably superior to Moltke, but we shall never know, since he never had an opportunity to command in battle or war.

Baron Colmar von der Goltz was one of a number of German military thinkers who emerged from that institution of genius —the German General Staff—during its heyday, under Moltke and Schlieffen. In his two best known works, *The Nation in Arms* and *The Conduct of War,* he refers frequently—if somewhat vaguely—to the theory of war, and to its principles. He may not deserve to be included in the intellectual company on this list, other than as a representative of an extremely prolific and thoughtful group of German writers from the General Staff. His work had great influence in Germany, in France, and particularly in Britain.

Ferdinand Foch was a disciple of both Clausewitz and Ardant du Picq. He probably understood Clausewitz as well as anyone ever has—certainly better than most Germans. Paradoxically, he misread his countryman, Ardant du Picq. He did try to think and write in scientific, theoretical terms, and there was much that was sound in his approach to analyzing military history. However, his influence and his devotion to the moral significance of *l'offensive à outrance* came close to ruining the French Army at the outset of World War I. But his leadership in the recovery from that near-disaster was brilliant.

Giulio Douhet was the first and most important theorist of air warfare. It matters not that he—like many other early ardent adherents of air power—greatly exaggerated the potential of the military aircraft of his time. Nor does it matter that this World War I Italian Army officer, turned military aviator, was no more prescient than many of his contemporaries in Britain, France, Germany, Russia, or the United States in forecasting the role of aviation in war. What distinguished him from the others was his ability in his book, *Command of the Air,* published in 1921, to put together a coherent, consistent theory of air warfare, which correctly anticipated (even if it overestimated) the dominant role of airpower in all subsequent wars. Douhet's name is often linked with the contemporary air warfare apostles of Britain and the United States: Marshal of the Royal Air Force Sir Hugh Trenchard, and U. S. Major General William Mitchell. However, even in their own countries, neither of these men had nor deserved the influence that Douhet exercised upon airpower developments and trends, continuing through the twentieth century.

J.F.C. Fuller

John F. C. Fuller was the greatest military thinker of this century, and probably the most important since Clausewitz. It is interesting that in his earlier writings he tended to downgrade Clausewitz, but in later years he began to recognize that his own approach to military theory was essentially Clausewitzian. He was immodest enough to compare himself (and Clausewitz) with Copernicus, Newton, and Darwin. He did not much overstate the case. Fuller was the first important armored warfare tactician and theoretician as a combat staff officer in World War I. He was the first to codify the Principles of War as they have been known for most of this century. Underlying this seminal production was a conviction that there must be laws of combat, or a science of war. Fuller knew that there should be more content and more scientific rigor to a theory of combat than just the Principles of War, but he never quite succeeded in formulating such a theory.

In 1911 then-Captain John Frederick Charles Fuller of the 43d Regiment, Oxfordshire Light Infantry, came to the conclusion that a war would soon break out in Europe. To prepare for this he began very seriously to study military history and the British official manual on military doctrine, the 1909 edition of *Field Service Regulations.*[6] In this latter book he read that British officers should understand "the fundamental principles of war [which] are neither very numerous nor in themselves very abstruse." Fuller then searched through the book for a list and discussion of these important foundations of British military professionalism. He looked in vain. In disgust he wrote that the manual was "grammar without an alphabet."

However, Fuller did heed the admonition, he intensified his study of military history, particularly the campaigns of Napoleon, seeking insight on the basic principles of war. Two years later, while a student at Camberley, the British Staff College, he suggested to his instructors that the *Field Service Regulations* should be modified to provide student officers with some guidance about these all-important principles. He was, as his biographer tells us, "reprimanded for attempting to amend rather than study *Field Service Regulations*."[7]

During his subsequent brilliant career in World War I, Fuller kept thinking about the need for a more systematic, scientific approach to the study of war, founded on basic principles. In 1916 he wrote:

> It is an extraordinary thing [that] whilst every science is run on a few definite principles, war today [1916] should be run on the dice-box of luck. . . . We can predict certain events in war as surely as Darwin could in life, directly he grasped the fundamental principle of evolution. However we have no military Darwin as yet; let us hope the Germans will not discover one.[8]

The following year Fuller, then the chief planner for the new British Tank Corps in France, was responsible for the first important use of tanks at the Battle of Cambrai. He continued in this position to the end of the war. After the war he became an instructor at the Staff College at Camberley, where he redoubled his efforts to get the British Army to base its doctrine not on lip service to some anonymous and unspecified principles of war, but rather on an understanding of truly fundamental principles.

He was successful. In 1921 a new issue of *Field Service Regulations* was produced, and included, with only slight modifications, the eight Principles of War that Fuller had advocated. It is perhaps instructive to compare Fuller's 1921 Principles with the official list of the US Army as included in the US Army's current edition of *Field Manual 100-1:*

Table 2-1

The Principles of War

FULLER	FM 100-1
Objective	Objective
Mass	Mass
Offensive	Offensive
Surprise	Surprise
Security	Security
Movement	Mobility
Economy of force	Economy of force
Cooperation	Unity of Command
	Simplicity

It will be seen that the lists are virtually identical except that the US Army adds "Simplicity" and substitutes "Unity of Command" for "Cooperation" and "Mobility" for "Movement." (In my opinion, "Maneuver," which was used in earlier American texts, is a better summary word than either "Movement" or "Mobility.")

In subsequent years Fuller wrote extensively on armored warfare, military theory, the science and philosophy of war, and on military history in general. Despite his brilliance—or perhaps because of it—Fuller was never fully understood or liked by the majority of his fellow officers in the British Army. He continued to write and to criticize with acid pen and tongue, after he was retired as a relatively youthful major general. He was not called back to active duty in World War II, prompting French General Charles de Gaulle to ask:

> But what about your best soldier, General Fuller? He was the prophet, we only followed him, . . . You will find prophesized in his books everything the Germans did with tanks. I have often wondered why he is never used.[9]

An indication of Fuller's approach to military history analysis —and the application of the Principles of War—will be found in his comments about one of the best known, but probably apocryphal, quotations of the Duke of Wellington:

> Do not let my opponents castigate me with the blather that Waterloo was won on the playfields of Eton, for the fact remains geographically, historically and tactically, whether the great Duke uttered such undiluted nonsense or not, that it was won on fields in Belgium by carrying out a fundamental principle of war, the principle of mass; in other words by marching on to those fields three Englishmen, Germans or Belgians to every two Frenchmen.[10]

Frederick W. Lanchester

A fellow countryman and contemporary of Fuller was also concerned about the application of the Principle of Mass on the battlefield. This was an early aeronautical engineer, Frederick William Lanchester, who wrote an article entitled "The Principle of Concentration," which was published in October 1914 in the British journal, *Engineering*.[11] That article has had profound impact on the evolution of a theory of combat.

Like Fuller, Lanchester's ideas about the Principle of Concentration (or Mass) were based upon his analytical reading of military history. This is somewhat ironical in view of the fact that probably a majority of the people who have exploited Lanchester's ideas have rejected the relevance of history to modern warfare.

Lanchester's initial formulation of this concept of warfare was designed to deal with conceptions of force strength and concentration of forces, rather than with force attrition. This is noteworthy because most modern applications of Lanchester's work deal essentially with battlefield attrition. Yet, the article mentions loss or attrition only as an incidental aspect of Lanchester's comparisons of the strengths of opposing forces under arbitrarily standardized conditions. His primary concern was with the relationship between numerical strength and fighting (or effective) strength. Stating this distinction is not intended to suggest that Lanchester would have denied that the application of his work to attrition was a logical product of the concepts. It is merely to point out that Lanchester stated some rather general force-strength relationships under two different kinds of circumstances, and then emphasized (and re-emphasized) that "superior morale or better tactics or a hundred and one other extraneous causes may intervene in practice to modify the issue, but this does not invalidate the mathematical statement [regarding relative force strength]."

In his article, Lanchester formulated, using historical examples, a concept of warfare that could be expressed in two slightly different but parallel differential equations. The following are Lanchester's differential equations (using the same symbols as in Lanchester's article).

Linear Law: $\frac{dr}{dt} = Nrb$ Opposing sides know only general locations of targets and cannot concentrate fire. Sometimes called the "unaimed fire" equation.

$\frac{dr}{dt} = Mbr$

Square Law: $\frac{db}{dt} = Cr$ Opposing sides know precise locations of targets and can concentrate fire. Sometimes called the "aimed fire" equation.

$\frac{dr}{dt} = Kb$

Where: b is for the blue side and r is for the red side; N, M, C and K are constants.

In essence, the Lanchester equations show the effects of force concentration upon the loss rates of two opposing sides in a simple, uncomplicated combat situation under two general conditions of combat: (a) when one or both of the sides have only a general knowledge of the location of the other (as in a meeting engagement, or as in the case of an attacker against defenders concealed behind prepared or fortified defenses), and (b) when one or both sides have accurate information of the location of the other (as, for instance, a defender in most prepared and fortified defense situations, or two forces opposing each other on a broad, flat desert).

For purposes of attrition calculation, the Linear Law shows the rate of change of each force with respect to time (in other words, the effect of casualty attrition), as a constant times the product of the two strengths of the opposing forces. The Square Law shows the rate of change as a constant times the strength of the opposing side only, the side that has the advantage of observation.

As a military historian I have some problems with Lanchester's historical examples,[12] but in general he has not distorted or misused his examples. What has bothered me more as a military historian, however, is the fact that it is impossible to make his equations fit actual historical statistical data.[13] That has not, however, deterred analysts from using the equations as the basis for attrition assessment in many of the models or simulations of combat in use in the United States and NATO today. I shall return to the Lanchester equations in Chapter 15 and show how they can be reconciled with historical statistical data.

Summary

Of the twelve men briefly identified above as important military theorists since Napoleon, three are particularly important as general theorists; Jomini, Clausewitz, and Fuller. All three were significantly influenced by the example of Napoleon, and also were stimulated by their own substantial battlefield experience, as well as by extensive readings in military history. Each of these three in his own way came close to capturing the essence of a theory of combat, but none was satisfied that he had accomplished what he had set out to do. In the next chapter we shall examine the work of one of them and shall discover that he succeeded better than perhaps he realized.

Chapter 3

Clausewitz's Theory of Combat

Perceptions and Interpretations

J.F.C. FULLER WROTE: "In my opinion Clausewitz's level is on that of Copernicus, Newton, and Darwin . . ."[1] I agree whole-heartedly with that assessment. In fact, in the realm of military theory, it could be suggested that at a time when the sophistication of military science was equatable with the physical science of the time of Copernicus, Clausewitz not only laid the groundwork for all subsequent theoretical military thought—as Copernicus did in his different field—but then went further and stated the fundamental law for combat theory in a fashion comparable to Newton's postulation of the fundamental theory of gravitation nearly two centuries after Copernicus.

Many of the scholars and military analysts who have studied and written about Clausewitz have concluded that he eschewed rigid quantitative approaches. One widely accepted assessment of Clausewitz goes so far as to say of him: "He distrusted set theories of war based upon mathematical computations or geometric patterns."[2] The author then provides some quotations from Clausewitz to support the statement.

My own studies of Clausewitz, and of the nature of combat, have led me to the conclusion that such statements reflect a profound misunderstanding of the theory of war that Clausewitz produced, and presented in incomplete, but nonetheless coherent and consistent form in *On War*. This is no abstract issue of interest and importance only to historians. Rather, I am asserting a truth that can lead to a new, forward-looking theory of combat essentially based upon Clausewitz's deterministic, predictive, mathematically based theoretical concept. While this is an iconoclastic interpretation of Clausewitz and the thrust of his masterwork, *On War,* the interpretation makes sense when the chronological and environmental context within which Clausewitz wrote the book are taken into consideration.

In the first place, as Clausewitz observed, he was dealing with concepts and relationships not easily manipulated by the mathematical tools of his time. This accounts for the descriptive and qualitative content of *On War*. Had Clausewitz been able to employ modern mathematical and analytical tools, including computers, it is likely that he would have more explicitly provided quantitative treatment. He stated his principles and concepts without explicit mathematical expressions because that was what the state of the art in his time permitted.

In the second place, the book was still in draft at the time of Clausewitz's death and was never really finished in the form he desired. Thus, it is inevitable that there will be some inconsistencies, and even apparent contradictions, in some of the statements found in the book. There are additional possibilities for apparent confusion and contradiction since Clausewitz used some terms that may be interpreted differently by different readers.

If this is so, some readers may ask, then why I can be so certain that my interpretation of terms used by Clausewitz is more consistent with his intent than are the possibly contrary interpretations of others. I have no evidence other than a general, internal consistency to be found in the philosophical and theoretical concepts presented by Clausewitz. I endeavor to interpret his terms and his apparent contradictions in a fashion conformable to that consistency, not in a fashion that would be contradictory.

Clausewitz's Approach

Clausewitz looked at and wrote about many aspects of war, but his logical analytical approach focused on two of these aspects: (a) the activities of war, and (b) its characteristics. To get them out of the way (but not to forget them) let me summarize his view of the three interlocking characteristics of war:

War is an activity involving violence and passion.
War is subject to the vagaries of human behavior.
War is essentially subordinated to politics.

Clausewitz perceived two fundamental activities in war: (1) the actual hostilities, or fighting, and (2) the preparation for and support of the waging of war. He wrote little about this second activity, devoting most of his attention—and his book—to the waging, or fighting, aspects of war.

The waging of war, Clausewitz believed, also had two distinct aspects: the higher control and direction of combat, and combat itself. His approach to the higher control and direction of war was fundamentally philosophical, with little mathematical or quantitative consideration. Here he was dealing with issues we today would refer to as national strategy, and its various components, such as political, psychological, social, economic, and military. His approach to combat, on the other hand, was essentially theoretical, scientific, and in concept highly mathematical. In his systematic approach he saw that combat theory was logically divisible into the two related areas of strategy and tactics. Today many military theorists tend to subdivide strategy, as Clausewitz saw it, into military strategy (the overall direction of war) and operations (the control of large forces in a theater of war).

In order to provide some background for a discussion of his basic theory of combat, I will survey what Clausewitz wrote in *On War* about his philosophy of war.

Clausewitz's Philosophy of War

One of the three most profound theoretical statements that Clausewitz made about war had to do with his philosophy of war. This was his statement of the relationship of war to politics.

War as a Continuation of Politics. This theme is too well known to need elaboration here. I merely wish to remind the reader that this is perhaps the most fundamental element of Clausewitz's philosophy of war. War is, and must always be, subservient to politics. He states this many times and in many ways.

"Absolute" War in Theory and War in Practice. In theory, Clausewitz points out, war is an act of violence to be carried out to the utmost limits of the lethal capabilities of the opponents. In practice, however, war will be carried out only to the degree of violence consistent with the politics motivating the opponents. This is mainly because war is an instrument of policy, but also because of the realities that led him to develop his concept of friction. From this duality of theory and practice emerge two more significant characteristics of war.

War can be Total, or War can be Limited. War can be conducted with as much force as is possible—thus approaching the theoretical absolute war—in order to overthrow an opponent, if that is the aim of policy. Or it can be carried out in more limited fashion for the purpose of achieving lesser policy goals.

Ends and Means in War. When the ends of war are total (i.e., the overthrow of the opponent, or survival against such an effort), the means will be violent to the utmost capability of the contestants. If the ends of war are less than overthrow of the enemy, then the means will be less violent.

The Activities of War. As already noted, Clausewitz divides the activities of war into two principal categories: fighting, or combat; and preparation for fighting, or administration.

In sum, Clausewitz thought in theoretical terms, and saw war as having both quantitative and qualitative aspects. He also made it very clear that the general philosophy of war—dealing primarily with strategy—was essentially qualitative, and probably not amenable to quantitative analysis. On the other hand, when he was writing about tactics—in other words, dealing with actual fighting or combat—he saw much in terms of scale, degree, or quantity.

Clausewitz and Combat Theory

In the next few paragraphs I shall deal with the current relevance of six important combat theoretical concepts of Clausewitz, three of which show his interest in scale, dimension, or quantity. I shall start with the three that are not inherently quantitative. First, I consider his thoughts about "genius in war."

Genius in War. The principal reason for the apparent dichotomy in Clausewitz's thinking about the obvious scalar or dimensional nature of a theory of combat, and the hopelessness of quantifying some aspects of war—and particularly the vagaries of human behavior and human nature—was his recognition of the overwhelming importance of leadership in battle. Like Napoleon, Clausewitz referred to the quality of leadership as "genius." Since he saw no way of quantifying genius, he thought it was fruitless to try to develop rules for generalship, which was really a manifestation of unquantifiable genius.

Clausewitz is correct on the importance of genius and the impossibility of preparing rules for generals of differing levels or qualities of genius. It is also probably impossible to quantify genius, but it is possible to fit genius into a concept of relative combat effectiveness, and this concept in turn can sometimes be used to establish an approximate value for genius. I have used this approach to calculate the relative combat effectiveness of the Confederate Army to the Union Army at the Battle of Antietam at about 1.6. In one of his most profound statements about the strategy of the Civil War, President Abraham Lincoln assessed Northern and Southern soldiers as equal in combat quality.[3] If one agrees with Lincoln in this—as I do—the 1.6 ratio of the combat effectiveness of the Confederate Army to the Union Army at Antietam must be indicative of the relative generalship capabilities of the opposing commanders, Lee and McClellan: 1.6 to 1. Or, if Lee was a 10.0 then McClellan was a 6.0.

Destruction of the Enemy. Some British and American critics have dismissed Clausewitz as a "bloodthirsty Prussian" because of his emphasis on the importance of striving for the destruction of the enemy, and for such statements as "of all the possible aims in war, the destruction of the enemy's armed forces always appears to be the highest," and "We . . . emphasize that the violent [or "bloody"] resolution of the crisis, the wish to annihilate the enemy's forces, is the first-born son of war." Similar thoughts abound in the book; in fact, Clausewitz devotes an entire chapter to this idea of destruction.

It must be remembered, however, that at the point where he first expresses the idea of destruction of enemy forces, Clausewitz qualifies this by saying "Whenever we use the phrase, destruction of the enemy forces, . . . we mean . . . they must be put in such a condition that they can no longer carry on the fight." Elsewhere he points out that this can also be accomplished by destroying the enemy's will to fight.

Speed and Direct Approach. When Clausewitz's critics note his emphasis on destruction, and read his statement, for example, that it is essential "to act as swiftly as possible [and] therefore to permit no delay or detour without sufficient reason," they see him as advocating a bludgeon instead of a rapier, and of having no understanding of such strategic concepts as that which Liddell Hart called "the strategy of the indirect approach."

This is simply reading Clausewitz out of context, and failing to recognize the many other things he said about the art of war —and particularly about genius in war.

It is abundantly clear from *On War* that Clausewitz understood maneuver, and he understood surprise—of all kinds—at least as well as any other military theorist. His discussions of the brilliant strategic maneuvers of Frederick and Napoleon demonstrate this. He also understood the principles we now call Objective, Simplicity, and Mass. Next we turn to the thoughts of Clausewitz on the quantitative aspects of combat theory.

Defense. I have earlier suggested that his statement about the relationship of war to politics was one of the three most important of the concepts of Clausewitz, as I see them. The second is his statement that "Defense is the Stronger Form of Combat." In several places, and in varying words, Clausewitz emphasized that point throughout *On War*.

This statement implies a comparison of relative strength. It is essentially scalar and thus ultimately quantitative. Clausewitz did not attempt to define the scale of his comparison. However, by following his conceptual approach it is possible to establish quantities for this comparison. Depending upon the extent to which the defender has had the time and capability to prepare for defensive combat, and depending also upon such considerations as the nature of the terrain which he is able to utilize for defense, my research tells me that the comparative strength of defense to offense can range from a factor with a minimum value of about 1.3 to maximum value of more than 3.0.

It must be noted, however, that Clausewitz emphasizes the fact that defense is essentially negative in nature, and cannot win wars. (The first of my Timeless Verities [see Chapter 1] is consistent with Clausewitz's views on the essentiality of offensive action for success in war.)

Friction in War. Next I would like to mention an idea of Clausewitz that is often quoted, but not very well understood. This was his concept of "friction in war." Although he mentions this concept several times, it is best expressed in the following passage.

> Everything in war is very simple, but the simplest thing is difficult. The difficulties accumulate and end by producing a kind of friction that is inconceivable unless one has experienced war. . . . Countless unforeseeable minor incidents . . . combine to lower the general level of performance, so that one always falls far short of the intended goal. . . .
>
> Friction is the only concept that more or less corresponds to the factors that distinguish real war from war on paper. . . . None of [the military machine's] components is of one piece: each part is composed of individuals, every one of whom retains his potential of friction [and] the least important of whom may chance to delay things or somehow make them go wrong. . . .
>
> This tremendous friction . . . brings about effects that cannot be measured, just because they are largely due to chance. . . .
>
> Action in war is like movement in a resistant element. Just as the simplest and most natural of movements, walking, cannot easily be performed in water, so in war it is difficult for normal efforts to achieve even moderate results.[4]

Clausewitz thought and expressed himself in quantitative terms, as did the man he most admired and hated: Napoleon. He obviously thought of friction in war as a factor degrading combat performance, but he went on to say that it could not be measured. However, as in the cases already noted where Clausewitz was reluctant to assign specific values to analysis, modern quantitative historical analysis suggests that at least tentative values can be given to the effects of friction at different levels of military unit aggregation. Because of these modern developments, this concept of friction is perhaps more important in military theory than even Clausewitz realized, and I shall return to it later. Now let me turn to the concept of Clausewitz that I consider to be the essence of his quantitative approach to combat theory.

The "Law of Numbers"

It has been obvious to most soldiers and scholars who have studied *On War* that it is the most profound book on military theory ever written. We know, of course, that it is an unfinished work, and we suspect that had he been able to complete it in the fashion that he planned, he might have been able to integrate its many brilliant thoughts and concepts into a single, comprehensive theory. But he did not, and all of us who have attempted to distill that coherent theory from the book have been frustrated.

Nevertheless, it has long been evident to me that one of the most important passages in *On War* was Clausewitz's discussion of numbers. Let me quote the essence of the passage I call The Law of Numbers.

> If we . . . strip the engagement of all the variables arising from its purpose and circumstances, and disregard the fighting value of the troops involved (which is a given quantity), we are left with the bare concept of the engagement, a shapeless battle in which the only distinguishing factor is the number of troops on either side.

> These numbers, therefore, will determine victory. It is, of course, evident from the mass of abstractions I have made to reach this point that superiority of numbers in a given engagement is only one of the factors that determines victory. Superior numbers, far from contributing everything, or even a substantial part, to victory, may actually be contributing very little, depending on the circumstances.

> But superiority varies in degree. It can be two to one, or three or four to one, and so on, it can obviously reach the point where it is overwhelming.

> In this sense superiority of numbers admittedly is the most important factor in the outcome of an engagement so long as it is great enough to counterbalance all other contributing circumstances. It thus follows that as many troops as possible should be brought into the engagement at the decisive point.

Whether these forces prove adequate or not, we will at least have done everything in our power. This is the first principle of strategy. In the general terms in which it is expressed here it would hold true for Greeks and Persians, for Englishmen and Mahrattas, for Frenchmen and Germans.[5]

Just as important as the actual numbers—or perhaps more important—are the variable factors describing the engagement, which must be "stripped out" for analysis. Clausewitz also states specifically that the fighting value, or effectiveness, of a military force is a given quantity (i.e., quite measurable), and he implies clearly that the quality of forces will vary from nation to nation and among units within national forces. Finally, he tells us that his formulation of the relationship of numbers to victory is historically timeless and applicable in any geographic setting. I interpret the Law of Numbers to be a clear, unambiguous statement of a mathematical theory of combat, which Clausewitz asserts is valid throughout the course of history.

It is necessary to reconcile this interpretation of the Law of Numbers with the passages in Book Two of *On War* where Clausewitz argues with himself the twin questions of whether war is a science or an art, and whether or not war is amenable to theory. It is necessary also to reconcile this deterministic statement with the many references throughout *On War* to the role of chance in war, which has led many of his readers to assume that Clausewitz saw war as a random process with unpredictable results, rather than the mathematical process implied so clearly in the above quotation.

I had been considering how to reconcile these different interpretations for several years when something occurred that erased all of my lingering doubts about Clausewitz's approach to the theory of combat. This was a presentation at a conference of The Military Conflict Institute in April 1984. The speaker was talking about chance in war, and he quoted Clausewitz as one who emphasized that the outcome of battles was determined by chance. Suddenly a light flashed.

Despite some passages in *On War* that could be interpreted that way, Clausewitz did *not* think of chance as a roll of the dice determining victory or defeat. As is clear, for instance, in his famous quotation on "friction" (see page 27) he looked upon chance much as he did friction: one of many factors contributing to the confusion and chaos of battle. Indeed, the two concepts of chance and friction obviously overlapped in his mind.

To Clausewitz the word chance meant that there will always be problems in battle that a commander cannot possibly foresee, problems that arise either because of the "innate perversity" of inanimate objects, or of nature, or of man himself. Even though not individually foreseeable, these problems of chance are things that a commander can—if he is ready—deal with and control by means of his "genius" in the same way in which his genius will enable him to overcome the even less predictable actions and reactions of his opponent.

Suddenly what Clausewitz had written about chance became understandable and fully reconcilable with his Law of Numbers. The outcome of the battle will be determined by the genius of the commander in bringing to the critical point on the battlefield a force superior in numerical combat power; by his genius in being adaptable, and taking advantage of the "circumstances of the combat," including most of the variables of combat (not excepting friction and chance), and by his genius in assuring the highest value (quality) of his troops.

The light flashed again. Even though Clausewitz did not specifically say so, and even though he might not even have recognized the fact at the time of writing, his Law of Numbers is, indeed, a synthesis of a comprehensive theory of combat. Although Clausewitz never expressed that law as a formula, it is stated so clearly, and in such mathematical terms, that such a formula was unquestionably in his mind, and probably not subconsciously.

Here is how I derive the equation. First I show Clausewitz's concept of battle outcome as a ratio:

$$\text{Outcome} = \frac{N_r \cdot V_r \cdot Q_r}{N_b \cdot V_b \cdot Q_b}$$

Where: N = numbers of troops
V = variable circumstances affecting a force in battle
Q = quality of force
r = red force identifier
b = blue force identifier

If that is a valid relationship—as Clausewitz asserts, and I maintain fervently—then the following equation can be written for the Combat Power, P, of each of the opposing sides:

$$P = N \times V \times Q.$$

Just as Newton's physics can be summarized by the simple formula, $F = MA$, so too can Clausewitz's theory of combat be summarized in an equally simple formula: $P = NVQ$.

Chapter 4

The Three-to-One Theory of Combat

President Lincoln, Military Strategist and Theorist

THE SEARCH FOR a mathematical theory of combat was particularly evident in the mid-nineteenth century when advances in science brought about by experimentation and measurement seemed to make it possible to express all knowledge in precise mathematical formulas. One of the prevalent theories of combat was based on the dictum that an attacker needs a three-to-one strength superiority over the defender in order to win. One of the earliest expressions of this theory of which I am aware is found in the writings of Abraham Lincoln.

In the first two years of the American Civil War, President Abraham Lincoln found himself increasingly involved in the military decision-making process. This was in large part because he was—often with good reason—dissatisfied with the way in which his principal military subordinates were doing their jobs. At first the militarily untutored Lincoln was frustrated by the fact that when he tried to control operations, he could not do any better than his military subordinates had done or were doing. However, he was learning, and two of the most important things he learned are relevant to this book.[1]

In the first place, Lincoln learned that he did not have the training or experience to tell his military subordinates how to do routine military tasks. This led him to call upon and to use the military experience and capabilities first of a Henry W. Halleck, and later of a Ulysses S. Grant.

Secondly, experience taught Lincoln that his logical and intuitively strategic mind could grasp and deal with strategic problems better than most of his generals, and as well as the best. It was this recognition that led him, after the examples of Vicksburg and Chattanooga, to recognize and to utilize the strategic genius of Grant.

Before he finally selected Grant as his general in chief, Lincoln wrote to Halleck one of the most amazing documents ever penned by a chief of state. In his letter of 19 September 1863 to General Halleck, Lincoln revealed his sure grasp of military strategy and of some fundamentals of military theory—to say nothing of providing us with what is possibly the first true example of military operations research. That letter is quoted in full below:

Executive Mansion
September 19, 1863

Major General Halleck:

By General Meade's despatch to you of yesterday it appears that he desires your views and those of the government as to whether he shall advance upon the enemy. I am not prepared to order, or even advise, an advance in this case, wherein I know so little of particulars, and wherein he, in the field, thinks the risk is so great, and the promise of advantage so small.

And yet the case presents matters for very serious consideration in another aspect. These two armies confront each other across a small river, substantially mid-way between the two capitals, each defending its own capital, and menacing the other. General Meade estimates the enemy's infantry in front of him at not less than 40,000. Suppose we add fifty per cent to this for cavalry, artillery, and extra-duty men stretching as far as Richmond, making the whole force of the enemy 60,000.

General Meade, as shown by the returns, has with him, and between him and Washington, of the same classes of well men, over 90,000. Neither can bring the whole of his men into a battle; but each can bring as large a percentage in as the other. For a battle, then, General Meade has three men to General Lee's two. Yet it having been determined that choosing ground and standing on the defensive gives so great advantage that the three cannot safely attack the two, the three are left simply standing on the defensive also. If the enemy 60,000 are sufficient to keep our 90,000 away from Richmond, why, by the same rule, may not 40,000 of ours keep their 60,000 away from Washington, leaving us 50,000 to put to some other use? Having practically come to the mere defensive, it seems to be no economy at all to employ twice as many men for that object as are needed. With no object, certainly, to mislead myself, I can perceive no fault in this statement, unless we admit we are not the equal of the enemy, man for man. I hope you will consider it.

To avoid misunderstanding, let me say that to attempt to fight the enemy slowly back into his intrenchments at Richmond, and then to capture him, is an idea I have been trying to repudiate for quite a year.

My judgement is so clear against it that I would scarcely allow the attempt to be made if the general in command should desire to make it. My last attempt upon Richmond was to get McClellan, when he was nearer there than the enemy was, to run in ahead of him. Since then I have constantly desired the Army of the Potomac to make Lee's army, and not Richmond, its objective point. If our army cannot fall upon the enemy and hurt him where he is, it is plain to me it can gain nothing by attempting to follow him over a succession of intrenched lines into a fortified city.

Yours truly,
A. Lincoln

This may be the most remarkable military document ever written by a civilian. It reveals the thinking process of a highly logical mind—a mind clearly unmilitary, but equally clearly familiar with the fundamentals of strategy and with the basic principles of war.

The Three-to-One Rule of Thumb

In his letter to Halleck Lincoln based much of his argument on the thesis that the inherent battlefield superiority of defensive posture is such that a military planner or commander can count on defensive success if he has at least two-thirds the strength of the attacker. This, of course, is the corollary of the proposition that a commander or planner can count on an attack being successful if he has a three-to-one superiority over the defender. This is a rule of thumb so widely accepted that it has become virtually a military principle, and, indeed, a rudimentary theory of combat.

It is worth noting that this three-to-one rule or principle was a very new concept in Lincoln's time, and that his statement of its corollary in his letter to Halleck was, I believe, the first time the concept appears in serious military literature. The historical record shows that before the introduction of the conoidal bullet in the rifled musket (which occurred in most armies in the decade just prior to the Civil War) the advantage of defensive posture was substantially less than was the case in the Civil War and all subsequent wars.[2]

As a gross measure for campaign planning the three-to-one rule is undoubtedly useful and stands up fairly well under historical scrutiny. As a basis for forecasting battle outcomes, however, it is less reliable. So, let us examine the three-to-one rule more carefully. There is, in fact, (unlike Clausewitz's law of numbers) *less* here than meets the eye.

Table 4–1

The Three-to-One Model of Combat

PERSONNEL STRENGTH RATIO	ATTACKER SUCCESS CERTAIN	OUTCOME UNCERTAIN	DEFENDER SUCCESS CERTAIN
Attacker to Defender Strength Ratio	300% or more	200%	150% or less
Defender to Attacker Strength Ratio	33% or less	50%	67% or more

The three-to-one rule is shown as a model of combat. There is a spectrum of numerical strength ratios, which is divided into three zones. On the left, where the attacker's ratio to the defender is 300% or more, is the zone in which the model predicts certain attacker success. On the right, where the attacker's superiority is 150% or less, is the zone in which the defender's success is presumed certain. In between, in the area in which the attacker's superiority is between 300% and 150%, is a zone of uncertainty.

Unfortunately, historical statistics tell us that in the overwhelming majority of cases in modern war, the attacker to defender strength ratio is around 200%, thus in the zone of uncertainty. This simple model is not very helpful in these cases. What is worse, there have been enough important battles in which the outcome has not matched the model to raise serious questions about it. Let's look at two well-known battles of the Civil War, and then at a less well-known example from World War II.

Historical Examples of the Three-to-One Rule

At the Battle of Gettysburg, 76,000 Confederates attacked 90,000 Union troops. This gave the Union defenders a 116% strength superiority over the Confederate attackers, enough to guarantee Union success according to the three-to-one model. Yet it can be, and has been argued seriously that the Confederates would have won the battle if: Confederate General Ewell had been more energetic late on the first day; or Confederate General Longstreet had been more energetic on the second day; or Union General Warren had not miraculously saved Little Roundtop from the Confederates on the second day. Although many (perhaps most) historians do not believe that Union success was certain, the fact is the Union won.

When the Battle of Antietam opened, General McClellan had a 300% strength superiority over Lee, a superiority he retained for most of the day, until the final division of Jackson's corps arrived on the battlefield in the afternoon. The model says McClellan's success was certain, but he didn't win. At the end of the day, the forces actually engaged in the battle were 59,000 bloody and exhausted Union troops, opposed by 37,000 bloodier and more exhausted Confederates, a 160% Northern superiority, or a 63% Southern inferiority. This is at the lower end of the zone of uncertainty, almost to the point where defender success was certain; and, of course, the defenders had been successful, since they had not been driven off the field. Yet again, there are many historians (and again, perhaps most) who believe that if Burnside had not allowed himself to be held up at the bridge, ever since known by his name, the Union would have won, despite McClellan's timidity or stupidity in holding out his 20,000-man reserve. In other words, the model was wrong at the outset and inconclusive at the close of the battle.

Finally, let's look at a bloody four day battle in Italy at Lanuvio, south of Rome, in May–June 1944, between the 34th American Infantry Division and the German 3rd Pazer Grenadier Division. The Americans—flushed with victory from their breakout from the Anzio beachhead—had nearly a three-to-one strength superiority, and more than a three-to-one firepower edge over the Germans, who had been battered back in the three previous days from their positions overlooking Anzio. American success was certain according to our three-to-one model, but, the Americans were stopped cold by the Germans. The model was wrong again.

Why was it wrong in these examples? It was wrong because it considered only raw strength numbers, and ignored the other two general considerations mentioned in Clausewitz's Law of Numbers: the circumstances of the battle and the respective quality of the opposing forces.

Actually, despite the arguments of the historians, the three-to-one model was probably right in the case of Gettysburg. So long as General Meade was willing to stand and fight, the quality of his troops and the strength of his defensive positions, enhanced by terrain favorable to defense, meant that Lee probably had no chance of winning that battle. The critical considerations were the will and ability of General Meade, the strength of the Union defenses, and the nature of the terrain. The model ignores these considerations; it was right only by happenstance.

At Antietam the critical considerations were: the pusillanimity of General McClellan and his lack of control over the battle; the stupidity of General Burnside; and the determination and skill of Generals Lee, Longstreet, and Jackson. The model ignored these and thus failed in its predictions.

At Lanuvio the critical considerations were again those that Clausewitz called the circumstances of the battle, and the value of the troops. As to the battle circumstances, the Germans had fallen back to previously prepared fortifications, in terrain favorable to the defense. They had mobility superiority over the Americans in terms of proportion of armored vehicles to infantry. A first-rate German division was fighting against an average American division. The model could not deal with any of these things. Instead of American success being certain, as the three-to-one model suggests, a more sophisticated analysis would show that the attackers could not win.

The three-to-one model of combat was better than previous formulations, but it did not always work very well. Nevertheless, this initial effort to formulate a quantitative expression for victory conditions in combat was highly significant as the forerunner of more complex theories.

Chapter 5

The Soviet Approach to a Theory of Combat

Soviet Military Capability

MODERN RUSSIANS ARE as convinced that there are some immutable laws and relationships in warfare as their predecessor, D.I. Mendeleyev, was with respect to a theory of atomic structure, which led him to develop the first periodic table of elements. While Soviet military research is clouded with secrecy, enough is known to describe the Soviet approach to a theory of combat. There can be no doubt about the importance of this effort.

The Russians are not ten foot tall super soldiers. Nor are they backward, untutored, unimaginative peasants who do not understand how to flush a toilet.

Generalizations can be dangerous oversimplifications if one is attempting to establish precise parameters and bases for detailed, specific comparisons. They are, however, useful in the portrayal of a broad, impressionistic picture. Let's apply some generalizations to the current Soviet armed forces, before looking at specifics.

The Soviet military establishment is highly professional at the top. Soviet officers are well-trained; their military educational program is more intensive and rigorous than that of the United States Army. It probably has the most efficient general staff system in the world today. This system is based to a considerable extent upon the German Army General Staff as it existed in the early twentieth century, but is possibly even more efficient, if probably less imaginative. However, Soviet officers, at least at the top levels, are encouraged to be imaginative. Major emphasis in training and doctrine is placed on surprise, mobility, and the seizure of the initiative in battle.

Soviet weapons are good. On the average they are slightly less advanced technologically than ours, but they are generally simpler, easier to use and maintain, and much more numerous. The Soviets know and use the most modern and advanced technologies. Maybe they are less technologically advanced than we are, but in practical terms (as demonstrated, for instance, in the technology of equipment fielded in meaningful numbers) the differential is inconsequential, perhaps even in their favor.

Although Soviet military literature as well as the educational and training systems preach the military virtues of imagination and initiative, the political and social systems tend to induce rigidity and conformity and to discourage initiative. Soviet military training tends to be selective and cautious. The result is that rigidity often seems to prevail over the espoused military virtues.

At lower levels and in the ranks, it is probable that rigidity and conformity overpower imagination and initiative. Although education in Russia is good, it is likely that the average Russian soldier is more stolid and less susceptible than ours to being trained or inspired to flexibility and imagination in use of weapons. Soviet training emphasizes the basics to achieve uniformity and adequate performance at the lower combat unit levels from crew or squad to battalion. Although nominally encouraged, initiative at the lower echelons is mainly directed at better accomplishment of assigned tasks. The Soviet system neither wants nor could withstand a group of junior-level Pattons. That type of initiative, if it exists, is almost certainly reserved for senior commanders. However, Soviet soldiers are tough! They do what they are told. Russians traditionally have been good defensive soldiers, who can also perform well in offensive warfare under good leadership.

On balance, then, our major potential enemy is formidable, though far from unbeatable. The Soviet-German War of 1941 –1945 showed clearly that the Soviets can be both dangerous and vulnerable. Quantitatively, and in a very gross and average sense, the Germans had a better than two-to-one superiority over the Russians in battlefield skill. However, the Russians outnumbered the Germans by more than three-to-one, and they won the war. It is doubtful if today the West–East average qualitative superiority is anything like the two-to-one advantage the Germans had—if, indeed, there is any superiority at all.

The Soviets view war, and the preparation for war, as a science. This perception leads them to conclude that war can be studied, quantified, and somewhat predicted. As a result, what we call operations research is not an awesome subject studied by military scholars or "whiz kids," but rather something they practice and use in force planning and field operations. Their approach is that of engineers, applying science pragmatically.

The Soviets study carefully the military thinking and accomplishments of Western armies. They copy us in some things; they prefer their own methods in others. Some of our concepts and procedures they apparently find literally laughable, but they ignore nothing that we do. In this they are following the example of total objectivity, which was one of the hallmarks of the German General Staff in its heyday.

It is not easy for us to find out what the Soviets are doing in military affairs, because they are so secretive in their efforts to protect their procedures, weapons, and activities from Western eyes. However, it really doesn't matter much. Even if theirs was an open society like ours, we would probably pay little more attention to the details of their military system and its operations than we do currently. Despite Soviet secrecy, there is a tremendous mass of published and available materials that tells us a great deal about the Soviet military establishment. This is particularly true in military literature, largely because the upper levels of the establishment cannot communicate with the rank and file without such publications. It is a rich literature, particularly in military history, and we can learn from it if we choose.

Just because the Soviets follow certain practices and have certain ways of thinking and acting is no reason for us to copy them. Their military establishment is good, but so is ours. Nevertheless, while it is not necessary to copy them to be as good as, or better than, they are, it behooves us to pay attention to what they do. While it is useful to be aware of their weaknesses, it is even more important to know and understand everything that contributes to their capabilities. Unfortunately, we Americans too often pay only lip service to the old admonition "Know the enemy." For the most part, only a small and dedicated band of scholars and intelligence specialists are aware of these things.

Soviet Use of Military History

My own concerns regarding this arcane subject of understanding the Soviets are to a great extent focused on their interest in military history and their reasons for this interest. It is apparent from the bulk of Soviet publications on combat operations of World War II that considerable work has been done and is being done to make the details of the experience of that war available and useful to the current Soviet military organization. The importance of analyzing and profiting from historical experience is emphasized frequently and strongly by the military leaders of the Soviet Union in Soviet military literature. For example, General P. G. Grigorenko[1] of the Frunze Academy in a book entitled *Methodology of Military Scientific Investigation* (Moscow, 1959), indicated clearly that Soviet operations research for military planning purposes relies extensively upon analysis of historical data, particularly data from World War II operations on the Eastern Front. They have sizable organizations that study the lessons of history for their application to future warfare.

While the Soviets do not make their official publications and research results readily available, the extensive military literature they produce (numerous periodicals and 300-odd books on military affairs annually) reveals much of the general emphases and results of Soviet military historical research. Even a cursory review of this literature provides an awesome picture of the kinds of results they are achieving, and the influence of these results on evolving doctrine, strategic planning, and force planning.

In the May and June 1981 issues of the *Military History Journal,* a list of 197 military history topics selected by the Soviet General Staff, the Military History Institute, and the faculties of the major Soviet military academies (war colleges) was published for study during the decade of the 1980s. This was an *official* announcement of a major decision by the senior military intellectual authorities of the Soviet Union, in a widely read, widely circulated, official journal of the Soviet Armed Forces. The authors and readers are military professionals who treat the use of military history as an integral part of their work, not just a hobby, or something reserved for off-duty relaxed reading.

The purpose of this intensive study, ongoing as these words are written, was stated as follows:

To research laws governing development of military theory and practice and to prepare concrete proposals on how to use historical military experience to solve contemporary military problems.

I have already mentioned the Russian scientist Dimitri Mendeleyev, who established one of the most important theoretical foundations of modern physics when he published the first periodic table of the elements in 1870, a theory enabling him—and others since—to predict the discovery of elements at that time undreamed of. Soviet military theorists are seeking a "periodic table" of military combat.

The Soviet View of Military History

The Soviet view of military history is best understood by reading the views of a high ranking Soviet officer and military theorist. This section presents excerpts of an article "Contemporary Problems of Military History," written by Marshal V. Kulikov and published in the *Military History Journal*, December 1976. Marshal Kulikov was then Chief of the Soviet General Staff and is now (1987) Commander of the Warsaw Pact Forces. Kulikov stated:

Military science, including a broad knowledge of military history, plays a leading role in strengthening the defense capabilities of the Soviet Union, and in improving the armed forces and heightening their combat readiness. The Institute of Military History of the Ministry of Defense, which was created by a decree of the Central Committee of the Communist Party of the Soviet Union, has made an important contribution by expanding the theoretical level of scientific research in the field of military history.

Soviet military science has always depended heavily on Soviet military experience. By analyzing the history of the Soviet Union and of other states, and exploring the experiences of past wars, military history reveals the way in which military events have tended to obey the fundamental laws of war. This understanding permits military science to interpret present problems and approach future ones correctly.

Knowledge of military history also plays an important role in improving the professional competence of military cadres. It helps develop flexibility in military thinking, a deeper understanding of the complexity of warfare, and the habit of making sound decisions on the basis of combat experience.

In addition, military history is an effective tool in the ideological and historical-patriotic education of the people, and in molding the patriotic and internationalist character of Soviet citizens.

In order to relate the results of military historical research to contemporary requirements, it is necessary to select and analyze those aspects of diversified combat experience that can answer the questions posed by today's military needs, and those that have implications for the future.

A comprehensive analysis of past wars, including the changes that have occurred recently in the military field, demands from military historians, philosophers, sociologists, and economists an increase not only in methodological expertise. Military historians should constantly study and be aware of contemporary theories of military art, *their practical applicability, and the future require-ments that may result from them.*[2] Military theoreticians, in turn, must be well acquainted with military history.

The current level of the development of the science of military history calls for wide use of mathematical methods, including computers. Such techniques are essential for the proper utilization of the huge amounts of very rich archival material, which is the fundamental source for military history research.

The close connection between military history and current problems facing the armed forces should be the touchstone of research done by military historians.

The prime task of research in military history remains the qualitative analysis of World War II experience. However, this should not be limited to strictly military problems, but should encompass such matters as the political, economic, social, and ideological aspects of warfare.

It should be noted that, up to this time, research on World War II has paid insufficient attention to the Stavka of the Supreme Command, the General Staff, and the staffs of the various services and arms, and to their efforts to command and control the armed forces, both in the war as a whole and in individual campaigns and operations. There is also not enough research on the work of army group commanders and their staffs (or fleet commanders and their staffs) in preparing for and carrying out various operations, or of commanders and staffs at tactical levels in organizing and conducting battles.

Since the Soviet officer corps includes many officers without combat experience, military history research in the field of tactics becomes extremely important. Special research is necessary to exploit the combat experience of generals, admirals, and other officers, so that today's officers can learn the actual working methods of commanders, staffs, and political branches during the preparation for an operation and during various combat situations. All this should be presented not only from the point of view of tactical necessity but with consideration for the moral and psychological elements that count so much in war.

The following problems in military art that emerged with heightened importance during World War II need more thorough evaluation:

the creation and utilization of strategic reserves

planning and conducting strategic and operational regrouping of forces

surprise

breakthrough

the organization and conduct of meeting engagements

assault crossing of rivers

encirclement, and the destruction of encircled troops

achievement of high rates of advance

the organization and conduct of operations in extreme northern latitudes, in forested and mountainous terrain, and in deserts

partisan operations and their cooperation with operations of regular forces.

Also insufficiently researched are the moral and psychological factors in war, the use of weapons and equipment by crews and commanders of small units (or ships) in various combat situations, and combat operations in various theaters of war and during different seasons. Scientific historical research in this field could be quite useful in the further improvement of military technology and in finding more effective methods of troop training.

World War II experience includes a great deal of material on the organization of defense at various levels and on actual defensive operations in both main and secondary sectors. This, too, deserves analysis and study, for it would help the officer corps in a thorough analysis of all the problems related to contemporary defense.

In developing contemporary military theory, one cannot limit oneself to the experiences of past wars alone. It is also necessary to study the present structure of the Soviet forces, their training and maneuvers, and the development of current military thought.

It is necessary, as well, to study in depth the main tendencies in the development of military art in the leading capitalist states, and especially their experience in commanding large formations composed of ground air, and naval forces in various theaters of operations in World War II, and to discover the major trends in the development of their armed forces in the postwar years. It would be of great interest to study the theory and practice of combat operations in local wars conducted by imperialists, and to review them not only from the aggressor's point of view, but from the point of view of the victims of aggression.

The results of the study of past wars can be of appreciable use only if they reach a wide military audience and are consistently introduced into the operational training of commanders and staffs at all levels.

The creative minds of military historians should search constantly for new topics for military history research. It is essential that the old and already proven methods of historical research be skillfully combined with contemporary technology in order to expedite and facilitate the process of scientific research, especially in the use of vast stores of statistical material. This approach would advance the quality and effectiveness of research, so its results could be better used in practical work within the armed forces.

Soviet Application of Historical Studies

The Soviets do not limit themselves to using military history for the formulation of general doctrinal concepts.[3] They use the results of their historical studies to provide their military men with the tools that enable them to put their doctrine into practice.

Drawing primarily from the records of "The Great Patriotic War,"—the Eastern Front of World War II—the Soviets have dissected and synthesized the details of engagements in such a way that operations in various categories may be assembled, averaged, and expressed quantitatively in terms of coefficients that will permit predictions of likely outcomes of each category, under given circumstances. At the heart of the Soviet military planning and analysis process is a concept of "correlation of forces and means" discussed in some detail below.

This concept of correlation of forces is the basis for a total process of static and potentially dynamic force comparison and is applied at the various levels of command. The averages or expected values derived from historical research are systematically catalogued and computerized so that they can be manipulated easily and rapidly by field commanders since the circumstances (and thus the factors) of each problem situation vary. The results of this process are objective, empirically based, and adaptable readily to modern data processing methods.

The Soviets believe that war can be studied scientifically to determine its basic nature, and that fundamental laws can be deciphered through careful scrutiny. The Soviets believe that there are predictable causes for the outcomes of battles. The Soviets seek an understanding of the essence of war through analysis of historical events and identification of the various factors that contribute to battle outcomes. They believe that careful association of factors with the influences they had on the outcomes, and the melding of these factors with similar ones from other actions, can provide insights of substance for assessment of current operational and force development problems.

The Soviets do not exclude professional judgment, but they focus primarily upon historical analogy and quantitative analysis. For them, each serves the other. History provides data. Qualitative and quantitative analysis makes the data understandable. Objectivity comes from comprehensiveness rather than selectivity in the historical research. "Norms" are derived for all manner of questions that the process must satisfy: ammunition expenditure rates, casualty rates, rates of advance and withdrawal, coherence in force behavior. Once approved, the norms enjoy organizational acceptance until proved wrong. Then they will be recalculated as new experience provides new raw data. There are two key factors: first, avoidance of drawing too much from any single historical event (as Americans tend to do in their rare uses of military history); second, continuous updating of the data bases through research and continuous refinement of norms in the inductive process.

Soviet military structure tends toward greater rigidities and conservatism than its counterparts in the West. Decisions at the lower echelons must be made in close accordance with the policies of the leadership. The Soviets recognize, however, that unless there is adequate guidance for subordinate commanders and staffs, too many problems would necessarily be referred back to higher headquarters, or to Moscow, for resolution. The existence of norms, derived from objective assessments of numerous historical military engagements and approved by the highest authority, provides just such guidance. In planning at tactical and operational levels there is no need for debate over whether this or that historical event has any relevance to the problem at hand. The characteristics of the current problem can be fed into a computer already stocked with approved historical norms. The computer will search its files, pick out a match and very rapidly issue the essentials of operations orders or other action documents for the staff.

The magnitude of the Soviet effort in pursuit of a theory of combat is impressive. They school their officers in the scientific method far more thoroughly than we do. Quantitative analytical techniques are taught throughout their military educational system; these are not just a specialty of a few officers. The Soviets have dozens of officers with doctoral degrees in military science conducting research and publishing treatises on all aspects of war.

Soviet planners apply the data derived from historical research to their operational plans. They press hard to avoid leaving anything to chance. They do not see themselves as practioners of an art. They are scientists and engineers applying the scientific process.

Correlation of Forces and Means

The ultimate expression of the Soviet application of military history to contemporary military science is in what they call the "correlation of forces and means." This is both a mathematical model of combat and a theory of combat. The reader is enjoined, as he continues into the following chapters, to note how closely the Soviet concept of a theory of combat, based on historical analysis and expressed in a mathematical model, matches my own approach. Here, in slightly abridged form, is the official statement of this concept.[4]

The Correlation of Forces and Means is an objective indicator of the *fighting power* of opposing sides, which permits a determination of the degree of superiority of one of them over the other. The correlation of forces and means is determined by means of a comparison of existing data on the quantitative and qualitative descriptions of subunits, units, combined units and armaments of one's own forces and those of the enemy. Correct calculations and an evaluation of the correlation of forces and means assist in making well-founded decisions during training and during an operation and in the timely creation and maintenance of the necessary superiority over an enemy in selected sectors. An analysis of the correlation of forces and means also permits one to make a deeper investigation into the essence of operations, battles and engagements which have been carried out.

Correlation of forces and means is determined on strategic, operational and tactical levels. It is usually calculated for the entire zone of combat operations in the main and other sectors during preparation for an operation. An estimate of the quantity of forces and means necessary for accomplishing set missions in the main and other sectors is made, the combat composition and grouping of troops and also their modes of operation are elaborated, and a maneuver aimed at maintaining a favorable correlation of forces and means during the operation is stipulated on the basis of the established correlation of forces and means.

A correlation of forces and means was determined during the Great Patriotic War for personnel and for the number of combined units (divisions, brigades, battalions), tanks and self-propelled guns, artillery pieces and mortars (usually by caliber), antitank weapons and aircraft. Each side's provision of ammunition and fuel was also taken into account. The *combat and numerical strength* of our own groupings of forces which had been drawn upon for the accomplishment of the combat mission and the enemy's opposing groupings of forces formed the initial data for the estimation. This method of calculating the correlation of forces and means is also useful for today's conditions, especially if troop formations, armament, and military equipment with roughly identical *combat capabilities* are compared. A battalion, special forces company, squadron, or ship is taken as a tactical computational unit, and a division, individual brigade or regiment of a service of the armed forces is taken as an operational unit. The numbers of personnel, missile launchers, nuclear ammunition, tanks, artillery pieces and mortars, aircraft, and ships are compared at each command echelon.

In a case where combat capabilities differ significantly, coefficients of comparability of combat potentials that have been estimated beforehand are used. If, for example, the combat capability of a 122mm howitzer (of a battery or division or a motorized rifle battalion) for inflicting damage on the enemy is taken as the unit and the combat capabilities of other subunits of one's own forces and those of the enemy are compared, then it is possible to arrive at coefficients of comparability of combat potentials which may be used to estimate and compare the combat capabilities of any grouping for forces of each side.

For a more objective determination of the correlation of forces and means, the following are also taken into account: the peculiarities of organization of each side's forces, their levels of combat training, the national composition of the forces, their levels of combat training, and their moral and fighting qualities, the capabilities of reconnaissance forces and means, the tactical and technical data on armament and military equipment, experience in conducting combat operations, firmness in troop control, material and equipment provision, the nature of the terrain and the engineering equipment for it.

Those factors which lend themselves to a mathematical expression are compared with the aid of one or another of the coefficients, while the rest are expressed in terms of "superior" or "inferior." Modern computer equipment is used for speeding up the computation of the correlation of forces and means. Possible changes in the correlation of forces and means during combat operations can be determined with the aid of modeling.

We must not underestimate a potential foe that is able so skillfully to integrate the past, the present, and the future.

Chapter 6

Toward an American Theory of Combat

The Application of Science to War

IN GENERAL, AND with only a few significant exceptions, until very recently American military theorists have shown little interest in the concept of a comprehensive theory or science of combat. While most Americans who think about such things are strong believers in the application of science to war, they seem not to believe, paradoxically, that waging war can be scientific, but that it is an art rather than a science. Even scientists concerned with and involved in military affairs, who perhaps overemphasize the role of science in war, also tend to believe that war is a random process conducted by unpredictable human beings, and thus not capable of being fitted into a scientific theoretical structure.

That aspect of the paradox relating the application of science to war became increasingly pronounced during and since World War II. This has been manifested in two principal fashions: the application of technology to the design and development of implements of war, and the study of a wide variety of combat phenomena through military operations research.

American scientists have been generally successful in the first of these activities: the application of technology to weaponry. This success, however, has not produced the results that might have been anticipated. Despite the unquestioned lead of the

United States and its allies in technology, the Russians, though technologically relatively backward, have been able to keep up with us and to produce comparable weapons as rapidly as we have. Moreover, some of our new weapons have been disappointing in terms of actual performance versus expected performance, and the very high costs of new weapons have prevented production of the numbers that military men have considered to be adequate.

The experience of American scientists in operations research has been, if anything, even more frustrating. Despite brilliant success at solving individual problems, operations research has not been able to verify its accomplishments or to distill them into a coherent theory. In fact, the opposite may be true because the results of operations research tend to be confusing without an overall theory to place them into context. The situation is particularly disappointing in the field of combat modeling. Elegant mathematical formulae abound, purporting to describe the battlefield operations and interactions of weapons and forces in detail from duels between individual combat soldiers, through engagements between small units, to battles involving larger aggregations of units. Thousands of computers are in use in the American defense research community, operating combat models and simulations, producing results designed to provide useful insights to planners and commanders on how to achieve success in battle. Unfortunately there is a major problem: no two sets of results agree. The combat models are not validated, and there is a general lack of confidence in them.

Problems With Combat Models

An event in 1977 brought home to a number of people in the American defense research community the fact that there must be something seriously wrong with the American operations research effort in the field of combat models and simulations. This was a conference on models, which took place at Leesburg in northern Virginia near Washington, in the fall of that year. Incompatability among combat models and the inability to get similar results from them even if they were used to analyze the same scenario were deplored by several of the speakers at that conference. Clearly many of these inconsistent and incompatible models must give wrong results. But which were unreliable? No one, in fact, could be sure that they were not all unreliable. Two or three speakers suggested that this state of anarchy would continue until someone produced a theory of combat.

Among those who pondered the results of this conference were two highly respected mathematical modelers, both based on the West Coast, who got together to compare their notes. These were Mr. Lawrence Low of SRI International, who had been the moderator of the Leesburg meeting, and Dr. James Taylor, a professor in the Operations Research Department of the U.S. Naval Postgraduate School, in Monterey, California. Both were aware of work I had been doing in analysis of the results of historical combat experience. They knew that I had been seeking patterns in combat experience in World War II, and in the adaptation of that historical research to the development of a model of historical combat. It occurred to them that an historical approach such as mine might provide the basis for the development of the theory of combat asked for so plaintively at Leesburg.

I had attended the Leesburg conference, and so I was pleased to accept an invitation from Low and Taylor to join them in March 1978 at the Naval Postgraduate School for three days of discussions. From that informal meeting emerged an effort to try to accomplish what Jomini and Clausewitz had tried to do a century and a half earlier, what Fuller had tried to do earlier in this century; and what the Russians are trying so intensively to do at this very time. We agreed to work together toward the formulation of a theory of combat.

The Military Conflict Institute

From the original meeting early in 1978 emerged an informal group of people calling themselves the Committee to Develop a Theory of Combat. This has now been formalized into The Military Conflict Institute, chartered as a non-profit organization, headed by Dr. Donald S. Marshall. Its purpose is to foster a scientific understanding of the nature of military conflict, and its first goal is to produce a theory of combat.

From the outset there was a consensus among those of us involved in this effort that it made sense to base the development of a theory of combat upon an inductive approach through the analysis of actual combat experience. We felt that there were four strong reasons for this.

First, the future does not emerge from a vacuum, but is always an extrapolation of the past. Second, the reactions and behavior of human beings in response to the stimuli and situations of combat have not changed over history, despite changes in the implements of battle. Third, projections of the future, in terms of the performance of the new products of modern technology in battle, and their interaction with human behavior, can be estimated best by relating test and experiment data to trends evident in past conflicts. And fourth, it should be possible, with a large, reliable data base, to perceive patterns and logical relationships in the transformation of input data to quantified outcomes determinable from battle statistics. This not only could provide insights into the interactions of inputs and variables, and thus permit reasonable quantification of factors effecting combat, but it could also lead to an overall theory of combat.

We visualized a program with two broad objectives.

First, we would analyze modern combat experience in order to:

Identify major processes that occur in combat;
Identify major factors that influence combat outcomes;
Define cause and effect relationships among:
    Combat force elements
    Battle processes and factors;
Relate combat elements at the outset of a battle to the quantified outcome of the battle.

Second, the results of this analysis would, in turn, be expected to provide:

A logical, coherent, consistent theoretical structure for developing, assessing, and validating combat models and simulations;
Improved defense decision-making by:
    Increasing confidence in model outputs;
    Increasing the utility of models as analytical tools;
    Facilitating model validation;
    Developing more reliable and realistic simulations for training;
    Creating a framework for consistent and reliable data bases.

Ours was, therefore, an inductive, as opposed to deductive, approach. Since the definitions of these terms in dictionaries and encyclopedias can be confusing, let me define them as I use them here.

Deductive reasoning proceeds from the general to the specific, as follows: An accepted general statement (which may be true or false) is applied to individual cases by syllogism. For instance: "All dogs are animals. This is a dog. Therefore this is an animal." When the general premise is true, deduction is certain. When the general premise is uncertain, deduction must be dubious.

Inductive reasoning proceeds from the specific to the general. Individual cases are studied by experiment or observation. The results of a number of experiments or observations provide a basis for the enunciation of a general principle. For instance: "All metals tested expand when they are heated. Therefore, all metals are likely to expand when heated."

One or more such principles of inductive reasoning leads the analyst to the postulation of an hypothesis. This hypothesis can become a workable theory only when the analyst is satisfied that he has examined most of the likely alternative hypotheses, or possibilities. It becomes a law when *all* possibilities have been examined. However, one cannot always be certain that all—or even most—possibilities have been examined, and the analyst must be aware that the next individual case may not be consistent with hypothesis or theory. Obviously, the more cases considered, the more reliable is the inductive process.

The remainder of this book will be devoted to presenting the story of relevant work I have undertaken with my colleagues in The Military Conflict Institute, or with other colleagues in a small, private research organization called the Historical Evaluation and Research Organization—which we usually modestly refer to by its acronym: HERO. The work of HERO has focussed on the compilation and analysis of military data, and on the refinement and use of the Quantified Judgment Model (QJM).

Among other things, we have attempted to gain a better understanding of those somewhat ephemeral aspects of combat, which are often referred to as "combat variables," "combat elements," and "combat processes." In an earlier work, I devoted considerable attention to combat variables.[1] Proceeding from that work, I have tentatively identified the elements I hope to see better defined within a theory of combat. These are:

Forces:	Units
	People
	Materiel

Circumstances:	Environmental
	Operational
	Behavioral

Doctrine:	Strategy
	Operations
	Tactics
	Technique

I have also tentatively identified the major combat processes as follows:

Effectiveness
Attrition
Movement
Command (including control, communications, and intelligence
  gence
Friction
Suppression
Disruption

Practical Value of a Theory of Combat

A theory of combat would provide a framework for assuring consistency in the modeling or simulation of combat, solving the problem described earlier in this chapter; that is, the lack of consistency in models. A theory of combat would not, by itself, provide assurance to decision makers and planners that their models are true predictors of the future, but such a theory would make it more difficult to base major policy decisions on dangerous assumptions and false conclusions, and would assure the provision of consistent, mutually comparable simulation outputs. Should two models, dealing with the same situation or scenario, provide different predictions, the reasons for such differences would be easily determinable, and then issues arising from the differences could be analyzed on their merits, not by intuition or guesswork.

A theory of combat would help analysts to understand human behavior in combat. It is doubtful if anything has baffled analysts and military planners more than the effect of human or behavioral factors upon battle outcomes. Napoleon has been quoted as saying that "the moral is to the physical as three is to one." Most modern military judgment would tend to accept some such relationship between moral (or behavioral) forces and physical facts and factors in combat. However, practically all of our combat models and simulations ignore behavioral considerations because analysts have not yet devised a satisfactory procedure for measuring the impact of human behavior in combat. If Napoleon was even close to right in regarding the relative importance of physical and behavioral factors (and later in this book I shall demonstrate that he was) then failure to consider behavioral factors in simulation and planning gravely endangers our national security.

A theory of combat would provide specific means for dealing with the influence of behavioral factors. This in turn would open many opportunities for solving problems that until now have been intractable, such as assessing the suppressive effects of fire (which can effectively inhibit hostile action, while doing relatively little physical damage) and determining the nature and effects of disruption.

A theory of combat would also provide a yardstick for the evaluation of military judgment, to the benefit of both military and civilian decision-makers. Men in uniform would no longer have to apologize for lack of documented support for their expressions of professional opinion based upon experience. Civilians could no longer criticize such opinions as being vague or intuitive. Documentation and corroboration would be found in the formulations of the theory of combat.

Should a professional military man present arguments not fully consistent with a theory of combat, he would have no reason to feel insulted if a civilian superior demanded that he provide documented support of his unorthodox military judgment. Indeed, he should be eager to demonstrate how he can improve the theory of combat.

At least equally important is the contribution to tactical doctrine that would flow from a theory of combat. At last soldiers would understand the relationships among the elements and among the processes of combat, and the interrelationships between elements and processes.

One practical manifestation of this improved understanding of the structure of combat would be transformation of the idea of "combat multipliers" or "force multipliers" from some vague, exhortatory concept to a real battle planning tool for commanders at all levels. A division commander, familiar with his own resources, and having a reasonable perception of the enemy's strengths and capabilities, would be able to calculate the effects of terrain, defensive posture, weather, mobility, and the like upon the possibilities of successfully accomplishing his mission. Similarly, he could calculate what the enemy commander could do to improve *his* chance of success. The Estimate of the Situation would then become a scientific process in its contribution to the art of decision making.

The transformation of force multipliers from vague generalities to concrete battle-planning instrumentalities will be as useful to leaders of brigades, battalions, companies, and platoons as to division commanders. This process will not change the art of war into a science. But it will mean that even the pedestrian commander will be able to do a workmanlike job of battle planning.

Human Behavior and Battle Outcomes

As suggested above, the fundamental problem in any effort to generalize and formulate theories of combat is the influence of presumably unpredictable human behavior on outcomes of battle. The key to developing theories of combat is unquestionably a systematic study of military history. To discern the common relationships among the various processes of combat requires careful review of the specifics of a large number of conflicts. But the perverse refusal of human beings to fit themselves into consistent patterns of behavior on the battlefield makes the search a long and difficult one. Until a method of determining such patterns can be established, the search for a theory of combat will never be satisfied.

The Process of Theory Development

Early in the life of the Committee to Develop a Theory of Combat, one member, Dr. Janice B. Fain, provided her colleagues with some thoughts on how we might be able to proceed.

With her permission I shall attempt to summarize some of her conclusions.

I have already noted there was a consensus that our approach to the development of a theory of combat was to be inductive rather than deductive. Dr. Fain's ideas about past theory development were, I think, convincing in demonstrating that this was not a traditional approach to theory development. This is always a chaotic process, but when viewed with the benefit of hindsight, one can discern seven key steps employed in theory development in past intellectual history, and then she showed the significance of these steps in the formulation of the modern theory of gravitation.

The steps are:

1. Observation: Accurate, detailed description of a phenomenon or phenomena.
2. Identification of Measurables: Identification of quantities that are characteristic of the phenomenon to be measured, and selection of the units of measurement.
3. Data Collection: Collection of a large and significant number of the measurables.
4. Data Analysis: Derivation of empirical relationships among the measurables.
5. Definition of Derivative Concepts: Some of the measurables may be found to occur together frequently; it may be convenient to re-name the group by a single name.
6. Formulation of General Principles (Hypotheses): Statement of general principles from which the empirical relationship can be derived.
7. Hypothesis Testing: Derivation of logical consequences of the general principles; for instance: "if A, then B." This is followed by experimentation to check the predictions from the theory.

Dr. Fain then summarized the development of modern gravitational theory in terms of her seven-step structure as follows:

1. Observation. There have been thousands of years of observing the night skies by curious human beings; observations have been recorded by such scholars as Hipparchus (ca. 150 B.C.), Ptolemy (ca. 140 A.D.), Copernicus (1473–1543), Brahe (1546–1601), Galileo (1564–1642), Kepler (1571–1630), and Newton (1642–1727) (and many others).

2. Identification of Measurables. In antiquity, stars and planets were catalogued by Hipparchus and Ptolemy, who did their measurements in terms of celestial latitudes and longitudes, and formulated a geocentric theory of relationships of sun, moon, stars and planets around a central Earth. This theory was accepted for more than a millenium until Copernicus produced his heliocentric theory.

3. Data Collection. Although Copernicus was able to make use of a thousand years of accumulations of observations to introduce his revolutionary heliocentric theory, the limits of human visual acuity would not permit any major enlargement or refinement of the basic data. Tycho Brahe, with the most advanced pre-telescopic instruments was, however, able to improve the measurement of planetary positions and motion. Early in the seventeenth century, and shortly after Brahe's death, the scope and precision of data collection were improved tremendously by the invention of the telescope,and its almost immediate application by Galileo.

4. Data Analysis. The work of Ptolemy and Copernicus were, of course, examples of data analysis. But significant post-Copernican analysis was done by Johannes Kepler, whose studies led him to postulate the laws bearing his name, concerning the nature of the orbits of planets around the sun and the relationship of the orbits to the sun, permitting for the first time reasonably accurate determinations of distances between and among the sun and its planets.

5. Derivative Concepts. The work of Kepler provides an excellent example of two derivative concepts: the relationship of elliptical orbits of the planets to the sun, and the importance of planetary periods as determinants of distance in solar system space.

6. General Principles. From the work of Kepler and Galileo, and from his own observations, Sir Isaac Newton was able to develop the fundamental principle or law that became the basis for all subsequent gravitational theory:

$$F = GMM'/d^2.$$

7. Testing. Since Newton's time, his law of gravitation has led to the discovery of new planets, and the prediction of planetary orbits have been confirmed by subsequent observation. Further, testing has led to modifications in the original theory to fit the observations and concepts of modern physics.

It is this process of inductive reasoning that I intend to follow throughout the remainder of this book in an effort to develop a coherent theory of combat. In the next chapter I present my basic definitions of terms. Following that, I formulate the basic structure of my theory in relation to Clausewitz's Law of Numbers. Then I apply the theory to the combat processes of effectiveness, movement, attrition, friction, and human behavior. Finally, I apply the theory to the problems of suppression and force multipliers. Interspersed among and within these chapters are examples of the compatibility of the theory with historical combat experience.

Chapter 7

Elements of a Theory of Combat

Setting the Stage

As A STARTING point for an explanation of a scientific theory, it is useful to define fundamental terms, to state and explain critical assumptions, and to establish—or limit—the scope of the discussion that follows. The definitions and explanations that follow are generally consistent with usage in the military and analytical communities, and with definitions that have been formulated for its work by The Military Conflict Institute. However, I have in some instances modified or restated these to conform to my own ideas and usage.

Definition of Military Combat

I define military combat as a violent, planned form of physical interaction (fighting) between two hostile opponents, where at least one party is an organized force, recognized by governmental or *de facto* authority, and one or both opposing parties hold one or more of the following objectives: to seize control of territory or people; to prevent the opponent from seizing and controlling territory or people; to protect one's own territory or people; to dominate, destroy, or incapacitate the opponent.

The impact of weapons creates an environment of lethality, danger, and fear in which achievement of objectives by one party may require the opponent to choose among: continued resistance and resultant destruction; retreat and loss of territory, facilities, and people; surrender. Military combat begins in any interaction, or at any level of combat from duel to full-scale war, when weapons are first employed with hostile intent by one or both opponents. Military combat ends for any interaction or level of combat when both sides have stopped fighting.

There are two key points in this definition that I wish to emphasize. Though there may be much in common between military combat and a brawl in a barroom, there are important differences. The opponents in military combat are to some degree organized, and both represent a governmental or quasi-governmental authority. There is one other essential difference: the all-pervasive influence of *fear* in a *lethal* environment. People have been killed in barroom brawls, but this is exceptional. In military combat there is the constant danger of death from lethal weapons employed by opponents with deadly intent. Fear is without question the most important characteristic of combat.

In this book, wherever I use the word combat, I am referring to *military* combat in the sense of the above definition.

The Hierarchy of Combat

In my definition I have referred to interactions and levels of combat. This is recognition of the fact that fighting between armed forces—while always having the characteristics noted above, such as fear and planned violence—manifests itself in different fashions from different perspectives. In commonly accepted military terminology, there is a hierarchy of military combat, with war as its highest level, followed by campaign, battle, engagement, action, and duel.

These six words, which designate levels of combat, are often used loosely and imprecisely. Since they are used frequently in the following pages and in the interest of precision, I define these terms as used in this book.[1]

A *war* is an armed conflict, or a state of belligerence, involving military combat between two factions, states, nations, or coalitions. Hostilities between the opponents may be initiated with or without a formal declaration by one or both parties that a state of war exists. A war is fought for particular political or economic purposes or reasons, or to resist an enemy's efforts to impose domination. A war can be short, sometimes lasting a few days, but usually is lengthy, lasting for months, years, or even generations.

A *campaign* is a phase of a war involving a series of operations related in time and space and aimed toward achieving a single, specific, strategic objective or result in the war. A campaign may include a single battle, but more often it comprises a number of battles over a protracted period of time or a considerable distance, but within a single theater of operations or delimited area. A campaign may last only a few weeks, but usually lasts several months or even a year.

A *battle* is combat between major forces, each having opposing assigned or perceived operational missions, in which each side seeks to impose its will on the opponent by accomplishing its own mission, while preventing the opponent from achieving his. A battle starts when one side initiates mission-directed combat and ends when one side accomplishes its mission or when one or both sides fail to accomplish the mission(s). Battles are often parts of campaigns. Battles between large forces usually are made up of several engagements, and can last from a few days to several weeks. Naval battles tend to be short and—in modern times —decisive.

An *engagement* is combat between two forces, neither larger than a division nor smaller than a company, in which each has an assigned or perceived mission. An engagement begins when the attacking force initiates combat in pursuit of its mission and ends when the attacker has accomplished the mission, or ceases to try to accomplish the mission, or when one or both sides receive significant reinforcements, thus initiating a new engagement. An engagement is often part of a battle. An engagement normally lasts one or two days; it may be as brief as a few hours and is rarely longer than five days.

An *action* is combat between two forces, neither larger than a battalion nor smaller than a squad, in which each side has a tactical objective. An action begins when the attacking force initiates combat to gain its objective, and ends when the attacker wins the objective, or one or both forces withdraw, or both forces terminate combat. An action often is part of an engagement and sometimes is part of a battle. An action lasts for a few minutes or a few hours and never lasts more than one day.

A *duel* is combat between two individuals or between two mobile fighting machines, such as combat vehicles, combat helicopters, or combat aircraft, or between a mobile fighting machine and a counter-weapon. A duel begins when one side opens fire and ends when one side or both are unable to continue firing, or stop firing voluntarily. A duel is almost always part of an action. A duel lasts only a few minutes.

The elements of the hierarchy of combat are summarized in Table 7-1.

The Conceptual Components of Combat

Just as there are different levels in the waging of combat, and largely because of those different levels, there are also different levels in conceptualizing combat. Traditionally there have been two major conceptual components or levels of combat: strategy and tactics.

About 1830 Clausewitz defined strategy as "the use of engagements to attain the object of the war." Tactics, he wrote, is "the use of the armed forces in engagements."[2] About the same time Jomini defined strategy as "the art of getting the armed forces onto the field of battle," and as comprising "all the operations embraced in the theater of war in general." Jomini went on to define tactics as "the maneuvers of an army on the day of battle; its contents, its concentrations, and the diverse formations used to lead the troops to the attack."[3] In theory the distinction between strategy and tactics was clear; in practice the line was slightly fuzzy.

As war became more complex, and as its scope expanded, early in the twentieth century, it became evident to military theoreticians, particularly those on the German General Staff, that strategy's scope was correspondingly expanded, dealing often with more than one theater of war, and even embracing such non-military considerations as economics and politics. This expansion, of course, was at the "upper end" of strategy. It also

Table 7-1

Hierarchy of Combat

LEVEL OF COMBAT	DURATION	UNITS INVOLVED	COMMON THREAD
War	Months–years	National Forces	National Goals
Campaign	Weeks–Months	Army Groups or Field Armies	Strategic Objectives
Battle	Days–Weeks	Field Armies or Army Corps	Operational Mission
Engagement	1–5 Days	Divisions-Companies	Tactical Mission
Action	1–24 Hours	Battalions-Squads	Local Objective
Duel	Minutes	Two Individuals, People or Mobile Fighting Machines	Local Objective

meant that the nature of the authority and responsibility for those concerned with the upper level of strategy at the national capital and in the headquarters of a commander in chief was very different from those of the theater and army commanders at the lower end.

The Germans began to refer to the lower level of strategy as "operations," a term that—according to General Hermann Foertsch in the late 1930s—was "frequently employed to indicate a sub-concept of strategy. Strictly speaking, operations are the movements of armed forces preparatory to battle, but the fighting itself is usually also included in the concept. There is no definite line of demarcation between the two in ordinary usage."[4] Foertsch then provided a diagram to help clarify the distinctions between tactics, operations, and strategy as seen by the Germans at that time. For the Germans warfare was comprised of three conceptual levels, divided by theoretically clear but practically fuzzy lines, as shown in Figure 7-1 below.

At the same time other theorists, particularly in Britain, had adapted a term used by Jomini, "grand tactics," to deal with the area of warfare the Germans called operations, and coined the term "grand strategy" to distinguish that form of strategic thinking applicable to the conduct of war at the highest levels of government. There were, however, no generally accepted definitions of grand tactics or grand strategy. Furthermore, it was clear that the concept of grand tactics was really part of the realm of strategy as originally visualized by both Jomini and Clausewitz.

In the United States after World War II a clearer understanding of the relationships of the upper levels of strategy emerged, through development of concepts of "national strategy" and "military strategy." This has led to a new set of definitions for strategy in general, and for its upper levels, as follows:

Strategy is the art and science of planning for the use of, and managing, all available resources in the waging of war by those in high levels of national and military authority.

National strategy is the art and science of developing and using political, economic, psychological, social, and military resources as necessary during war and peace to afford the maximum support to national policies and—in the event of war—to increase the probabilities and favorable consequences of victory and to lessen the chances of defeat. Art predominates over science in national strategy.

Figure 7-1

Relationship of Tactics, Operations, and Strategy

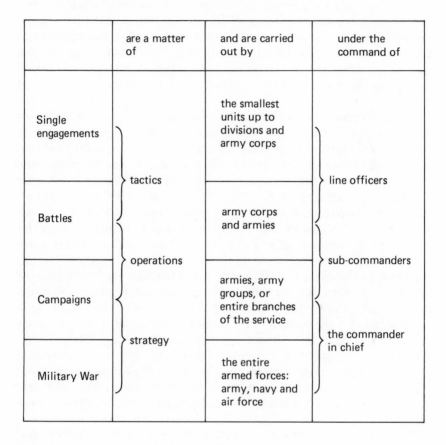

	are a matter of	and are carried out by	under the command of
Single engagements	tactics	the smallest units up to divisions and army corps	line officers
Battles	operations	army corps and armies	sub-commanders
Campaigns	strategy	armies, army groups, or entire branches of the service	the commander in chief
Military War		the entire armed forces: army, navy and air force	

Military strategy is the art and science of developing and employing in war military resources and forces for the purpose of providing maximum support to national policy in order to increase the probabilities and favorable consequences of victory and to lessen the chances of defeat. Science predominates over art in military strategy. The difference between military competence and military genius at the strategic level is greater artistry by genius. This definition covers a very broad range of the activities of warfare, from the global deployments of armed forces to the theater-level activities the Germans called operations.

Soviet military theorists have also devoted their attention to the relationship between the lower and intermediate levels of strategy by characterizing the lower level as the conceptual area of the operational art. To end fuzziness of distinctions, they arbitrarily define tactics as being that aspect of the art of war that is the responsibility of division commanders and lower; operational art is the responsibility of army and front (army group) commanders; strategy is the domain of higher commanders. This arbitrary distinction may have ended the practical fuzziness of the previous lines, but it tends to blur the concepts, since—as can be seen in the Foertsch diagram in Figure 7-1—it is not possible to make a firm distinction between the concepts of strategy, operations, and tactics simply on the basis of command levels.

Despite the theoretical problems clouding the concept of the operational art, the United States has recently (early 1980s) decided to adopt the concept, following the Soviet example perhaps more closely than would be desirable for conceptual clarity. A definition of operations, or operational art, generally consistent with that recently adopted by the U.S. Army, is as follows:

Operations involves the control and direction of large forces (usually armies or army groups) in combat activities within a single, discrete theater of combat. Operations can be considered a separate conceptual level of combat lying between strategy and tactics.

Thus, the classic duality of the conceptual components of combat as visualized by Clausewitz and Jomini has in the twentieth century become a trilogy in the current military doctrines of many major military powers. Having had the temerity to tinker with the classic definitions of strategy by Clausewitz and

Jomini, and in the process having inserted a whole new conceptual level of combat, I must now adjust their classic definition of tactics to fit into this trilogy.

Tactics is the technique of deploying and directing military forces (troops, ships, or aircraft, or combinations of these, and their immediate supporting elements) in coordinated combat activities against the enemy in order to attain the objectives designated by strategy or operations.

There is another word often used in relation to the conceptual components of combat: doctrine. Interestingly, the Germans have no such term in their military lexicon, apparently because of its imprecision. However, it is a useful word and concept, and the following definition attempts to limit its inherent imprecision:

Military doctrine is the combination of principles, policies and concepts into an integrated system for the purpose of governing all components of a military force in combat, and assuring consistent, coordinated employment of these components. The origin of doctrine can be experience, or theory, or both. Doctrine represents the available thought on the employment of forces that has been adopted by an armed force. Doctrine is methodology, and if it is to work, all military elements must know, understand, and respect it. Doctrine is implemented by tactics.

The Scope of the Theory

The discussion to this point has focused on combat as violent interactions of armed forces in lethal fighting. There has been no consideration of the origins of war, of the relationship of war to politics, or of the forms of conflict in which there is either no fighting, or specialized or unorthodox kinds of fighting. For instance, the fighting that takes place in an insurgency often does not fit neatly into the combat levels of campaigns or battles.

Yet, it is obvious that a theory of combat cannot be derived or developed in isolation from—or without consideration of—the various forms of international and intra-national conflict, or armed conflict that are obviously encompassed within the general phenomenon we call war. The range of these general hostilities is often called "the spectrum of conflict."

A diagram of the spectrum of conflict is shown in Figure 7-2.[5]

A diagram of the spectrum of conflict is shown in Figure 7-2.[5] The dimension across the chart from left to right is the level of violence in the conflict, from non-violent conflict on the left to the most violent form of conflict—nuclear war—on the right. Three important thresholds of violence are established. The violence threshold marks the transition from conflict without violence to the use of violence as an integral part of the conflict. The overt hostilities threshold marks the transition from violence perpetrated by informal groups, often operating covertly, to an overt employment of violence by armed forces. Finally, the nuclear threshold marks the transition from nonuse of nuclear weapons to their use, along with the lesser forms of warfare violence. The vertical dimension of the spectrum is the participant dimension. This is organized according to whether the conflict is between groups within a nation, between two nations, or among several nations. The participant dimension helps substantially to organize and to make more understandable the complex array of the various forms of conflict that occur.

The theory of combat which I am addressing in this book is related to the categories of: major conventional war; regional war; small war; minor hostilities, guerilla warfare, and insurgency/counter-insurgency (which is often, but not necessarily, guerilla warfare). To the extent that civil war is similar to war between two nations or coalitions, it would apply to civil war. Given the probability that major conventional war will precede any form of nuclear warfare, and could continue during and after the termination of nuclear warfare, it would apply at least to the conventional part of a nuclear war as well.

The scope of this theory of combat is generally similar to that to which Clausewitz, Fuller, and others devoted their attention. It might be argued that Clausewitz was also concerned with nonviolent conflict, but I would contend that he focused completely on the violence of armed conflict. Nevertheless, he did devote significant attention to a different dimension of conflict or war from that presented in my spectrum of conflict. This is the dimension involving the relationship between war and politics; of civilian concerns related to military concerns in war.

A simplified diagram of the complex relationship between the civilian and military segments of society in peace and in war is shown in Figure 7-3. Clausewitz focused his attention on the wartime aspects of that relationship, particularly with respect to

Figure 7–2

The Spectrum of Conflict

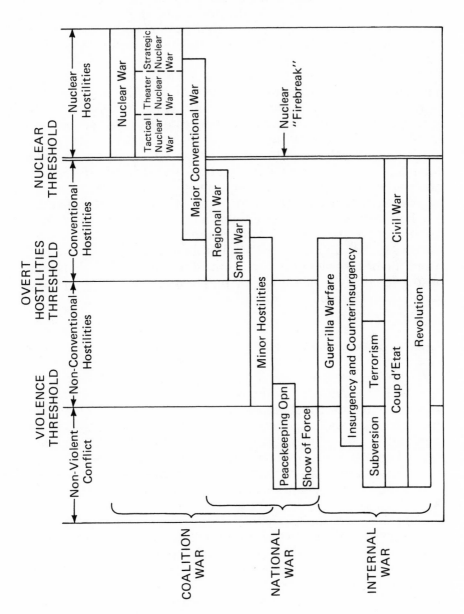

the interaction of the military high command and the civilian government and leadership.

This book, however, is concerned only with the fighting forces in contact and in combat with the enemy as illustrated at the very bottom of Figure 7-3. Yet another way of looking at the scope of a theory of combat can be seen in the spectrum of military theory in Figure 7-4.

The theory of combat in this book is concerned with military strategy, operations, tactics, and technique. This was the area with which Clausewitz was mostly concerned. His interest in the philosophy of war was primarily to establish the context for combat theory, and to make it clear to his readers (particularly military readers) that military combat and theories related thereto should not be considered in isolation. They are, he pointed out, intimately connected with civilian society, and under the control of national authority, which in most modern states is usually civilian authority. Clausewitz also noted the importance of that portion of the spectrum of military theory concerned with preparation for and support of combat, but then specifically excluded it from further consideration in his masterwork *On War*. This book also excludes consideration of preparation for and support of combat in order to focus on the combat itself.

Combat Theory and Nuclear War

In the spectrum of conflict (see Figure 7-2) there is a threshold between conventional and nuclear hostilities. There are two reasons why this threshold, sometimes called the "Nuclear Firebreak," exists and why it is very important. In the first place, the destructive power of nuclear weapons is so much greater than that of conventional weapons that even small nuclear weapons are many times more powerful than conventional weapons.

Weapons developments since 1945 have somewhat tended to narrow this gap in power or destructiveness from both directions. On the one hand, nuclear scientists have created nuclear devices with very low yields. On the other hand, there have been successful efforts to develop ever more devastating conventional weapons, some of which are approaching the destructive power of the low yield nuclear devices. Nevertheless, there does not appear to be any likelihood that this gap will be closed in the foreseeable future. The firebreak is likely to remain tangible.

Figure 7–3

Civil-Military Relationship in Peace and War

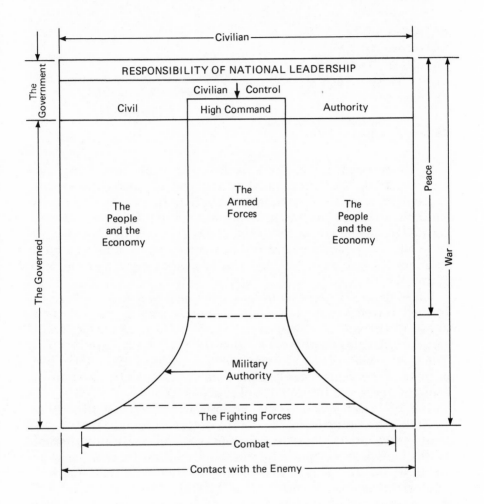

Figure 7–4

The Spectrum of Military Theory

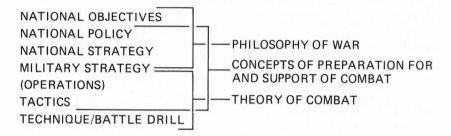

In the second place, there is fear that any use of nuclear weapons will lead inevitably to full use of nuclear weapons through a process of escalation. Whether this is true or not is unknown. Despite arguments from some that nuclear war can be limited, many do not believe this, and there is enough uncertainty to the prospects for controlling nuclear escalation to attach momentous import to the first use of a nuclear weapon in any future war.

There does not seem to be any certainty that in the event of limited introduction of nuclear weapons into a war—limited either in the size or power of the weapons or in the selection of targets or locales for their use—that the war can remain limited. The sizable body of literature on the use and limitations of the use of nuclear weapons reveals that there are at least two schools of thought about the limited use of nuclear weapons.

One of these schools—the pragmatists—believes that it is possible, through a combination of deterrence and tacit agreement between the warring opponents, to make limited use of tactical nuclear weapons in war, and to keep tactical nuclear warfare limited. This school believes, therefore, that tactical nuclear weapons are simply a logical continuation of the centuries-old trend toward bigger and better weapons, and that they can be used like any other weapons on an integrated conventional-nuclear battlefield.

The other school—the pessimists—maintains that, once tactical nuclear weapons are used by either side, there will be an inevitable escalation that will almost certainly lead to theater or strategic nuclear war in which large numbers of nuclear weapons of tremendous power will cause enormous destruction in the theater of war and in the homelands of the U.S. and the USSR, destroying civilization as we know it. This school points out further that even if there is only a slight probability of the ineluctable nature of this process, it would be madness to attempt to fight a limited nuclear war, either tactical or strategic.

Pragmatists point out that in World War II, in one conventional air raid on Tokyo (9–10 March 1945) more people were killed and injured (83,000 and 100,000 respectively) than in either of the two atomic bomb attacks of the war. At Hiroshima about 78,000 were killed and 70,000 injured; at Nagasaki the figures were 40,000 and 25,000. Certainly the power of modern nuclear weapons is not unimaginable; this power is measurable, and the effects are known. As to the destruction of civilization as we know it, the pragmatists rightly assert that this was also the effect of both World War I and World War II.

The pessimists respond that the casualties inflicted by the fire bombing of Tokyo were caused by hundreds of planes and thousands of bombs; while the losses at Hiroshima and Nagasaki were each caused by one weapon dropped from one plane, and that these were weapons that today are considered to be "low yield." They also maintain that even though some effects of individual nuclear weapons are measurable, there are some effects that have not yet been measured. The potential effect of the use of large numbers of high yield nuclear weapons on the world, on its populations, and on its environment is not well understood.

While there is much largely speculative literature on nuclear warfare, there is almost no experience. Without more practical knowledge there is little to be gained by going further in this book into nuclear warfare theory other than to note the likely impact of nuclear war on a theory of combat focused on conventional war. Three points are important. One, if the pragmatists are correct, a theory of combat based upon experience with conventional weapons is undoubtedly valid for limited nuclear warfare, particularly tactical nuclear war. Two, if the pessimists are correct, the applicability of any theory of conventional combat is doubtful. And three, because of its dangers, a nuclear war of any kind is an unlikely event, while the existence of a stable nuclear deterrence increases the probability of conventional war.

I do not intend, therefore, to consider within my discussion of a theory of combat the possible effects of strategic or theater nuclear war. It must be recognized, however, that nuclear war is quite likely to be preceded by a period of rising tensions, mobilization, minor hostilities, and major conventional war. It is also likely, depending on the effects of nuclear attacks, that conventional combat will continue during nuclear war itself. It is even possible that conventional conflict will continue after nuclear attacks stop, or during pauses between successive nuclear attacks. The madness that brought about a nuclear war in the first place could still be a cause for continued fighting to achieve the original goals. The theory of combat discussed in this book remains valid in the nuclear age because, unfortunately, men will continue fighting conventionally in any case.

Applicability to Air and Naval Warfare

In Chapter 2, I listed some twelve military theorists since the time of Napoleon whose writings have contributed—directly or indirectly, intentionally or accidentally—to the inchoate effort to produce a theory of combat. This was an arbitrary list, and there were unquestionably a number of other serious military scholars whose works would qualify them for consideration in such a list. It should be noted, however, that only one of the twelve I listed was a naval combat theorist, although mankind has been fighting on, in, and over the water almost as long as it has on land. Also, there was only one air combat theorist in the list.

It is likely that if the list were to be expanded to include all possible contributors to significant military theory, the proportion of naval theorists would not rise much above ten percent. The proportion of air theorists would probably be even smaller, in part because we have been able to fly and fight in the air for less than a century. Other than the reason noted above for the paucity of air theorists, I do not propose to speculate on why there have been so many more theorists for land warfare than for war at sea or in the air. In any event, there is reason to believe that a general theory of combat for land warfare is likely to be applicable—probably with some modifications—to both naval and air warfare.

The theory discussed in this book is intended to be applicable to that portion of modern conventional war called the Air-Land Battle. I define this as combat between ground forces supported by modern high-performance helicopters and fixed-wing aircraft. The theory does not address specifically the air-to-air combat or air interdiction roles of modern air forces. This is simply because

I have not yet gotten around to it. There is a large amount of historical data on air operations in World War II, Korea, Vietnam, and the Middle East. It remains to apply to this data the same disciplined and systematic approach taken with air-land combat data.

The theory presented in this book does not apply to naval warfare. That also is simply a matter of not yet being able to do the work. There is a large amount of data available on naval combat, but it, too, has yet to be analyzed systematically. The last person to define an historically based theory of naval combat was Alfred Thayer Mahan, and little has been done since his time.[6]

Time and funds permitting it is my intention to expand this theory of combat to cover all air and naval combat. In the meantime, the scope of this book is limited to air-land combat.

Definition of a Theory of Combat

Having exhaustively—but I hope not exhaustingly—explored the various aspects of combat that appear to be pertinent to a theory of combat, one last definition is necessary. I define a *theory of combat* as: the embodiment of a set of fundamental principles governing or explaining military combat, whose purpose is to provide a basis for the formulation of doctrine, and to assist military commanders and planners to engage successfully in combat at any level. Such a theory includes the following elements:

(1) Identifying the major elements of combat and the combat processes through which they operate and patterns in the interactions and relationships among them;

(2) Describing combat structures and patterns of interactions and relationships of variable factors that constantly shape or determine the outcome of combat;

(3) Expressing in quantitative terms the patterns so identified and described.

Please note that this is not a philosophy of *war*. As Clausewitz discusses at some length, even though the dominant feature of war is fighting, or combat, the amount and intensity of fighting varies greatly from one war to another, and there have been wars without fighting. The attention of this book is tightly focused, looking toward a *theory of combat*.

Chapter 8

The QJM Combat Power Formula

The Clausewitz Connection

IN CHAPTER 2 I presented Clausewitz's Law of Numbers, a simple but comprehensive theory of combat based upon a comparison of the relative numerical combat powers of two opponents, in which combat power for each was calculated as follows:

$$P = N \times V \times Q . \quad (1)$$

In this equation, N represents the number of troops in a military force, V the variable factors reflecting the combat circumstances affecting the force, and Q the quantified value for the fighting quality of the troops.

In this chapter, the Clausewitz equation will be transformed into the combat power formula, which is the basic equation of the Quantified Judgment Model (QJM). This will be done in three operations as follows:

1. Substitute Force Strength (S) for numbers of troops (N);
2. Elaborate and define the environmental and operational factors (V_f) which represent the effect of the circumstances of combat on the force;
3. Substitute relative Combat Effectiveness Value (CEV) for troop quality (Q).

This process will provide the basis for a modern theory of combat based on historical analysis and described by the QJM.

Substituting Force Strength for Numbers

In Clausewitz's time the quantity N was fairly simple and straightforward. Armies were composed largely of infantrymen equipped with muskets, plus a number of cannon (each worth perhaps ten infantrymen), and a number of cavalrymen who could be employed in battle either as dragoons (mounted infantrymen) or as a shock force; in either case (because of mobility) each was worth probably a little more than an infantryman in calculating a battle outcome. While the proportions of infantry, cavalry, and artillery varied somewhat from army to army, the relationships were sufficiently standard that a simple numeration of the total numbers of men in the forces gave a fairly accurate and consistent representation of the total firepower available to each side.

It is less easy today to make a simple numerical comparison of the firepower value of opposing forces in terms of numbers men or weapons because the calculation has been complicated enormously by the variety of weapons and the application of the internal combustion machine to the battlefield in mobile fighting machines, such as tanks and combat aircraft. It is necessary to substitute for personnel strength an expression that takes into account the firepower and mobility components of modern weapons and forces. This requires a method to relate and compare the lethality or effectiveness of different weapons.

Several different methods of comparing the relative lethality of weapons have been developed in recent years. Each provides a quantitative representation of the widely differing effects of the individual weapons types. Some of the most widely used measures of weapons effectiveness are firepower scores, the Weapons Effectiveness Index (WEI) and the TASCFORM methodology. The measure of weapon effectiveness used in the QJM is the Operational Lethality Index (OLI). However, the QJM, properly calibrated, could be based on any logical and reasonable measure of weapon effectiveness.

The OLI was developed originally to represent the comparative lethality of all weapons over the course of history.[1] A methodology was derived that could consistently calculate OLIs in terms of weapons' characteristics. It was used to compare the relative lethal effects of, for instance, spears, bows and arrows, rifled muskets, quick-firing artillery pieces, machine guns, and atomic weapons. It has been applied to most existing modern weapons, including tanks, aircraft, and missiles, and it can be applied to hypothetical future weapons.

Because of the varying ways in which weapons produce their destructive and damaging effects, and because of the different ways in which these effects can be applied, it will probably never be possible to arrive at a completely satisfactory method of measuring and comparing the effectiveness of weapons. In order to provide a common measure for weapons of different classes and roles, it is necessary to make some simplifying assumptions that are always arbitrary and sometimes at least partially incorrect. The OLI, however, provides a logical, reasonable, and consistent methodology for weapons' effects quantification.

The OLI compares the relative lethality of weapons against a theoretical target array of unarmored soldiers, standing in formation on an infinite plane surface, each occupying one square meter of space. The number of casualties that a weapon can inflict upon this infinite array of human targets in one hour is calculated by combining the following weapons' characteristics:

1. Rate of fire (RF): the number of times the weapon reasonably can strike at the target array in an hour.
2. Reliability (R): the probability that the weapon will function as designed when an attempt is made to strike the target array.
3. Accuracy (A): the probability that a specific intended target will be struck when the weapon functions properly.
4. Number of targets per strike (C): for most weapons this is related to the area of burst of a high-explosive shell. The method permits conversion of this effect to the damage that can be inflicted by a weapon employed against a point target, such as an individual soldier or a tank.
5. Range (Rn): a factor representing the extent to which the ability of the weapon to fire at varying distances increases the potential number of targets struck in the use of the weapon over time. For reasons of practicality, and to facilitate reliable comparisons among varying types of weapons, muzzle velocity is usually used in a conversion formula as a surrogate for range.

The product of the values for these five weapon characteristics is the Theoretical Lethality Index (TLI), expressed in casualties per hour. The formula is as follows:

$$TLI = RF \times R \times A \times C \times Rn . \quad (2)$$

The TLI is converted to an OLI by adjusting its value by appropriate weapon performance factors and by dividing the resulting product by a dispersion factor (DI). The weapon performance factors take into account, for example, the tactical mobility of such weapons as tanks, helicopters, and combat aircraft, and the protection provided by armor.

The increasing lethality of weapons over the past several centuries has had an effect upon combat formations that has made them less and less comparable to the assumed infinite array of targets in a density of 1 square meter per man. The effect has been increased dispersion. The actual average density of troops in combat formations has increased from an average of about 10 square meters per man in ancient armies, to about 27,500 square meters per man in World War II, and to about 35,000 square meters per man in the 1973 Arab-Israeli War. These are average density figures, since troops in units are not distributed over ground space uniformly, but in patterns of varying concentration. Based on the current doctrines of modern military forces, the average density in a conflict between modern forces in the 1980s and 1990s is likely to be about 50,000 square meters per man.

The effect of dispersion requires the conversion of the TLI scores of weapons to OLIs, to represent the actual operational effect of weapons against contemporary average troop densities. The dispersion factors that account for increased dispersion over history are shown in Table 8-1. The dispersion factors are normalized to the average density of troops in ancient armies.

Table 8–1

Dispersion Factor (DI)	
Ancient Armies	1
Napoleonic Era	20
American Civil War	25
World War I	250
World War II	3,000
1970s	4,000
1980s	5,000

The formula for the OLI is as follows:

$$OLI = \frac{TLI}{DI} \text{ (weapons performance factors). (3)}$$

Once an OLI has been calculated for each weapon, it is possible to add the individual weapons values to provide aggregate scores for units and forces. This is complicated by the fact that each type of weapon is affected somewhat differently by environmental and operational factors, such as terrain and posture.

To facilitate the consistent application of factors to different weapons, weapons are divided into six major classes:

1. Infantry Weapons, which include not only the small arms of individual riflemen, but also machine guns, mortars, and armored personnel carriers.
2. Artillery Weapons, some of which are towed, some self-propelled; some are traditional ballistic cannon; others are some form of rocket or missile.
3. Armor Weapons, mobile fighting machines that combine firepower, armored protection, and automotive mobility, and intended primarily for direct fire employment.
4. Air Support Weapons, mobile fighting machines based behind the ground-fighting troops, which fly over the battle to apply gunfire, rockets, and bombs to the combat.
5. Air Defense Weapons, guns and missiles designed primarily to protect ground-based troops from hostile air support weapons.
6. Anti-Armor Weapons, guns and missiles designed to protect forces from hostile armored weapons.

For every battle the OLI values of all weapons in each class are modified by the variable factors representing the effects of the circumstances of that particular battle upon that class of weapon. A value for Force Strength (S), analogous to the Clausewitzean N, is calculated by the following procedure:

$$S = (W_n \times V_n) + (W_g \times V_g) + (W_i \times V_i) + (W_y \times V_y) + (W_{gi} \times V_{gi}) + (W_{gy} \times V_{gy}) . \quad (4)$$

The symbols represent:
S   = Force strength
W   = The aggregate OLIs of the weapons in a category.
V   = Weapon effect factors

n = Infantry weapons identifier
g = Artillery weapons identifier
i = Armor weapons identifier
y = Air support weapons identifier
gi = Anti-armor weapons identifier
gy = Air defense weapons identifier

The S calculated in equation (4) is the modern equivalent of the Clausewitzean N. Substituting S for N, equation (1) can be rewritten at this stage as follows:

$$P = S \times V \times Q . \quad (5)$$

In this equation V is the combination of the effects of all of the circumstantial variables upon the combat employment of the force—as distinct from the application of the relevant variables to the weapons themselves in the calculation of S. The next step is to identify the variable factors that modify the force strength itself.

Defining Force Effects Variables

One of the three components of Clausewitz's Law of Numbers consists of what he called "the variables representing the circumstances of combat." There are many such variables, and their effects can differ greatly from one variable to another. Some of them are more or less physical in nature (like weather and terrain) and lend themselves relatively easily to quantification, at least conceptually. Other variables are behavioral in nature (like leadership, training, and morale) and are intangible. In between are some other variables that are in themselves intangible, and perhaps unquantifiable, but produce effects that can be measured. The latter category of quantifiable variables includes such things as surprise and relative combat effectiveness. Clausewitz quite properly chose to distinguish quality of the troops (Q) from the other circumstantial variable factors.

In the QJM, the circumstantial variables are divided into three major groups according to kind. The three kinds of variables are environmental, operational, and human behavioral. *Environmental variables* are those that occur because of nature. Environmental variables include weather, terrain, and season. Commanders have no influence over this kind of variable, and they affect both sides, although not necessarily equally. *Operational variables* are those that occur because of the actions of the combat forces. Operational variables include posture, mobility, air superiority, surprise, fatigue, and vulnerability. Commanders have great influence over these. And *behavioral variables* are those that exist because of the nature of the human participants in the combat. Behavioral variables include leadership, morale, training, and experience. Commanders have influence over these variables, but that influence must be applied at least in part before the battle. Factors representing behavioral variables are applied only to forces.

Factors representing both the environmental and operational variables are applied to weapons to calculate Force Strength (S) as in formula 4. Factors representing both of these kinds of variables are also applied to forces to represent the effects of battle circumstances on the forces. Historical analysis of combat has permitted factor values to be established for the environmental and operational force effects variables shown in Table 8-2.

Table 8–2

Forces Effects Variables

Environmental	Operational	Behavioral
Terrain	Posture	Leadership
Weather	Mobility	Training
Season	Vulnerability	Experience
	Fatigue	Morale
	Surprise	Manpower Quality
	Air Superiority	

The environmental and operational force effects variable factors are denoted by the symbol V_f, and substituted for V in the equation for combat power (5), as shown in equation (6) below:

$$P = S \times V_f \times Q. \quad (6)$$

Substituting Relative Combat Effectiveness for Troop Quality

In order to determine how troop quality (which is based upon the behavioral variables) affects the outcome of a battle, it is necessary to be able to compare the theoretical outcome of a combat event (in which troop quality is not considered) to the actual outcome of the same combat event (in which the relative troop quality has influenced the outcome). The theoretical outcome is described by the relative force strengths and force variables. The actual outcome of a historical battle or engagement is represented in the QJM by a results factor, which combines three measures of effectiveness as follows:

1. Mission Factor (MF), an "expert" judgment of the extent to which a force accomplished its assigned or perceived mission.
2. Spatial Effectiveness (Esp), a value representing the extent to which a force was able to gain or hold ground.
3. Casualty Effectiveness (Ecas), a value representing the efficiency of the force in terms of casualties, taking into consideration the strengths of the two sides, and the casualties incurred by both sides.

The three factor values are summed to obtain a measure of results (R) as shown below:

$$R = MF + Esp + Ecas . \quad (7)$$

Having calculated results for both sides, then the outcome of a battle or engagement is described as follows:

$$\text{Actual Outcome} = R_r/R_b . \quad (8)$$

The theoretical outcome of a battle is represented by the combat power ratio: P_r/P_b (in which quality of troops has not been considered). The actual outcome of the battle is represented by the ratio R_r/R_b. It might seem reasonable to expect that P_r/P_b should be the same as R_r/R_b for any battle. But this is rarely the case.

Clausewitz has already indicated the two principal reasons why the values of these two ratios will rarely be identical, even under the best of circumstances. First, the "fighting value of the troops," as he called it, is rarely identical. Second, there is always some element of chance or luck, particularly in the interactions of hundreds or thousands of troops on each side of the battle. In addition, it is impossible to achieve absolute accuracy in developing factors to represent the variables affecting the circumstances of the battle, particularly those relating to behavior.

The intangible behavioral considerations are combined into a single factor representing a relative combat effectiveness value (CEV). The CEV is the factor explaining the difference between the P/P (theoretical outcome) and R/R (actual outcome) ratios.

This relationship is expressed as follows:

$$CEVr = (R_r/R_b)/(P_r/P_b) . \quad (9)$$

The CEV is a ratio, and CEV_b is the reciprocal of CEV_r. To the extent data is available, it is possible by means of equation (9) to calculate the CEV for any historical battle.

The CEV for a force is the equivalent of the Clausewitzean Q, and for all practical purposes the two are identical. The CEV is used in this theory to represent relative combat effectiveness, and the final step in the transformation of the Law of Numbers to the QJM combat power formula is to substitute CEV for Q as shown in equation 10.

$$P = S \times V_f \times CEV . \quad (10)$$

Summary: The QJM and the Clausewitz Law

In Chapter 2, I showed the significance of Clausewitz's Law of Numbers, which he stated was applicable across all military history, and any place in the world. This chapter demonstrates that the QJM is an elaboration of the Law of Numbers, adapted to take into account modern weapons technology. In other words, the QJM is a theory of combat fully consistent with that which Clausewitz expounded.[2] The essence of the QJM as a theory of combat is as follows:

1. A military force goes into combat with an organization consisting of men and weapons, with the men employing the weapons to impose their collective will upon the enemy by means of firepower. The firepower of the force is quantified in terms of Operational Lethality Indexes (OLIs).
2. The aggregate OLIs for the weapons inventory of a force (W) is converted to Force Strength (S) by application of weapon effects variables (to each of six classes of weapons) as follows:

$$S = W \times V_w . \quad (9)$$

3. Force Strength is converted to Combat Power (P) as follows:

$$P = S \times V_f \times CEV . \quad (10)$$

Chapter 9

Illustration: 1940 Flanders Campaign

Significance of the 1940 Flanders Campaign

NOT LONG AGO, several of my colleagues and I collaborated on writing a book about "what might have been" in World War II if certain key decisions had been different in ten major battles of that war.[1] The first chapter of that book is about the May 1940 campaign in Flanders. That campaign is a good vehicle to illustrate the application of the QJM.

The Germans won an overwhelming victory over the French and British in this campaign, which led to the fall of France. There were several reasons for the German victory.

Perhaps the most significant reason why the Germans won was the fact that the French high command, after a tremendous and expensive national effort to build a nearly impregnable line of fortifications—the Maginot Line—along the frontier with Germany, actually deployed its forces as though the Maginot Line were not there. A German thrust across that frontier, such as had occurred in 1870 and 1914, could be stopped by a relatively small number of men in the fortifications. Thanks to the Maginot Line the French high command could have greatly reduced the number of reserves behind the fortifications, which was a substantial proportion of their military manpower. These troops could have been used elsewhere, or in an enlarged strategic reserve.

The French defeat in May 1940 has often been blamed—by

people who don't know any better—on the fact that French military men put too much faith in the defensive strength of the Maginot Line. In fact, it is just the opposite. The French were defeated mainly because they did not put enough faith in the strength of that line.

Instead of using Economy of Force (one of the nine Principles of War), which was possible because of the military manpower that could have been saved from the forces in and behind the Maginot Line, they deployed their forces equally along the frontier, leaving four armies behind the fortifications, when one—at most —would have been required. In other words, French deployment ignored the existence of the Maginot Line.

The Germans made no such mistake! Understanding well the terrible losses they would suffer if they attacked through the fortifications, they did not attack the Maginot Line. They went around it! By the time the French realized what was happening, the German blitzkrieg had broken through the Allied lines in Belgium and Flanders, and France had lost the war. If the French had had available in the breakthrough area one, or two, or three of the armies that were sitting idly useless in and behind the Maginot Line, they could at least have stopped the German thrust.

In my "might have been" chapter about that campaign, I set up an imaginary scenario that had the French making proper use of the Maginot Line. To do this I arranged in my scenario for General Weygand to replace General Gamelin *before* the war began, rather than afterward, and for him to choose young Brigadier General Charles De Gaulle as his chief of staff. I then described how—after making a proper assessment of the situation—Weygand and De Gaulle very quickly redeployed to the northwest three of the four armies behind the Maginot Line. Thus, in my revised version of history, when the German attack came, not only did the French have more troops available to meet the thrust, they also had reserves available for a pre-planned counterattack.

My previous historical analyses of the campaign made me confident that such decisions should have enabled the French to repel the German offensive, and even possibly to win a decisive victory. However, to be sure, I decided to "wargame" my scenario, using a simplified version of the basic QJM formula, which could be applied to the general, aggregated scenario quite readily. The following presents the results of this simplified wargaming.

Allied Force Strength

The numerical strength and composition of the forces actually available to the Allies in May of 1940 are summarized in a very aggregated way in Table 9-1.

To compute troop strengths into a force strength it is assumed that each combat aircraft was the equivalent of 100 soldiers, each with his share of supporting weapons (such as mortars, machine guns, and artillery). Thus, 1700 aircraft would have been the equivalent of 170,000 men. Comparisons of the fire-power values of the weapons involved (using the OLI methodology) reveal that this assumption, while arbitrary, is neither unreasonable nor capricious.

Table 9–1

Allied Force Composition, May 1940

Strength:	Anglo-French	2,000,000	
	Dutch	400,000	
	Belgian	600,000	
	Total	3,000,000	
Combat aircraft		1,700	
Tanks		3,600	
Anglo-French field armies:		9	
Anglo-French divisions:			
	Infantry	87	(c. 1,740,000 men)
	Armored	3	(c. 60,000 men)
	Fortress	13	(c. 200,000 men)
	Total	103	divisions (plus about 40 Dutch and Belgian division-equivalents)

Similarly, it is assumed that each Allied tank was worth 50 men and their share of supporting weapons. This means that the 3600 tanks were the equivalent of 180,000 troops. With the exception of the three armored divisions, the Allies allocated their tanks and planes more or less equally among their divisions and armies. The three armored divisions were also parceled out to the army groups.

On the basis of these assumptions about the manpower values of planes and tanks, the force strength of the Allies in thousands of manpower equivalents is shown in Table 9-2.

Table 9-2

Allied Force Strength (000s): May 1940	
Dutch	400
Belgian	600
Anglo-French Forces	
French fortress troops	200
Field Forces	
Manpower	1,800
Aircraft	170
Tanks	180
Subtotal Field Forces	2,150
Allied Total	3,350

Since the field forces were divided among nine field armies, the force strength of each army was about 240,000 manpower equivalents.

German Force Strength

An aggregated summary of the numerical strength of the German forces is shown in Table 9-3.

It is assumed that each German combat aircraft was roughly the equivalent of the Allied planes, or worth about one hundred men and their share of supporting weapons. Thus, the Luftwaffe force was the equivalent of 350,000 troops.

The German tanks were, on the average, inferior to those of the Allies. So it is assumed that each German tank was worth about forty men, plus their share of supporting weapons. Thus, the German tanks had a manpower equivalent of 103,040.

Table 9-3

German Force Composition: May 1940	
Manpower	2,460,000
Combat aircraft	3,500
Tanks	2,576
Field armies:	8, plus a panzer group (or panzer army)
Divisions:	
Infantry	104 (c. 2,080,000 men)
Panzer	10 (c. 200,000 men)
Mechanized	9 (c. 180,000 men)
Total	123 divisions

The Germans allocated their tanks exclusively to panzer and mechanized divisions, and then combined these divisions into one panzer group (General von Kleist), and one panzer corps (General Hoth). The Germans did not allocate their airpower to armies, but kept it under centralized control.

A summary of the force strength of the German forces, in thousands of manpower equivalents, is shown in Table 9-4. The approximate breakdown of these forces by Army group is shown in Table 9-5. The geographic allocations of the forces is shown schematically in Figure 9-1.

Table 9–4

German Force Strength (000s): May 1940

Field armies	2,080 (or 260 per army)
Panzer group (or army)	382
Panzer corps	101
Luftwaffe support	350
Total	2,913

Table 9–5

German Force Strength by Army Group: May 1940

Army Group B (2 armies plus panzer corps plus 30% airpower)	766
Army Group A (4 armies plus panzer group plus 60% airpower)	1,712
Army Group C (2 armies plus 10% airpower)	595

Variable Factors

Next, in order to apply the QJM it was necessary to consider the variable factors that affected the outcome of the battle significantly. There were two factors of principal importance: defensive posture and terrain. Both of these affect the strength of the defender. It was assumed that other variable factors more or less cancelled each other out on the two sides.

HERO analyses show that (other things being equal) a force in a hasty defensive situation has its force strength multiplied by a factor of 1.3; prepared defense enhances the force strength of a defender by a factor of 1.5; fortified defense has a multiplying effect of 1.6. An average value for a mixture of these postures would be about 1.4.

The multiplying factor in favor of the defender of the flat terrain of the Low Countries is about 1.1. The effect of the mixed terrain of the Ardennes and northeastern France is to increase the defender's force strength about 1.3 times. In the more rugged areas, like the Vosges Mountains, the terrain factor is about 1.5. Across the entire front, from North Sea to Switzerland, the average terrain factor would be about 1.2 for the defender.

Quality of Troops

Quantification of the quality of the troops is also based on extensive analysis by HERO, much of which is presented in Chapter 10. The analyses show that in their previous conflict (World War I), the Germans were better in ground combat than the Allies by a factor of about 1.2. In QJM terms the German Combat Effectiveness Value (CEV) relative to the allies was 1.2. In other words, 100 Germans in combat units were roughly the equivalent of 120 Allies in combat units. The factor turned out to be almost identical in World War II.

Overall Comparison

The next step is a general comparison of the opponents, as is shown diagrammatically in Figure 9-1. In terms of total force strength, and without consideration of variable factors, a comparison of Tables 9-2 and 9-4 shows that the Allies had a preponderance of 3350 to 2913, or 1.15 to 1.00.

However, when the comparison is based on combat power, the result is changed considerably. The general equation is as follows:

$$\frac{P}{P} = \frac{\text{German S} \times \text{Terrain Factor} \times \text{Posture Factor} \times \text{CEV}}{\text{Allied S} \times \text{Terrain Factor} \times \text{Posture Factor} \times \text{CEV}}$$

The Germans were the attackers, and the Allies were the defenders. In this chapter the combat power ratios are all calculated with the Germans in the numerator and the Allies in the denominator. The Allied combat power ratios are the reciprocals of the calculated German combat power ratios. The average terrain factor for the defender is 1.2 and the average defense posture

Figure 9–1

Overall Comparison

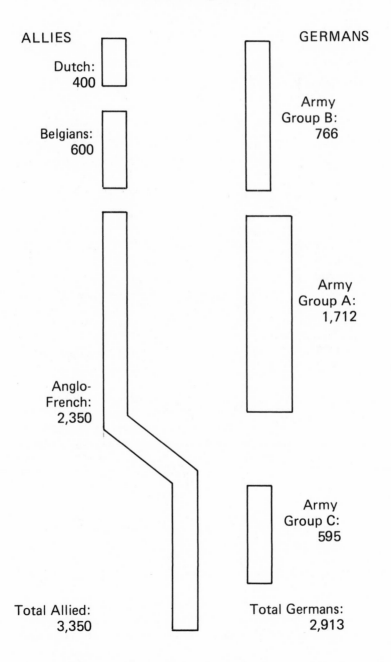

Figure 9–2

The Actual Force Comparison

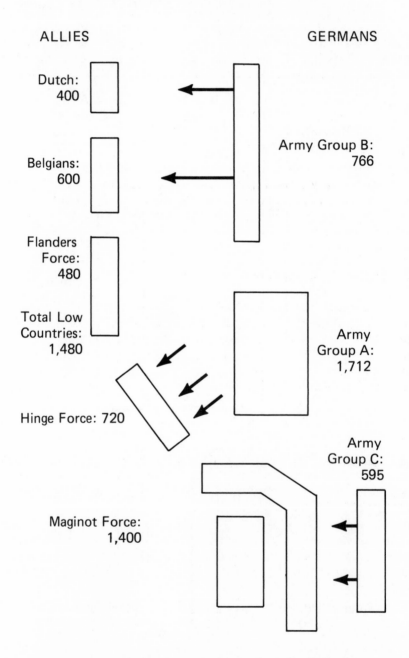

ALLIES

GERMANS

Dutch: 400

Belgians: 600

Army Group B: 766

Flanders Force: 480

Total Low Countries: 1,480

Army Group A: 1,712

Hinge Force: 720

Army Group C: 595

Maginot Force: 1,400

factor for the defender is 1.4. (The terrain and posture factors for the attackers are both 1.0.) Inserting these factor values and the German CEV of 1.2 gives the following equation:

$$\frac{P}{P} = \frac{\text{German: } (2913)\,(1.0)\,(1.0)\,(1.2)}{\text{Allies: } (3350)\,(1.2)\,(1.4)\,(1.0)} = \frac{3496}{5628} = 0.62 \ .$$

The German attack would obviously be stopped, according to this analysis, which gives the Allies a combat power ratio preponderance of 1.61 (the reciprocal of 0.62).

If both sides attack, the equation gives a slightly different result:

$$\frac{P}{P} = \frac{\text{G: } (2913)\,(1.0)\,(1.0)\,(1.2)}{\text{A: } (3350)\,(1.0)\,(1.0)\,(1.0)} = \frac{3496}{3350} = 1.04 \ .$$

There is a slight German preponderance (due to their greater CEV), but in the light of the crudeness and aggregation of the comparison any combat power ratio of less than about 1.10 must be considered inconclusive. This case is clearly a standoff, particularly because whichever side is forced on the defensive will immediately have a combat power preponderance, for the variable factors will then favor the defense.

The Historical Comparison

The Germans, of course, had no intention of making a general attack all along the line. They had amassed a powerful striking force in Army Group A, in the center of their line, and planned to make a penetration through the Ardennes. This situation is shown diagrammatically in Figure 9-2. The German plan and deployment requires an analysis of the battle in its three major sectors: (1) Low Countries, (2) Ardennes, and (3) the Maginot Line.

Low Countries. Army Group B was to make a holding attack against the Dutch, Belgians, and any Allied forces advancing into Belgium and Holland. It was their intention to make the Allies believe this was their main effort, and that they were initiating a new Schlieffen Plan. The Allies took the bait. Three Allied armies actually moved into Belgium, but only two were in contact very briefly with Army Group B. The Allied posture was a combination of hasty and prepared defense. The QJM analysis is as follows:

$$\frac{P}{P} = \frac{\text{G: } (766)\,(1.0)\,(1.0)\,(1.2)}{\text{A: } (1480)\,(1.4)\,(1.1)\,(1.0)} = \frac{919}{2279} = 0.40.$$

Obviously the German holding attack would be stopped under these circumstances by the Allied combat power preponderance of 2.48.

Ardennes. The Allied defensive posture was again a combination of hasty and prepared defense. The analysis:

$$\frac{P}{P} = \frac{\text{G:} \quad (1712)\,(1.0)\,(1.0)\,(1.2)}{\text{A:} \quad (720)\,(1.4)\,(1.3)\,(1.0)} = \frac{2054}{1310} = 1.57 \ .$$

The German preponderance of combat power is sufficient to assure a breakthrough, which in fact occurred.

Maginot Line. The Germans never had any intention of attempting a bloody, and essentially doomed, assault on the Maginot Line. All they wanted was to demonstrate with sufficient vigor so that they could hold the Allied forces in and behind the fortifications as long as possible. Had they really attempted an attack, the result would have been as follows:

$$\frac{P}{P} = \frac{\text{G:} \quad (595)\,(1.0)\,(1.0)\,(1.2)}{\text{A:} \quad (1400)\,(1.6)\,(1.3)\,(1.0)} = \frac{714}{2912} = .25 \ .$$

This comparison demonstrates most clearly the appalling waste of French forces deployed in the Maginot Line area, giving them a combat power preponderance of 4.0.

The analysis concludes that the overwhelming German attack in the Ardennes area would break through the Allied lines. This is what happened. As a result of the breakthrough, the Allied defensive effort collapsed.

The Hypothetical Comparison

In Figure 9-3 are the deployments resulting from the hypothetical DeGaulle plan to withdraw three armies from the Maginot area, and to use them in a counterattack against the northern army of German Army Group A. The principal difference between these deployments and those shown in Figure 9-1 is that in this hypothetical case an Allied group of four armies would have attacked eastward just north of the Ardennes, while the hinge just to the South would have been held by four more Allied armies in the rugged forests of the Ardennes. No reinforcements would be sent to the Low Countries, since their survival would

Figure 9–3

Hypothetical DeGaulle Plan

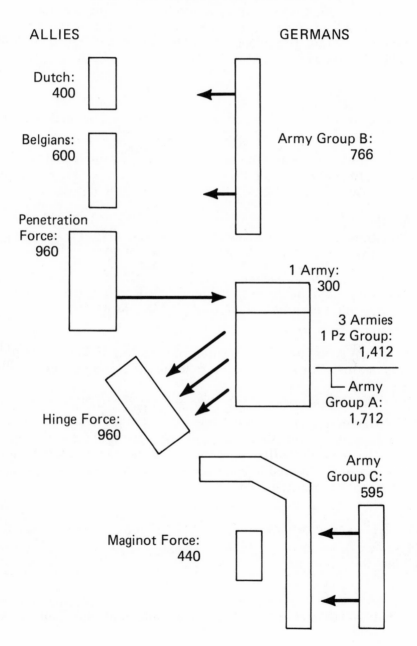

depend on the main battle in and around the Ardennes. Only one Allied army would remain to support the fortress troops in the Maginot Line. The German deployments remain unchanged, except that one German army would find itself thrown unexpectedly into a hasty defense posture by the Allied thrust north of the Ardennes. Thus, the hypothetical De Gaulle strategy gives four areas to analyze.

Low Countries. Here the Dutch and Belgians would, at first, have to fend for themselves against Army Group B. The analysis:

$$\frac{P}{P} = \frac{G: \quad (766)\,(1.0)\,(1.0)\,(1.2)}{A: \quad (1,000)\,(1.4)\,(1.1)\,(1.0)} = \frac{919}{1540} = 0.60 \ .$$

Again the German attack should be stopped by the Allied combat power preponderance of 1.68.

Northern Ardennes: The Allies took the offensive in the Northern Ardennes. Allowing for German airpower, diverted to support their threatened army, the analysis is as follows:

$$\frac{P}{P} = \frac{G: \quad (300)\,(1.3)\,(1.3)\,(1.2)}{A: \quad (960)\,(1.0)\,(1.0)\,(1.0)} = \frac{608}{960} = 0.63 \ .$$

The Allied combat power preponderance of 1.58 (the reciprocal of 0.63) would result in a clearcut Allied breakthrough.

Southern Ardennes. The German main effort of Army Group A, was against four Allied armies holding the Ardennes hinge. The analysis:

$$\frac{P}{P} = \frac{G: \quad (1412)\,(1.0)\,(1.0)\,(1.2)}{A: \quad (960)\,(1.4\text{x}1.3)\,(1.0)} = \frac{1694}{1747} = 0.97 \ .$$

The German attack would have been stopped under these circumstances, despite their preponderance in numbers and combat effectiveness. The Allies, making use of the terrain and of a mix of hasty and prepared defenses, would not have been overrun as they actually were in 1940.

Maginot Line: Although there would still have been no reason for the Germans to try to break through the formidable Maginot Line, the following analysis shows that they could not have done so:

$$\frac{P}{P} = \frac{G: \quad (595)\,(1.0)\,(1.0)\,(1.2)}{A: \quad (440)\,(1.6)\,(1.3)\,(1.0)} = \frac{714}{915} = 0.78 \ .$$

This rough and aggregated application of the QJM illustrates how quantitative assessment of combat can make sense out of historical combat and helps in thinking about future operational decisions. In the historical example, the resulting combat power ratios show clearly how the Germans defeated the Allies through a superior strategy and by applying the Principles of War, and not through better technology or a larger force. (Indeed, overall, they were outnumbered and their tanks were inferior.) In the hypothetical DeGaulle plan, the importance of using terrain and posture to the best advantage in accordance with the Principles of War is demonstrated. This analysis shows that the Allies could have won this campaign if they had placed enough reliance on the superiority of the tactical defense and fortifications to allow them to deliver a powerful operational attack against a selected portion of the German deployment.

Chapter 10

Relative Combat Effectiveness

Relative Combat Effectiveness and Force Quality

AN IMPORTANT AND unique feature of the QJM is that it includes an explicit, aggregated factor to account for those factors of combat that are generally intangible, but very identifiable, such as leadership, morale, training, experience, initiative, momentum, and chance. The effects of those intangible variables have to be determined by historical analysis because they cannot be detected from engineering tests of weapons or from field exercises. The real human factors of combat appear only during actual combat, when the element of fear is present. No model or theory of combat can be complete unless it can and does deal with these human factors. In the QJM, these are all represented by the concept of relative combat effectiveness and the quantitative expression of that concept, the Relative Combat Effectiveness Value (CEV).

In Chapter 8 I introduced the concept of the CEV. This concept is analogous to, but not quite identical with, Clausewitz's concept of "the quality of the troops." The CEV is a composite factor representing the total effect of all of the variables that have not been identified and quantified explicitly in the computation of combat power. The CEV includes the effects of all of the behavioral variables and the effects of those operational variables that have not yet been identified separately. In Table 10-1 a large set of variables included in the circumstances of combat are shown. This is not meant to be an exhaustive list, and additional variables could probably be added. However, the variables in Table 10-1 cover most of the important circumstances. As the list expands, the distinction between behavioral and operational variables tends to blur because some of the operational variables (surprise, for instance) include a large amount of the human element. That is the reason why this table differs from Table 8-2; there are ten additional operational variables, all with some behavioral element.

Table 10–1

Circumstantial Variables of Combat

Environmental	Operational
*Terrain	*Posture and Fortifications
*Weather	*Mobility
*Season	*Vulnerability
	*Air Superiority
Behavioral	*Surprise
Leadership	*Fatigue
Training	*Weapons Sophistication
Experience	Logistical Capability
Morale	Intelligence
Manpower Quality	Initiative
	Command and Control
	Communications
	Momentum
	Time and Space
	Chance
*Factor values established	Friction

Those variables in Table 10-1 for which factor values have been established in the QJM are marked with an asterisk. The remaining variables constitute the present composition of the CEV. It may be possible to isolate and quantify the individual effects of additional variables, and as this is done the composition of the CEV will be adjusted accordingly.

The variables included in the CEV are those that are difficult if not impossible, to quantify on a consistent basis. The CEV includes all of the human behavioral variables often referred to as "intangibles of combat." The CEV also includes several operational or composite operational/behavioral variables that have thus far resisted quantification. To the extent that the CEV includes the effects of operational variables, such as command and control, it differs from the quality of troops (Q) as defined by Clausewitz. However, this difference does not impair the use of the QJM because the CEV assures that the overall impact of all of the circumstances of combat is considered for each battle or engagement.

The CEV also includes the effects of chance and friction. There is an element of chance in all human activities, and friction is created by the interactions of hundreds of thousands of individuals on a battlefield. The calculated CEV for any one battle will include not only the influence of the quality of the troops and leadership on both sides, but also the influence of the ambient circumstances of chance and friction. The more battles for which the CEV for a unit is calculated, particularly against the same opponent, the more the ambient circumstances will tend to cancel out, and the closer the average CEV will approach the true quality of the force, or the Q of the Clausewitz equation.

Combat Outcome Diagram

The Combat Effectiveness Value (CEV) is defined as the ratio of the result ratio to the combat power ratio. This is shown in the equation below for the red side, CEV_r. The value for the blue side, CEV_b, is the reciprocal of CEV_r.

$$CEV_r = \frac{(R_r/R_b)}{(P_r/P_b)}.$$

If the outcome predicted by the combat power ratio is matched by the outcome expressed in the result ratio, the combat effectiveness of the two sides is equal. If the result ratio for one side is larger than its combat power ratio, this means that that side performed better than was predicted by the combat power ratio, and its CEV for that battle or engagement is greater than 1.0. If the result ratio is smaller than the combat power ratio, then the actual outcome was not as good as was predicted, and the CEV is less than 1.0.

Relationships between results and combat power can be presented conveniently in graphic form using the combat outcome diagram shown in Figure 10-1, for two sides, red and blue.

The origin is set so that the values of the two ratios are unity. The upper half of the diagram is the result ratio of side blue over side red; this is reversed for the lower half. Similarly, the combat power ratio in the right half is for side blue over side red, and is

Figure 10–1

Combat Outcome Diagram

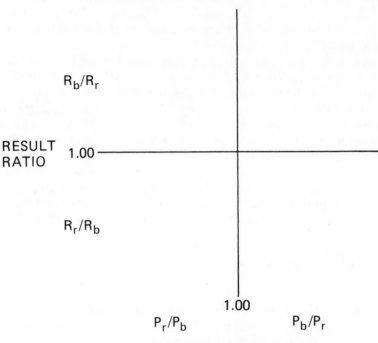

COMBAT POWER RATIO

reversed in the left half. This permits plotting the ratios for individual engagements consistently as having values over 1.00.

The meaning of each quadrant of the combat outcome diagram is shown in Figure 10-2. It is evident that if the result ratio and combat power ratio are reasonably consistent with each other, all of the engagement plots would fall into either the upper-right or lower-left quadrants. When they do not fall into either of these quadrants, the CEV becomes particularly significant.

As evident from equation 1, the CEV for an engagement is unity (or 1.0) when the actual result is the same as the predicted result, or the result ratio equals the combat power ratio. The locus of these points is a line passing through the origin and at a 45 degree angle to the horizontal axis as shown in Figure 10-3. This line includes all points with a CEV = 1.00, and is called the Equal Effectiveness Line.

In the upper half of the graph, the CEVs for forces whose engagement ratios intersect above or to the left of the Equal Effectiveness Line are greater than 1.0, the CEVs for forces whose engagement ratios intersect below or to the right of the line are less than 1.0. In the lower half of the graph, of course, the CEVs whose engagement ratios intersect below or to the right of the Equal Effectiveness Line are greater than 1.0; while the CEVs of the forces whose engagement ratios intersect above or to the left of the line are less than 1.00.

The combat outcome diagram will be used in the next chapter to present the phenomenon of diminishing victories in combat. The next step in this chapter is to explain how the concept of relative combat effectiveness emerged from analysis of World War II engagements.

German Excellence in Two World Wars

My early efforts to quantify combat were at first frustrated by an unexpected phenomenon. The results of the initial analysis of World War II data showed that the Germans were consistently better in that war than the Americans and the British, whether they were attacking or defending, whether they were winning or losing. This was an illustration, of course, of what Clausewitz had been referring to when he formulated his Law of Numbers: he stated that the quality of a force is a given quantity. It was not long before analysis of data from World War I battles demonstrated that the phenomenon of German combat effectiveness superiority in ground combat in World War II had been matched by a comparable superiority in that earlier war. I came to the conclusion that the United States Armed Forces should sponsor a study of this phenomenon, to see if anything could be learned from it. When I was unable to persuade either the Department of Defense or the Army to support such research, I wrote a book about it.[1]

Continued analysis of World War II combat data demonstrated that some German units were consistently better than others, and that one American unit in our data base, the 88th Division, consistently performed better than other Allied divisions in that data base[2] and was in fact of a quality comparable to better than average German opponents. From these findings, based upon performing analyses of a number of engagements, emerged the

Figure 10-2
Combat Outcome Diagram: Quadrant Meanings

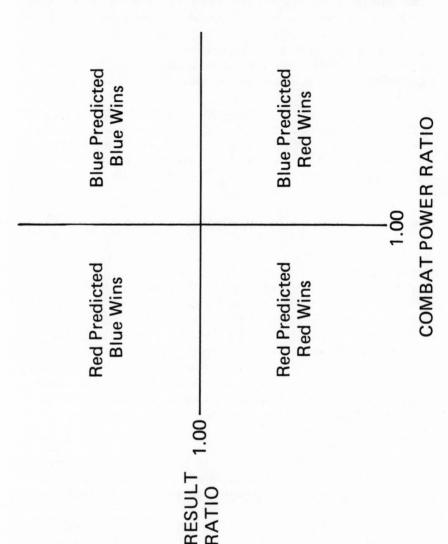

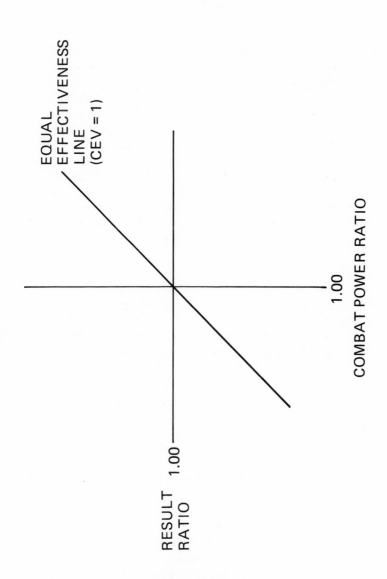

Figure 10–3

**Combat Outcome Diagram: Equal
Effectiveness Line**

concept of calculating the relative combat effectiveness of opponents by relating the result ratio to the combat power ratio.

Figure 10-4 is a scattergram showing the locations of the intersections of the combat power and result ratios for the eighty-one engagements of the initial World War II data base (sixty engagements in Italy in 1943–44, and twenty-one in Northwest Europe in 1944); a data summary of these is in Appendix A. These combat power ratios were calculated without consideration of any behavioral factors; that is, the intangibles were not considered. There are forty-nine engagements in the upper-right quadrant (Allied combat power superiority, Allied success); there are sixteen in the lower-left quadrant (German combat power superiority, German success): twelve are in the lower right quadrant (Allied combat power superiority, German success), and only one engagement is in the upper-left quadrant (German combat power superiority, Allied success). Two engagements in which the combat power was equal are also plotted; the Germans were successful in one of these, and the Allies were successful in the other.

Particularly significant were the twelve instances of clear-cut German success, despite an equally clear-cut Allied combat power superiority. (The lower-right quadrant.) It was from a graph such as this that I became convinced of the overall German ground combat effectiveness superiority over the Allies in World War II. Further analysis confirmed this conclusion.

In Table 10-2 are the results of the QJM analyses used to determine the relative combat effectiveness of most of the Allied and German divisions in the data base—those which participated in at least three of these eighty-one engagements. The combat power ratio (P/P) based on data in the records was calculated (including any factors for surprise) and compared with the result ratio (R/R). The CEV of each division with respect to its opponent in that engagement was then determined by dividing the result ratio by the originally calculated combat power ratio. A tentative CEV for each division was then applied against the CEVs calculated for each of that division's opponents, and a refined average CEV was calculated for each division.

In order to facilitate a comparison among the divisions, they were ranked in descending order of average CEV. The results are shown in Table 10-3. Nine of the first ten divisions were German. The U.S. 88th Division was rated fifth. This was the only Allied division in the data base to have a combat effectiveness value

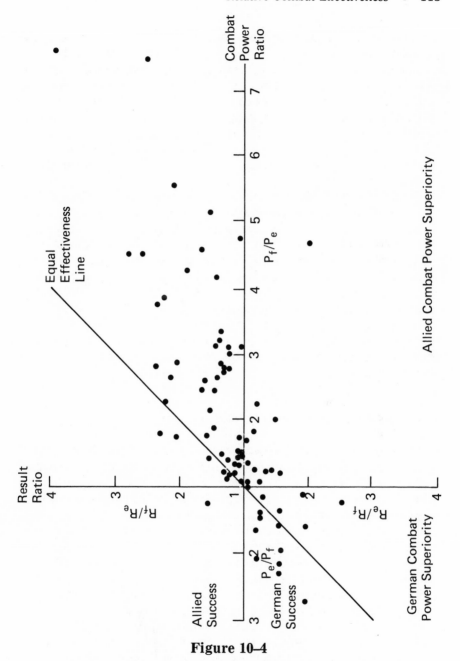

Figure 10–4

Combat Power and Result Ratios for 81 WWII Engagements

greater than 1.0 and comparable to the best of the German divisions.

The generally poor and unpredictable performance of the British 56th Infantry Division in Italy in 1943–44 is evident from the record of nine engagements in the data base. After these assessments were presented to officials in the British Ministry of Defence a few years ago, it was reassuring to learn that higher British headquarters in Italy in 1943 and 1944 had had a comparably low assessment of the division and had contemplated disbanding it.

On the other hand, both the American 3d Infantry Division and 1st Armored Division were held in high regard by their corps commanders and their opponents. The lower relative ranking of these divisions in Table 10-3 may result from the fact that several of their analyzed engagements took place after long periods of intense and protracted combat in very bad weather. The significance of this distortion can unquestionably be determined at some future time, since improved methods of quantification are now available and will permit a more refined evaluation of the effects of sustained combat, of weather, and of a steady casualty drain than did methods available to me when the above analysis was performed.

The Performance of the U.S. 88th Infantry Division

It did not at first seem reasonable that the relatively unknown U.S. 88th Infantry Division should have such a high combat effectiveness. However, the *Tagebuch* (War Diary) of the German Tenth Army revealed that by late 1944 the Germans were classing the 88th as a "shock troops" division. Also, when the 88th Division was committed to the battle line, the Germans shifted their reserves, anticipating a main effort in the 88th Division sector. Obviously, the Germans believed that the 88th Infantry Division was something special.

The 88th Division was one of fourteen new all-draftee divisions, activated in mid-1942 after the mobilization of all Regular Army, Organized Reserve, and National Guard Divisions. The activation and deployment schedule of these divisions is shown in Table 10-4. The 88th Division was the eighth of these divisions to be activated, in July 1942. It trained for one year at Camp

Table 10–2

CEVs of Selected Divisions in World War II

	NUMBER OF ENGAGEMENTS	AVERAGE CEVs
United States		
1st Armored	3	0.86
3d Infantry	4	0.86
4th Armored	8	0.73
34th Infantry	5	0.81
45th Infantry	11	0.72
85th Infantry	6	0.79
88th Infantry	4	1.14
Average		0.84
British		
1st Infantry	8	0.82
5th Infantry	3	0.61
7th Armored	3	0.83
46th Infantry	6	0.96
56th Infantry	9	0.60
Average		0.76
German		
H. Goering Panzer-Parachute	5	1.49
Panzer Lehr	4	1.02
3d Panzer Grenadier	17	1.17
4th Parachute	5	0.93
11th Panzer	4	1.31
15th Panzer Grenadier	11	1.12
16th Panzer	7	1.07
29th Panzer	3	0.82
65th Infantry	6	0.98
94th Infantry	8	1.38
361st Infantry	3	0.95
362d Infantry	3	0.98
Average		1.10

Grueber, near Muskogee, Oklahoma, and participated in the Louisiana maneuvers of the summer of 1943. It got very high marks from inspectors during its training and during the maneuvers, and as a consequence was the first of the new divisions to be

Table 10–3

C E V s o f S e l e c t e d D i v i s i o n s i n W W I I

Rank	Division		Average CEV
1	Herman Goering Panzer-Para	German	1.49
2	94th Infantry	German	1.38
3	11th Panzer	German	1.31
4	3d Panzer Grenadier	German	1.17
5	88th Infantry	American	1.14
6	15th Panzer Grenadier	German	1.12
7	16th Panzer	German	1.07
8	Panzer Lehr	German	1.02
9	65th Infantry	German	0.98
10	362d Infantry	German	0.98
11	46th Infantry	British	0.96
12	361st Infantry	German	0.95
13	4th Parachute	German	0.93
14	1st Armored	American	0.86
15	3d Infantry	American	0.86
16	7th Armored	British	0.83
17	1st Infantry	British	0.82
18	29th Panzer	German	0.82
19	34th Infantry	American	0.81
20	85th Infantry	American	0.79
21	4th Armored	American	0.73
22	45th Infantry	American	0.72
23	5th Infantry	British	0.61
24	56th Infantry	British	0.60

shipped overseas, in November 1943. The average elapsed time for the divisions to deploy was about twenty-three months, but the 88th Division deployed after only sixteen months of training. It was the first of the new divisions to go into combat, being committed to defensive positions about 50 miles south of Rome, on 1 March 1944.

On 11–12 May 1944, the 88th Division was committed to operation "Diadem," sometimes called the Rome Offensive or Rome Campaign. Beside the 88th Division was its sister division, the 85th Division. Figure 10-5 is a map showing the operations of the Rome Campaign. There are conflicting claims as to which American units were actually first into Rome on June 4. There is little doubt, however, that these were elements of the 88th Division.

During the three and a half weeks of the Rome Campaign the

Table 10–4

Activation and Deployment Dates of US Divisions

INFANTRY DIVISIONS	ACTIVATION MONTH	DEPLOYMENT MONTH	ELAPSED MONTHS
77th	March	March 1944	24
90th	March	March 1944	24
85th	May	December 1943	19
76th	June	November 1944	29
79th	June	June 1944	21
81st	June	June 1944	24
80th	July	June 1944	23
88th	July	November 1943	16
89th	July	January 1945	29
95th	July	July 1944	24
78th	August	October 1944	26
83rd	August	March 1944	19
81st	August	March 1944	19
96th	August	July 1944	23

performance of this green division was exceptional. The analysis upon which the assessment of the relative combat effectiveness of the 88th Division is based relates mostly to this period.

Why Was the 88th Division Good?

Both the Allied commanders and the Germans recognized the excellence of the 88th Division. The key question, with great significance for future U.S. Army doctrine, is *why* was it so good?

The most important factor appears to be leadership by the division commander. In other respects the 88th Division was similar to the other new divisions. Personnel policies were similar, and the 88th Division acquired no particular advantages in the officers and enlisted men assigned to it. The training programs were identical; they were established by Army Ground Forces for all new divisions. However, when one looks closely, there *were* differences in both leadership and training. These can

Figure 10–5

Rome Campaign
11-30 May–4 June
1944

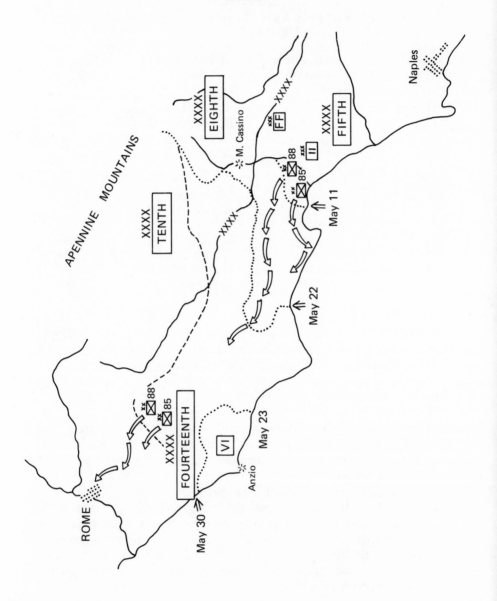

be mainly attributed to one man: Major General John Emmit Sloan, Commanding General of the 88th.

Sloan, a graduate of the U.S. Naval Academy at Annapolis in 1910, was 55 years old, and slightly over the arbitrary age limit that had been set for division commanders, when the 88th Division was activated. An exception was made by the Commanding General of Army Ground Forces, Lieutenant General Leslie J. McNair, to allow Sloan to command. This was based upon the recommendation of McNair's deputy, then-Brigadier General Mark W. Clark, who remembered Sloan as an outstanding instructor at the Command and General Staff School at Fort Leavenworth in the 1930s.

Sloan had little to do with the selection of other officers of the division and, of course, he could not exert direct personal leadership influence on the 13,000 enlisted men under his command. However, by example and by tireless supervision and guidance, General Sloan seems to have been able to instill his own high standards of conduct and leadership in all of the officers directly below him and, through them, in all other officers and noncommissioned officers of the division. This was manifested initially through zeal in training. The records show that leadership characteristics demonstrated in the 88th Division included

Aggressiveness
Attention to detail
Strict discipline
Inspirational talks and messages
Personal presence in the front line
Being sure subordinates had what they needed to do the job
Making sure every assignment was carried out properly, including those not immediately related to military procedures
Requiring strict adherence to established standards for military courtesy and proper uniform
Prompt relief of any subordinate who could not or would not do his job
Making friendly gestures to establish rapport with subordinate commanders
Tactical skill
Grasping and communicating the "big picture" and role of each unit in overall objectives.

Such characteristics, of course, were not at first appreciated by the enlisted men. In fact, during the training period in the United States, Sloan was considered to be an unnecessarily strict disciplinarian—a martinet who demanded smart salutes and buttoned buttons in a way that did not seem terribly important to the soldiers.

That being the case, it is interesting to see what, in retrospect after combat, the soldiers later considered important in the leadership they had received from Sloan, through the intermediate ranks of officers. Here are the major characteristics of 88th Division leadership, as perceived by its veterans:

Personal presence in the front lines
Discipline
Courage
Aggressiveness

As they remember it now, the opinions of the soldiers with respect to Sloan began to change after the first few weeks of battle. They were proud to be in a division that they now knew to be an excellent, outstanding unit, and they realized that the man primarily responsible was Sloan.

During lulls in battle, and during rest periods, the division trained. One reason why his division ranked right up with the best of the German divisions was that Sloan carried out rear-area training programs and demanded standards of performance very similar to those characteristic of the Germans, while showing similar interest in, and concern for, his men. He also demanded of his officers a professionalism comparable to that of the Germans. Replacements were soon imbued with the spirit of the division. When the division was out on the line Sloan still insisted upon smart salutes and buttoned buttons, and got them from proud soldiers.

The excellence of the 88th Division, and the potential to learn from its experience how to prepare leaders and train soldiers, was revealed by the QJM analysis, which established the exceptional CEV of this division.

The example of the 88th Division and comparisons of that division with other units of three armies, illustrates the importance of one of Clausewitz's three general measures of combat outcomes: the value of the troops. The analysis also supports his view that the value of the troops is indeed "a given quantity," which can be measured in the equation of battle.

Perhaps equally important is the fact that the performance of the 88th Division demonstrates that a commander who has an understanding of the components of a theory of combat can make use of that understanding to influence battle outcomes. By dedicated professionalism, inspiring leadership, and very hard work, General Sloan was able to raise his division (at least on the basis of the data available to us) to a combat performance capability 43% higher than that of the average of the other American divisions in our sample. In other words, in the equation of battle, the 88th Division had the advantage of a factor of 1.43. Remember that factor: 1.43! We shall see how important it is!

Relative Combat Effectiveness in the Arab-Israeli Wars

The experience of the 1967 and 1973 Arab-Israeli Wars offers additional evidence of the validity of the concept of relative combat effectiveness. Two important facts emerged from this evidence: (1) the relative stability of CEVs from one conflict to another, and (2) the implicit recognition of CEVs by force allocation. The CEVs for the Israelis versus their Arab opponents in the wars of 1967 and 1973 are shown in Table 10-5.

Table 10–5

Israelis CEVs versus Arabs in 1967 and 1973 Wars

	JORDANIANS	EGYPTIANS	SYRIANS	IRAQIS
1967	1.54	1.75	2.44	—
1973	1.88	1.98	2.54	3.43

This illustrates the stability of the CEVs for these sets of opponents. The rank ordering of the Arab state forces relative to the Israelis remained unchanged from 1967 and 1973, and the absolute values of the CEVs had also remained very close, but the relative combat effectiveness of the Israelis over all of their Arab enemies had increased somewhat between the two wars. There is little doubt that this increase was due to higher standards of professionalism in the Israeli Army than in the Arab armies.

Implicit validation of the CEVs is given by the actual allocation of Israeli troops in the 1973 October War. This war provides a rare instance in which it is impossible to deduce a value for the CEV from the allocation of forces because, in general, all other things were equal.

It is generally agreed that on both the Suez front in the south and the Golan front in the north, the opponents in the 1973 war fought each other to a standstill. The Arabs had taken the offensive initially and had much the better of the first phases of the campaign. The Israelis, after a remarkable recovery from the initial shock of surprise, assumed the offensive and had much the better of the later phases. At the end of the war the opponents were in a condition of relatively stable military balance on both fronts.

The two forces were about even except for relative combat effectiveness. Their force compositions were about the same, they fought over the same terrain in the same weather and each had spent about the same time attacking and defending. The only real differences were in numbers and the relative combat effectiveness of the forces. This was recognized by the Israelis in allocating their forces between the Suez front and the Golan front. Table 10-6 illustrates the Israeli and Arab strengths during this war.

Table 10–6

Personnel/Strengths in the 1973 Arab–Israeli War

Front	Israeli Strength	Arab Strength	Ratio of Arab to Israeli Strength
Golan	60,000	150,000 (Syrians)	2.50
Suez	120,000	240,000 (Egyptians)	2.00

The Israelis showed that they had a good idea of their combat effectiveness relative to their Arab opponents. In the north they had sufficient strength so that their CEV of 2.50 relative to the Syrians would be enough to offset the Syrian strength ratio of

2.50. In the south they had sufficient strength—about half that of the Egyptians—so that their CEV of about 2.00 relative to the Egyptians also was sufficient to produce a stalemate.

This is not only evidence of the validity of the CEVs computed using the QJM, but it also is a good example of the importance of knowing one's combat effectiveness relative to potential opponents.

Chapter 11

Diminishing Returns in Combat

Economy of Force and Relative Combat Effectiveness

IF THE ANALYSIS of historical combat is to be useful for fighting future warfare, it must be capable of helping the commander manage the battlefield operations of his forces. One of the most important Principles of War is Economy of Force. This instructs the commander to use only that force necessary to avoid defeat at non-decisive points in a given situation in order to accomplish his mission by massing superior strength at the decisive point. The trouble is that it is difficult to determine beforehand just how much force is necessary to achieve a given combat result, and how much is required to avoid defeat. One of the tests of combat leadership is the ability of a commander to assess the strength necessary to hold the non-decisive areas, in order to have adequate force where the decision will be reached. The application of the relative combat effectiveness value (CEV) to historical combat can provide some insights of great value to future commanders in dealing with this problem.

There is evidence from historical combat that, after a given ratio of combat power is reached, the addition of more forces provides less in terms of results than would otherwise be expected. In other words, the marginal value of an increment of combat power is less than the marginal value of the incremental results achieved. This is, of course, a statement of the familiar law of diminishing returns. What is new is that it can now be demonstrated that it not only applies to combat as well as to other human undertakings, but that its dimensions can also be determined.

If this is so, then a doctrine calling for military commanders to apply maximum, or overwhelming, force to assure decisive results could be counterproductive when considered in a larger context. The idea would be to apply at each place on the battlefield or in the theatre of operations just the right amount of force to get the job done. But then, an old soldier would suggest, add a bit more at the decisive point to allow for errors in calculations and for unexpected circumstances.

Economy of Force and Diminishing Returns

I did not appreciate the relevance of the relationship among diminishing returns, economy of force, and relative combat effectiveness during my early efforts to find some basis for measurement of the CEV. At first my comparisons seemed to indicate that the German superiority over the Allies could be expressed in terms of a CEV factor of 1.20, or a German ground combat effectiveness superiority of about 20%. Later, as more data was accumulated, and I became more certain of the validity and procedures of the QJM, the increasing numbers of the plots of the P/P and R/R intersections for the Allies below the equal effectiveness line, seemed to indicate that the German CEV might be greater than 1.20, perhaps closer to 1.25 or 1.30.

Although at first it did not appear to have any relationship to the apparently increased value of the German CEV, there was something else intriguing about the scattergram showing the plots of the first eighty-one World War II engagements analyzed by the QJM (see Appendix A). In not one instance where the Allied combat power ratio superiority exceeded 2.00 did the result ratio have a higher, or even equal, value. The same was true of the smaller number of instances in which the German combat power superiority exceeded 2.00; in all of these the result ratio was smaller. And this was true for the best of the German and the Allied divisions. I suspected that this was due to some as yet obscure manifestation of the law of diminishing returns.

Reanalyzing the Data

Relatively recently I decided to try another approach to the analysis of the data for these engagements. By this time the HERO/QJM data base for west European operations in World War II had expanded to ninety-three engagements. I decided to use the combat outcome diagram introduced in Chapter 10 as a basis for examining the evidence that the law of diminishing returns applies to combat. Figure 11-1 is a combat outcome diagram in which the equal effectiveness line is plotted, and in which a new line representing relative combat effectiveness is also plotted.

The relative effectiveness line is parallel to the equal effectiveness line, but displaced on the x-axis by a distance equal to the plotted value of the CEV of the side in the numerator of the result ratio and combat power ratio. The relative effectiveness line is the locus of the intersections of the result ratio and combat power ratio for combat engagements involving the military force having this CEV, relative to another military force. If there were no deviations from the average results, all engagements between these two military forces would plot on the relative effectiveness line.

This will seldom be the case. It is more likely that any individual engagement will appear to one side or the other of the relative effectiveness line. Figure 11-2 shows three possible positions for the results of an engagement between two forces in which the combat power is constant.

The interpretation of the significance of these three locations has to do with whether the military forces in the numerator of the ratios have been applied more efficiently or less efficiently than those of the opponent. That is, whatever amount of combat power has been applied to achieve the desired result, it has been applied with average efficiency, or with greater or less than average efficiency.

At Point A, the relationship is the expected one for the two sides. The result ratio at Point A equals the product of the CEV and the combat power ratio. In this case, the military forces both fought with expected, or average, efficiency. At Point B, however, the result ratio is greater than the product of the CEV and combat power ratio, and the military force of the numerator has fought more efficiently than expected—in comparison with the opponent —from its CEV value. And, at Point C, the result ratio is less than the product of the CEV and the combat power ratio, and thus the

Figure 11–1

Combat Outcome Diagram

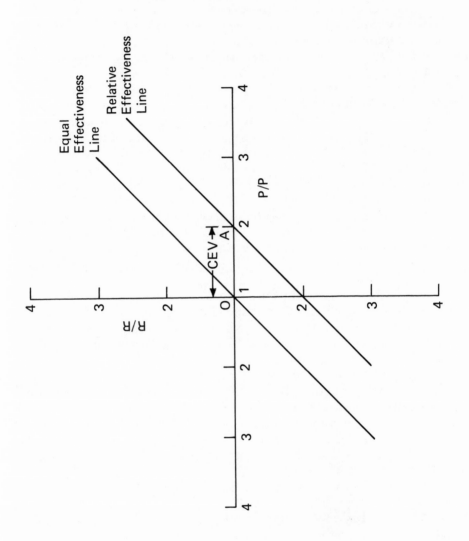

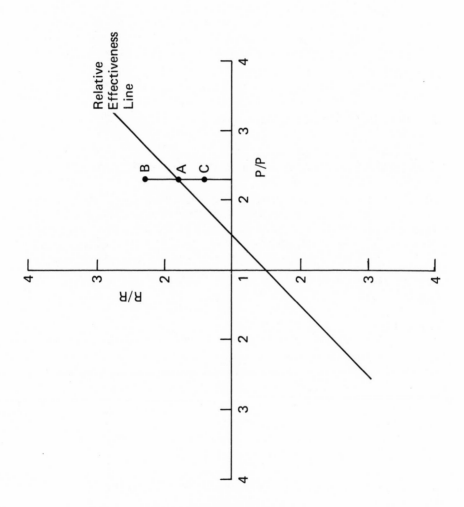

Figure 11–2

Combat Outcome Diagram

military force has fought less efficiently (compared to its opponent) than expected. The distance between Points A and C, therefore, is a measure of the relative inefficiency of the force in that particular engagement compared to average performance. Similarly, the distance from A to B is a measure of improved efficiency for the force in a particular engagement.

Since this is the case, it should be possible to describe the efficiency of a military force by determining the way in which the results achieved compare to the combat power attained as the combat power ratio increases from 1.0 to higher values. This is the procedure that will be used to demonstrate the phenomenon of diminishing returns.

Diminishing Returns in World War II

Combat engagement data from World War II and from the Arab-Israeli Wars are used to describe the relationship between combat power and results. The first step is to examine the evidence of ninety-three engagements from World War II. Then the same procedure is used on fifty-two engagements from the Arab-Israeli Wars.

The ninety-three World War II engagements used in this analysis are listed in Appendix A and include the initial eighty-one engagements discussed in Chapter 10. There are seventy-six engagements in which the Allies had superior combat power and seventeen engagements in which the Germans had superior combat power.

In order to demonstrate the behavior of the Allied forces as the combat power ratio varied, the seventy-six engagements in which the Allies had combat power superiority were arrayed in fifteen combat power classes. The results are shown in Table 11-1.

For the seventy-six engagements in which the Allies had combat power superiority the results indicate a definite decrease in efficiency as the combat power ratio gets larger. As the combat power ratio increases above 2, the results do not increase proportionately. For values of combat power ratio over 4 there is only a slight increase in results.

The data for the seventeen engagements in which the Germans had combat power superiority is shown in Table 11-2. The same trend is present. For combat power ratios from 1 to 2, the gain in

Table 11-1

WWII Allied Combat Superiority

Comparisons of Combat Power [P/P] and Result Ratios [R/R] for 76 WW II Engagements with Allied Combat Power Superiority (by Combat Power Ratio Classes)

P/P CLASS	NUMBER OF ENGAGEMENTS	CLASS P/P	AVERAGE R/R
1.00–1.19	7	1.06	1.02
1.20–1.39	13	1.28	1.07
1.40–1.59	9	1.49	1.20
1.60–1.79	4	1.75	1.43
1.80–1.99	3	1.86	1.55
2.00–2.19	3	2.10	1.25
2.20–2.39	4	2.27	1.71
2.40–2.59	2	2.48	1.56
2.60–2.79	6	2.65	1.63
2.80–2.99	6	2.85	1.69
3.00–3.49	4	3.09	1.22
3.50–3.99	4	3.71	2.03
4.00–4.99	7	4.50	1.55
5.00–5.99	2	5.32	1.80
6.00–7.99	2	7.50	2.70
	76		

results is roughly proportional. For combat power ratios over 2, the gain in results is less than expected.

The combined results for all ninety-three engagements, as shown in Tables 11-1 and 11-2 are plotted on a combat outcome diagram, with the results as shown on Figure 11-3. The relatively slight, but still consistent, superiority of German ground combat effectiveness is shown graphically in Figure 11-4, when the data from Tables 11-1 (Allied P/P preponderance) and 11-2 (German P/P preponderance) are both plotted together (with a common origin) in the upper-right quadrant of a combat outcome diagram. While the shapes of the two curves are close to identical, that for the side with the higher CEV (the Germans) rises slightly more rapidly.

A test was then made, following the same general procedure, to see the effects of making comparisons in terms of attackers and

Figure 11–3

Combat Outcome Diagram: 93 WWII Engagements
(averaged in P/P classes)

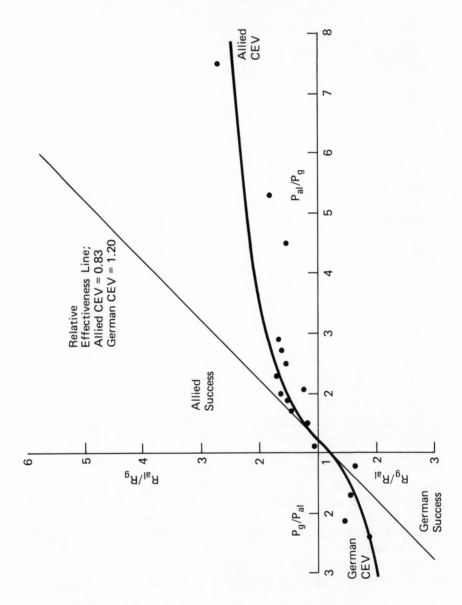

Table 11–2

**Comparisons of Combat Power and
Result Ratios for 17 WW II Engagements
with German Combat Power Superiority
(by Combat Power Ratio Classes)**

P/P CLASS	NUMBER OF ENGAGEMENTS	CLASS P/P	AVERAGE R/B
1.00–1.49	9	1.25	1.61
1.50–1.99	4	1.73	1.57
2.00–2.49	3	2.15	1.43
> 2.50	1	2.70	1.92
	17		

defenders. In our sample of ninety-three World War II engagements there were sixty-one instances of the attacker having a higher combat power ratio, and thirty-two in which the P/P of the defender exceeded 1.0. Since the attackers were usually the Allies, and the defenders usually the Germans, it was expected that the results would be similar to those summarized in Figure 11-4, but with a lesser CEV preponderance for the defender. Table 11-3 shows the results of organizing the engagement data in combat power classes as was done in Tables 11-1 and 11-2. Figure 11-5 shows the results when this data, both the attacker and defender, is plotted in the upper right quadrant of a combat outcome diagram.

It is clear that the results were not exactly what was expected. The curve for the attacker is quite similar in shape to those for the Germans and the Allies in Figures 11-3 and 11-4. But the curve for the defender is quite different. It rises at least as rapidly as the curve for the attacker, but then quite abruptly falls off, and is almost flat, with little or no rise in R/R as the P/P gets higher and higher. (In fact the data could be interpreted as indicating a slight fall-off in R/R as P/P increased.) Before attempting to draw conclusions from these somewhat surprising results, it will be desirable to analyze similar data from the 1967 and 1973 Arab-Israeli Wars.

Diminishing Returns in the Arab-Israeli Wars

Using the same technique, a total of fifty-two engagements from the 1967 and 1973 Arab-Israeli Wars were examined. (These and key data elements are listed in Appendix B.) The

Figure 11–4

Combat Outcome Diagram: 93
WWII Engagements
Comparative Plot of German and Allied CEV's

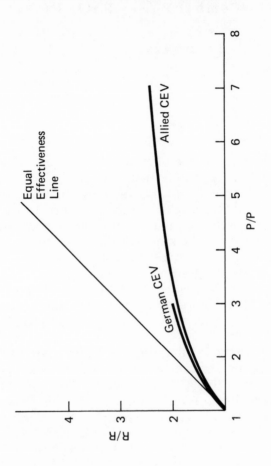

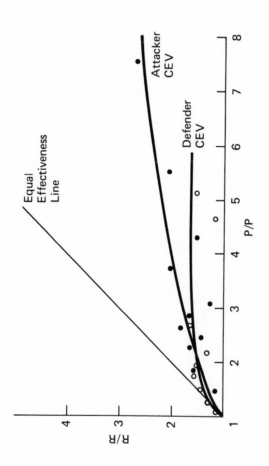

Figure 11–5

**Combat Outcome Diagram: 93
WWII Engagements
Comparative Plot of Attackers
and Defender CEV's**

Table 11–3

Comparisons of Combat Power and Result Ratios for 93 WWII Engagements, for Attackers and Defenders (by Combat Power Ratio Classes)

P/P Class	No of Engagements	Class P/P	Av. R/R
Attackers Superior P/P			
1.00–1.19	6	1.06	1.03
1.20–1.39	11	1.29	1.20
1.40–1.59	8	1.49	1.16
1.60–1.79	4	1.75	1.43
1.80–1.99	2	1.84	1.58
2.00–2.19	2	2.15	1.55
2.20–2.39	4	2.27	1.68
2.40–2.59	1	2.46	1.46
2.60–2.79	4	2.67	1.70
2.80–2.99	6	2.85	1.69
3.00–3.49	3	3.09	1.29
3.50–3.99	4	3.71	2.03
4.00–4.99	3	4.30	1.53
5.00–5.99	1	5.52	2.09
6.00–7.99	2	7.54	2.70
Total	61		
Defenders Superior P/P			
1.00–1.19	4	1.06	1.17
1.20–1.39	7	1.27	1.29
1.40–1.59	3	1.49	1.44
1.60–1.79	2	1.71	1.58
1.80–1.99	2	1.91	1.54
2.00–2.49	5	2.19	1.32
2.50–2.99	3	2.65	1.64
3.00–3.99	1	3.10	0.99
4.00–4.99	4	4.65	1.19
5.00–5.99	1	5.11	1.51
Total	32		

results are shown in Figure 11-6 which is a scattergram showing the locations of the intersections of the combat power and result ratios of the engagements. This is similar to the scattergram for

Table 11–4

Comparisons of Combat Power and Result Ratios for 52 Arab-Israeli War Engagements for Israelis and Arabs (by Combat Power Ratio Classes)

P/P Class	No of Engagements	Class P/P	Av. R/R
	Israeli Superior P/P		
1.00–1.19	3	1.10	2.38
1.20–1.39	5	1.28	2.55
1.40–1.59	3	1.47	3.00
1.60–1.79	2	1.63	2.31
1.80–1.99	3	1.91	3.15
2.00–2.29	3	2.14	2.75
2.30–2.59	1	2.56	2.75
2.60–2.89	5	2.79	3.19
Total	25		
	Arabs Superior P/P		
1.00–1.19	3	1.14	0.39
1.20–1.39	4	1.32	0.46
1.40–1.59	1	1.51	0.48
1.60–1.79	3	1.72	0.73
1.80–1.99	1	1.98	0.32
2.00–2.49	4	2.23	0.88
2.50–2.99	1	2.52	0.33
3.00–3.49	2	3.07	1.49
3.50–3.99	5	3.77	1.32
4.00–7.99	3	6.63	1.56
Total	21		

World War II shown in Figure 10-4. There were twenty-five engagements in which the Israelis had superior combat power and twenty-seven in which the combat power of the Arabs was superior. The engagements in which the Israelis had superior combat power are represented by the plotted points and the curve on the right of the P/P = 1 axis. The results of the twenty-six engagements in which the Arabs had superior combat power are represented on the left of this axis.

An analysis was then performed similar to that done for the World War II engagements. Comparisons of the P/P and R/R ratios

Table 11–5

Comparisons of Combat Power and Result Ratios for 52 Arab-Israeli War Engagements, for Attackers and Defenders (by Combat Power Ratio Classes)

P/P Class	No of Engagements	Class P/P	Av. R/R
Attackers Superior P/P			
1.00–1.19	1	1.14	2.49
1.20–1.39	5	1.29	2.14
1.40–1.59	2	1.46	3.18
1.60–1.79	5	1.68	1.36
1.80–1.99	2	1.88	3.22
2.00–2.49	3	2.15	2.62
2.50–2.99	4	2.78	3.13
3.00–3.49	1	3.07	1.85
3.50–3.99	2	3.66	1.96
4.00–4.49	1	4.38	1.71
Total	26		
Defenders Superior P/P			
1.00–1.19	5	1.12	1.17
1.20–1.39	4	1.31	0.97
1.40–1.59	2	1.50	1.56
1.60–1.79	0	—	—
1.80–1.99	2	1.98	1.68
2.00–2.49	4	2.22	0.98
2.50–2.99	3	2.64	2.17
3.00–3.49	1	3.07	1.33
3.50–3.99	3	3.84	0.89
4.00–7.99	2	7.75	1.58
Total	26		

are shown in Table 11-4. A plotted comparison of the CEVs is shown in Figure 11-7. This analysis shows the same general phenomenon found for the World War II engagements. For combat power ratios of 1 to 2, for either side, the results are roughly consistent with those expected from the relative CEV for the two sides. As the combat power ratios of either side approach, then exceed 2, the results fall far short of the expected results. Clearly, the law of diminishing returns applied in these fifty-two engagements.

As was done with the World War II data, an analysis was made of the manner in which diminishing returns affected the result ratios of attackers and defenders in the two Arab-Israeli wars. (See Table 11-5.) In twenty-six of the fifty-two engagements in this set of data, the attacker had a combat power preponderance, and in twenty-six the defender had a preponderance. However, in only seventeen of these engagements were the Israelis on the defensive; they were attacking in the remaining thirty-five engagements. In nine of these seventeen engagements, the Israelis had a P/P of less than 1.00, they were successful in defeating the numerically superior Arab forces in only three of these. In eight instances, the Israelis had a P/P ratio greater than the attacking Arab forces even though they were outnumbered in each of these, in all these cases, they translated a superior combat power ratio into a preponderant R/R ratio. Figure 11-8 shows the resulting plot of the CEV curves.

As with the World War II comparison, it will be seen that the law of diminishing returns affects the attacker in a fashion very similar to what we have seen for national forces. And also like the World War II comparison, the effect of diminishing returns upon the defender is much more abrupt and severe than for the attacker. There seems to be a point, not far beyond a combat power ratio of 2.0, where no amount of additional defensive force will substantially add to the defender's capability. Now what does all of that mean?

Diminishing Returns and Economy of Force

Several important things about combat can be learned from the plotted curves. It is obvious that the law of diminishing returns applies to combat. The old military adage that the greater the superiority the better, is not necessarily true. In the interests of economy of force, it appears to be unnecessary, and not really cost-effective, to build up a combat power superiority greater than two-to-one. (Note that this is not the same as a numerical superiority of two-to-one.) Of course, to take advantage of this phenomenon, it is essential that a commander be satisfied that he has a reliable basis for calculating relative combat power. This requires an ability to understand and use "combat multipliers" with greater precision than permitted by U.S. Army doctrine today (See Chapter 19). In particular, it requires that a commander be able to estimate the relative combat effectiveness of U.S. Forces compared to that of his opponent's forces.

Figure 11–6

Plotted Combat Power and Result Ratios, 1967–1973 Arab-Israeli War Battles

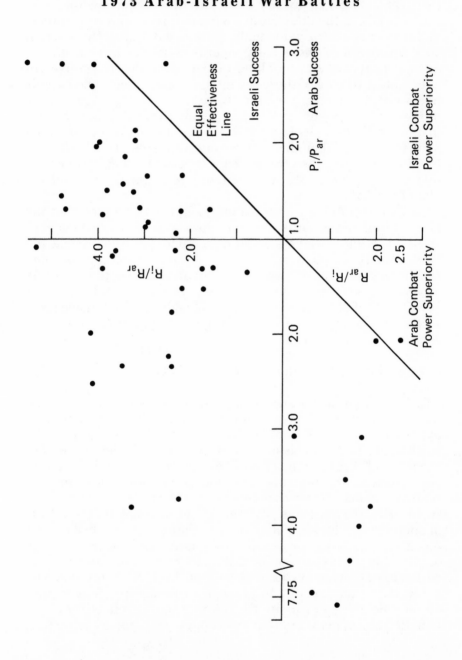

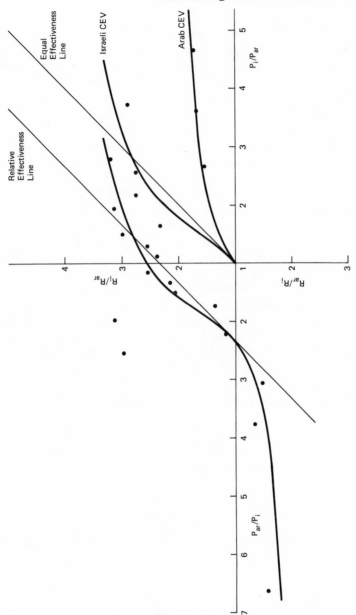

Figure 11–7

**Combat Outcome Diagram: 52 Arab-Israeli
War Engagements (1967, 1973)
(Averaged in P/P Classes)
Comparative Plot of Israeli and Arab CEV's**

Diminishing returns from greater combat power have considerable implications for the application of that most misunderstood of the so-called classical Principles of War, Economy of Force, sometimes called Economy of Forces.

A recent evaluation of J.F.C. Fuller[1] by British scholar Dr. Brian Reid gives an example of the misunderstanding. "The expenditure of force in battle was . . . determined by the law of economy of force, which in tactical terms meant the husbanding of reserves." The author then says that "Economy of force was, in Fuller's opinion, the product of *mobility*." He continues: "There is a constant tension between the law of economy of force and velocity in war. Fuller's principles of control, direction, determination, and mobility do not harmonize, but accentuate this tension." Reid then tries to prove his point by saying: "Those generals who actually employed economy of force, notably Montgomery, actually *reduced* the velocity of war." And this is buttressed by a quotation from the British official history of World War II, as follows: "Ever mindful of the casualty rates in the 1914–1918 war, Field Marshal Montgomery was determined to achieve his object with the minimum of loss and the exercise of good generalship." Reid then comments that "audacity and adventurousness did not fit into Montgomery's philosophy of war. Economy of force and velocity in warfare, in the long run, are not compatible. It was a dilemma that Fuller never satisfactorily solved."

While these extended quotations from Dr. Reid's article may be right on target so far as Montgomery is concerned, they display a common misperception of the Principle of Economy of Force, and the reason that it is a Principle of War. They also do a serious disservice to J.F.C. Fuller and his concepts.

In what I consider to be the best official summation of the principles of war, that in the 1954 issue of the US Army *Field Manual FM 100-5*, "Economy of Forces" is defined as follows: *"Minimum essential means must be employed at points other than that of decision.* To devote means to unnecessary secondary efforts is to violate the principles of both mass and the objective. Limited attacks, the defensive, deception, or even retrograde action are used in noncritical areas to achieve mass in the critical area."

When viewed in this light—and not as the "husbanding of reserves" or caution to avoid casualties—Economy of Force is clearly related to Fuller's other principles, and is fully consistent

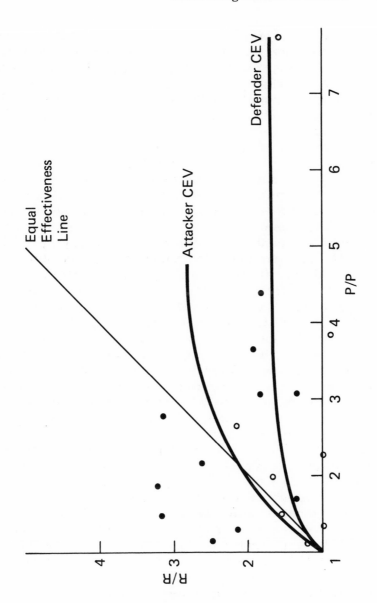

Figure 11–8

**Combat Outcome Diagram: 52 Arab-Israeli
War Engagements
Comparative Plots of Attackers
and Defender CEV's**

with both mobility (or maneuver) and velocity in warfare. Economy of force as practiced by Napoleon (from whose example Fuller derived the concept) was far from a form of caution; it was deliberate but carefully calculated audacity, permitting him time and again to defeat numerically superior forces. It was achieved by employing mobility to maneuver, and utilizing velocity to achieve superior strength at a decisive point, before the enemy was able to take advantage of the use of economy of force elsewhere.

` How does this relate to the finding, discussed above, that the law of diminishing returns applies to the battlefield?

Recognition of the operation of the law of diminishing returns will permit leaders who may not have the genius of a Napoleon nonetheless to emulate him confidently by calculating the proper amount of combat power to apply at a critical point. The Germans did this well in World War II; outnumbered on all fronts, they nonetheless were frequently able to assemble just enough combat power to win clear-cut offensive as well as defensive victories. It will be noted from the earlier examples that the Germans rarely assembled forces with a combat power ratio exceeding 2.00. The Israelis, possessing an even greater relative combat effectiveness superiority over their enemies, and not so severely outnumbered, did not have to calculate so closely. Nevertheless, in those very few instances where the Israelis massed combat power ratios greater than 2.00, they hardly did any better than when the combat power ratio was somewhere between 1.20 and 1.50.

It is obviously better for a commander to err on the side of concentrating too much power, than on calculating so closely that there might not be enough. Nevertheless, the application of the QJM, by demonstrating the applicability of the law of diminishing returns, means that commanders should no longer operate on the principle that more is always better. Understanding the applicability of the law of diminishing returns permits commanders to use the Principle of Economy of Force more wisely, both when outnumbered and when numerically superior.

Diminishing Returns for Attacker and Defender

The law of diminishing returns was as evident in the analyses of attackers and defenders for both World War II and the Arab-Israeli Wars as it was for the national force analyses of those wars. However, the different curves in Figure 11-5 and 11-8 show that the effect on the attacker is quite different from the effect on the defender. The curve tells us some very interesting things about the relationship of attackers to defenders in modern battle.

The extreme flatness of the defenders' curve in both data samples suggests that the law of diminishing returns is even more applicable to the defender than to the attacker. Once the force deployed in a defensive position has achieved the strength adequate for the task, the defender gains little or no advantage by adding more troops. There might appear to be an obvious limit to the applicability of this observation because successful defense depends on the force strength ratio. Also, the practical limits for amassing greater forces in a constrained area are at least as strict for the attacker as for the defender. Nevertheless, the significance of this observation is that it suggests that the defending commander has greater leeway in allocating elements of his force to reserves, or in utilizing them for other tasks, once he has provided adequate strength for the defense of his main position or positions. This, of course, is another manifestation of the Principle of Economy of Force. It also is at least part of the explanation of why General Lee was able to hold General Grant at bay outside of Richmond and Petersburg for so many months.

When there is not a great disparity between the relative effectiveness of attacker and defender, the defending force can achieve optimum effectiveness with a smaller increase in strength than can the attacker, until the defender achieves the optimum combat power suitable for the defensive position. After that, as noted above, the defender gains little from adding more strength. Again our Civil War provides two interesting examples: the build ups of the opposing armies at Gettysburg in the summer of 1863, and their build ups outside of Petersburg nearly a year later.

The application of the law of diminishing returns is less stringent for the attacker than for the defender. To the extent the terrain and general situation permit, an attacker can increase his chances of success—even though uneconomically—by adding to his combat power. In relating this observation to the first of the two examples noted above, Lee had no resources for building up his power at Gettysburg beyond what he had committed on 3 July 1863. But, in relation to the second example, Grant did have the capability for building up his strength outside of Petersburg and Richmond, which is what brought the two armies to Appomattox.

Friction and Challenge

It is relatively easy to demonstrate the applicability of the law of diminishing returns, but it is more difficult to explain why that law applies. On the basis of my past studies of combat, and quantifications of combat variables, I believe that the phenomenon is due to one of two considerations, and probably a combination of both of them: friction and challenge.

In Chapter 14 I shall demonstrate that the Clausewitzian concept of friction in war has an influence on combat results, particularly attrition. I have no doubt that friction is one of the reasons the relative value of results becomes proportionally less as the combat power ratio increases.

There is another possible reason for the declining proportionality of results to combat power. This is the response of a force of inferior strength to the challenge posed by such inferiority. Up to some point—which might be called a "breakpoint," but which has yet to be either identified, defined, or quantified—the psychological pressure of coping against odds unquestionably stimulates the weaker force to intensified efforts. There is, of course, no such pressure upon troops or commander of a clearly superior force.

Diminishing Returns and the QJM

No less significant than these new insights into the relationship between combat power and battlefield results is what this analysis tells us about the Quantified Judgment Model. The shape of the combat power ratio curve versus that of the result ratio suggests that the greater the combat power ratio, the less reliable for calculating CEV is a direct, linear comparison of the P/P combat power ratio with the R/R result ratio. In the past I assumed that the relationship was linear. However, as noted at the outset of this chapter, I had found some inconsistency in comparing CEV calculations when the combat powers of the opponents were not very different, with similar calculations when the power superiority of one side was substantial. As a result of the recent analysis described above, it is now clear that the combat effectiveness superiority of Germans over Western Allies during most of World War II was probably very close to 20% or perhaps slightly less (say 18–19%). Indications that the

German superiorities might have been as high as 30% or more were inferred as a result of the increasing ability of the Allies to bring superior forces to bear as the war went on. But, as we have discussed above, these superior forces could not, in fact, have been expected to be as efficient in results obtained as forces of marginal combat power superiority. The same phenomenon seems to apply generally for the Arab-Israeli war comparisons.

Even more significant, however, than the ability to refine reliable and consistent CEV calculations from data of historical combat, is what this analysis tells us about the QJM. In the past HERO and I have been able to claim, on the basis of unequivocal historical evidence, that the QJM is generally validated with respect to results of World War II and Arab-Israeli Wars combat. These wars, of course, were fought under very different circumstances, with very different weapons, and in very different geographical settings.

The QJM was designed to normalize battlefield situations by: (a) the identification and quantification of all variable factors that influence the outcome of a battle or engagement, and then (b) applying these factors in such a way that a given combat power ratio could be calculated, and could be relied upon to yield a given result. This recent analysis again confirms the fact that when behavioral factors such as relative combat effectiveness are *not* taken into consideration, a given combat power ratio cannot be counted upon to yield consistent results. In fact, the different curves show that in a comparison of opposing forces, the results can be quite different for the same ratio of combat power superiority where behavioral factors are not considered. But when the behavioral considerations are accounted for in a comparison of combat power to results, the relationship is consistent. Furthermore, not only are there clear patterns of national force effectiveness, the relationship of combat power to results applies with equal consistency to attacker-defender comparisons.

This is why the application of the behavioral and non-behavioral factors in the QJM to historical combat data has provided historically consistent results, over a thirty year historical period, in different battlefield circumstances. These results also demonstrate the QJM's internal validity in representing both physical and qualitative considerations affecting combat data. This, of course, conforms with what Clausewitz wrote in concluding his Law of Numbers: the concept is valid over history, and in all regions of the world.

Chapter 12

Advance Rates in Combat

Movement and Advance Rates

ONE OF THE most important outcomes of combat is the movement of the engaged forces in terms of advance or advance rate. For the attacker, movement or advance means seizing an assigned terrain objective or breaking through the defender's lines. For the defender, movement (usually called retrograde movement) means being forced out of a defensive position. Movement is thus usually good for the attacker and bad for the defender.

Movement in combat is measured in terms of the opposed advance rate of the attacker. Opposed forward movement involves proceeding, often through or over obstacles, in the face of enemy fire, while at the same time coping with the terrain and the weather and the road net and the other environmental factors that influence how fast a military force can move. Merely the presence of an enemy, even before contact, usually requires an attacker to move cross-country, forsaking the relative ease of movement along the roads.

Unopposed movement cannot be ignored by planners or theorists, but is not as difficult to assess as opposed movement. This chapter is concerned solely with opposed advance rates in combat.

Historical Advance Rates

Analysis of historical advance rates reveals that the average speed of opposed advance may possibly have increased very slightly since the American Civil War but certainly not as much as the capability of the technology would seem to permit. Advance rates are a function of many factors, not the least of which is that the defender is endeavoring to prevent the attacker from advancing.

In order to see if faster vehicles lead to faster advance rates for an attacker, it is useful to examine historical campaigns noted either for speed or for the long distance of movement, or both. Table 12-1 presents advance rates for thirty-three nineteenth and twentieth century campaigns that meet the stated criteria, selected mainly because they are relatively well known.

Inspection of Table 12-1 reveals no striking pattern of increase or decrease in opposed advance rates. The fastest rate on the list was accomplished by horse cavalry in the Battle of Megiddo in 1918. In this battle British cavalry moved slightly more rapidly, over more difficult terrain, than did General Tal's tanks a half century later in the Sinai Desert. Napoleon's advance rate to Moscow in 1812 of about 14 kilometers per day was faster than the advance rate of 10 kilometers per day achieved in 1941 by Hitler's armored forces in their blitzkrieg. It appears from a superficial look that faster vehicles do not necessarily guarantee faster advance rates.

But will these quick conclusions hold up under more rigorous examinations? Unfortunately the examples in Table 12-1 involve so many different variables, and are so few in number that they cannot be examined in a truly scientific manner to take into consideration the differences in terrain, circumstances, qualities of the opposing forces, intensity of opposition, durations of the operations, and the like. However, we can look at them from three different perspectives, and reach some fairly firm conclusions about trends in advance rates over the past two centuries.

First, let's look at the operations by chronological era, as in Table 12-2. We find that the average advance rate of the eight campaigns from the Napoleonic wars (all, incidentally, advances by Napoleon, not by his enemies) was 17 kilometers per day. For the five campaigns of the mid-nineteenth century, the average rate was significantly slower, 12 kilometers per day. The average

Table 12–1

Advance Rates in Some Selected
Nineteenth and Twentieth Century Campaigns

CAMPAIGN	DISTANCE (KM)	DAYS	ADVANCE RATE (KM/DAY)
*Marengo, 1800	350	31	11
*Ulm, 1805	475	22	22
*Jena, 1806	140	6	23
*Friedland, 1807	210	9	23
Danube (Aspern), 1809	405	30	14
Russia, 1812 (Smolensk)	680	57	12
Russia, 1812 (Moscow)	1160	85	14
Lutzen-Bautzen, 1813	300	20	15
Vicksburg, 1863	190	19	10
Savannah-Raleigh, 1865	1010	121	8
*Appomattox, 1865	100	6	17
*Sadowa, 1866	230	18	13
*Metz-Sedan, 1870	390	30	13
Marne, 1914	560	28	20
Caporetto, 1917	160	20	8
Gaza III, 1917	150	39	4
Somme II, 1918	110	16	7
*Megiddo, 1918	167	3	56
*Flanders, 1940	368	12	31
**Barbarossa, 1941 (Smolensk)	700	24	29
Barbarossa, 1941 (Moscow)	1160	122	10
Malaya, 1941–42 (K. Lumpur)	484	29	17
Malaya, 1941–42 (Singapore)	790	65	12
*Luzon I, 1941–42	216	15	14
Caucasus, 1942	775	34	23
Normandy Breakout, 1944	880	32	28
Luzon II, 1944	230	26	9
*Manchuria, 1945	300	6	50
N. Korean Offensive, 1950	560	42	13
UN Offensive, 1951	790	42	19
*Sinai, 1967	220	4	55
*Samaria, 1967	80	3	27
*Golan, 1967	35	2	18

*"Quick wins;" complete victory or irrevocable decision in 30 days or less.
**Discounts time lost in the Kiev excursion.

advance rate for the five World War I operations was, somewhat surprisingly, faster than either the Napoleonic or mid-nineteenth century rates, 19 kilometers per day. For World War II the average rate was only slightly higher than the World War I, 22 kilometers per day. And for the post World War II period, five examples from the Korean and Arab-Israeli wars, the average rate again showed a slight increase, to 26 kilometers per day.

Table 12–2

Mean Advance Rates for Selected Campaigns by Era

Historical Era	Number of Campaigns	Average Advance Rate (km/day)
Napoleonic Wars	8	17
American Civil War and Franco-Prussian War	5	12
World War I	5	19
World War II	10	22
Post World War II	5	26

Thus, without further analysis, the thirty-three examples suggest that, despite a dip in the mid-nineteenth century, advance rates have increased by about one-half since the time of Napoleon.

If, however, we look at the advance rates by duration (Table 12-3) and then look at the distribution of the examples among the eras, there must be considerable doubt whether advance rates have, in fact, increased at all over the past two centuries. What does the data tell us? There were four examples that lasted five days or less and the average rate of advance was 39 kilometers per day. There were five examples that lasted from six to twelve days, with average rates of 29 kilometers per day. Thirteen examples lasted between thirteen and thirty days, and the average daily advance rate of these was 15 kilometers. There were seven examples of thirty-one to sixty days with an average rate of 16 kilometers per day. Finally, four of the examples lasted from sixty-five to one hundred and twenty-two days, with an average daily rate of 12 kilometers.

It is thus very clear that the longer the campaign, and the

Table 12–3

Rates of Advance by Campaign Duration

					By Era				
Duration	No. of Campaigns	Av Days	Av Dist	Av Rate	Nap.	Mid-19th	WW I	WW II	Post-War II
0–5 days	4	3	121	39	0	0	1	0	3
6–12 days	5	8	257	29	2	1	0	2	0
13–30 days	13	21	342	15	3	3	3	4	0
31–60 days	7	40	598	16	2	0	1	2	2
61–122 days	4	98	1030	12	1	1	0	2	0

greater the distance to be covered, the lower the advance rate. And this seems to be true regardless of the means of locomotion —foot, horse, truck, or tank. Small, highly mobile forces can go quite rapidly for a few days. A relatively rapid rate can be sustained even by combined arms forces for as long as two weeks. But, for periods of one to two months, or distances of 350 to 600 kilometers, the rate stabilizes at about 15 kilometers per day, and declines only slightly for longer distances and shorter periods. And note that these generalizations appear to apply equally to all five of the periods of the past two centuries, and to all of the means of locomotion of those forces in those periods.

The relatively more rapid rate for the five campaigns of the post-World War II examples is explained by the fact that three of these were very brief, rapid advances of Israeli armored forces in the 1967 Six Days' War. The slightly more rapid rate of the World War I examples, in comparison with those of the preceding and following periods, is explained by the fact that one of the five examples of that period was the Battle of Megiddo, where General Allenby's horse cavalry sustained—for a very short period —the highest rate in our sample.

Thus, if the thirty-three examples in our sample suggest any increase in advance rates over the past two centuries, it has been an increase so slight as to be negligible. It is clear that factors other than means of movement influence the advance rates most significantly. Differences in advance rates are indicative more of road conditions, weather, intensity of hostile opposition, and the presence of enemy fortifications than they are of whether the troops moved by foot, horse, or machine.

Advance Rates Versus Force Ratios

A different approach to advance rates is shown in Table 12-4, which lists a group of fourteen relatively recent breakthrough operations analyzed by HERO a few years ago. Breakthrough operations are characterized by the attacker penetrating the defensive position of the defender and then moving against negligible resistance into the defender's rear area.

In Table 12-5, the same fourteen breakthrough operations are listed in descending order of advance rate, and three different force ratios are presented to show their relationship with the advance rates. The first ratio is simply the ratio of attacker personnel strength (N) to defender personnel strength. The second ratio compares the Force Strength (S) of each side. The third ratio compares the combat power (P) of each side, with the relative combat effectiveness values (CEVs) included in the calculation.

Examination of the data in Table 12-5 reveals no relationship between the advance rates for these breakthrough operations and the personnel strength ratios or force strength ratios. However, with some exceptions, there appears to be a positive correlation between the advance rates and the combat power ratios. This is consistent with the QJM approach. Only after the circumstances of the battle and the quality of the troops have been taken into account, will a force ratio be indicative of the outcome of combat.

The findings from Tables 12-1 and 12-5 refute two common assumptions regarding advance rates: that they are directly proportional to strength or firepower ratios, and that they are directly proportional to vehicular speed. Although the data set is small and more research is needed, the evidence indicates that advance rates are not directly proportional to personnel strength ratios, force strength ratios, or vehicular speeds.

Other conclusions that may be drawn from these data sets are as follows:

High rates of advance seem to be sustainable only for short periods of time.

Rates of cavalry-type units (the troops mounted on horses or fast moving armored vehicles) seem to be higher than those of infantry or combined armed forces—but still only for *short periods of time.*

Table 12–4

Rates of Advance in Breakthrough Operations

Operation	Width of Front (km)	Depth of Penetration	Days to Breakthrough	Advance Rate (km/day)
Megiddo, 1918	24	70	2	35
Flanders, 1940	9	10	2	5
Ukraine, 1941	65	120	5	24
Malaya, 1941	8	10	1	10
Leningrad, 1943	13	7	7	1
Kursk-Oboyan, 1943	16	35*	7*	5
Belgorad-Kharkov, 1943	7	26	3	9
Normandy, 1944	11	21	3	7
Manchuria, 1945	12	160	8	20
No. Korea, June 1950	40	50	3	17
Sinai-Rafa, 1967	21	35	1	35
Sinai-Abu Ageila, 1967	18	20	1	20
Syria-Qala, 1967	5	7	1	7
Syria-Tel/Fahar, 1967	3	5	1	5

* Breakthrough not achieved.

Table 12–5

Breakthrough Rates of Advance versus Force Ratios

Operation	Advance Rate (km/day)	Personnel Strength Ratio	Force Strength Ratio	Combat Power Ratio
Megiddo, 1918	35	2.81	2.99	5.20
Sinai-Rafa, 1967	35	1.00	1.45	4.19
Ukraine, 1941	24	0.88	1.17	3.36
Manchuria, 1945	20	1.96	4.00	3.16
Sinai-Abu Agelia, 1967	20	1.04	0.94	3.12
Korea, June 1950	17	1.58	1.73	3.20
Malaya, 1941	10	0.58	2.06	2.52
Belgorad-Kharkov, 1943	9	4.67	5.03	1.57
Syria-Qala, 1967	7	1.39	2.27	4.47
Normandy, 1944	7	4.20	7.34	4.10
Flanders, 1940	5	1.07	2.42	2.70
Kursk-Oboyan, 1943	5	0.69	0.79	1.31
Syria-Tel Fahar, 1967	5	1.43	1.79	4.74
Leningrad, 1943	1	4.00	4.83	1.51

Both infantry and cavalry rates tend to decrease and to con-
verge over long periods of time. Advance rates over longer
times seem to be very similar for both the nineteenth and the
twentieth centuries, for horse cavalry, for modern armored
vehicles, for foot soldiers, or for combinations of these.

Means of locomotion do not appear to have had great influence
on advance rates of forces moving over extended periods of
time.

Opposed advance rates appear to be determined by combinations of such factors as logistic capabilities, the terrain, the
strength of the defender and his fortifications, personnel
fatigue, and the missions of both sides.

The Need for an Advance Rate Methodology

There is no commonly accepted methodology for predicting
likely advance rates for a conventional war between NATO and

the Warsaw Pact, or any other kind of war. There is general agreement only that in a future war between NATO and the Warsaw Pact, the Pact forces will do all the advancing, at least at the outset. Agreement stops at that point. Using exactly the same inputs for force strengths and the physical circumstances of combat, some models calculate that the Warsaw Pact troops can advance at rates up to 50 kilometers or more per day. Other models say that the Soviet movement will be substantially less than 20 kilometers per day. The difference, in terms of NATO ability to hold long enough for reinforcements to arrive from the United States, Great Britain, and France, would be defeat or victory. But we don't really know which is correct.

In many combat models in use today in the United States and NATO, the advance rates are a function of the relative personnel or force strengths of the two sides. In other models, the advance rates are determined entirely by the methods used in the model to represent terrain. Advance rates in some models are outputs from smaller models that also have dubious methodologies. Other than the QJM, few models (if any) use historical experience as the basis, or starting point, for estimating opposed advance rates.

Although it is generally assumed by most model designers and users that both advance and attrition rates are proportional to force ratios, this cannot be true. If casualty rates and advance rates both were directly proportional to force ratios, then advance rates and casualty rates would both increase as force ratios increased. Yet, historical experience shows that casualty rates decline as the rate of advance increases. The reason for this is that troops on both sides use their weapons less when they are moving often and rapidly, than they do in a slow-moving battle.

Nor is there any general agreement as to how to deal with the distinction between opposed advance rates in the heat of battle and unopposed administrative movement, or operational advance against negligible opposition. It has been demonstrated that opposed advance rates are not directly proportional to personnel strength or force strength ratios in historical combat.[1] Under most circumstances, of course, the relative capability of the opposing sides to bring firepower to bear has *some* influence on advance rates, or at least in determining a threshold related to fire superiority and the ability to move. This influence is recognized in the QJM approach by relating certain standard advance rates to values of the combat power ratio.

Some analysts, however, suggest that military history experience is not relevant to advance rates in modern war. They insist that changes in the technology and machinery of war make it meaningless to compare the advance rates of forces equipped with the antiquated trucks and tanks that Generals Bradley and Patton directed across Europe in the 1940s with the rates that could be achieved in the 1980s by a modern force equipped with much faster tanks, trucks, and helicopters. However, even if the doubters are right and even if new rates are very different from those of the past, it is illogical to assume that the relationships between advance rates, circumstantial factors, and force ratios will totally contradict past experience. It is difficult to believe that the historical experience shown above, which was true between 1800 and 1973—despite tremendous changes in technology—has suddenly become invalid.

Combat Advance Rate Verities

These historical trends and examples set the stage for stating some hypotheses that are so thoroughly substantiated by historical experience that I call them the fifteen "combat advance rate verities."

1. *Advance against opposition requires local combat power preponderance.* In order to be able to undertake successful offensive operations, and to advance against opposition, a military force must have combat power superiority. This is simply a question of whether or not advance is possible, and has nothing to do with *rate* of advance. It should also be noted that superiority in numbers, even superiority in firepower, is not enough to assure combat power preponderance, and thus to achieve the ability to advance. For instance, a numerically inferior force, but one that is more effective in using its weapons and equipment and in coordinating its activities, can often advance against a more numerous force. The Germans demonstrated that against the Russians in World Wars I and II, as have the Israelis against the Arabs on a number of occasions in their several wars. Combat power superiority means a preponderance of power (not mere numbers) when due consideration is given not only to firepower and effectiveness, but also to the advantages that defensive posture gives to a defender, and to the effects of such factors as terrain and weather upon mobility and performance.

Assume, for instance, that an attacking force of 10,000 men has a relative combat effectiveness double that of a defending force of 13,000 men. In other words, the attacker is outnumbered by the defender by a ratio of 1.3:1.0. The Germans often had such an effectiveness preponderance over the Russians during World War II, and often attacked more numerous Russian defenders. Assume further that, under the given set of combat circumstances, defensive posture multiplies the force strength of the defending force by a factor of 1.40. In this situation, the attacker would still have a combat power preponderance of 2.00:1.82 (10,000 times 2.00, divided by 13,000 times 1.4). This would be a combat power ratio of 1.1:1.0 in favor of the attacker. In this case, an attacker outnumbered by a ratio of 3.00:4.00, but with a combat effectiveness superiority of 2:1, could still expect to advance, providing the other considerations discussed below are not unfavorable to advance.

On the other hand, if this same defender is in a strong fortified position (multiplying his force strength by a factor of 1.6), and in terrain favorable to defense (a multiplying factor of 1.5), then the combined multiplying factor of defensive posture and favorable terrain would be 2.4. In this case, the equation is $(10,000 \times 2)/(13,000 \times 1.6 \times 1.5) = 1.00:1.56$. The defender has the combat power preponderance; the attacker cannot advance. In these circumstances, the attacker would have to outnumber the defender by a factor of at least 1.30 in order to have enough combat power superiority to be able to advance. In this case the combat power ratio would be calculated as follows: $(2.00 \times 13,000)/(10,000 \times 1.50 \times 1.60) = 1.08:1.00$.

Alternatively, if the defender has a combat effectiveness superiority of 2.00, and his strength is multiplied by combined terrain and defensive posture factors of 2.00, then the attacker would need a numerical superiority exceeding 4:00:1.00 in order to have enough combat power to be able to advance. The equilibrium equation would be $40,000/(10,000 \times 2.00 \times 2.00) = 1.00$. With a 4:00/1:00 ratio the attacker cannot advance, but if he outnumbers the defender by more than 4.00:1.00, advance will be possible because of a preponderance of combat power.

2. *There is no direct relationship between advance rates and force strength ratios.* While a preponderance of combat power is essential for an attacking military force to be able

to initiate and sustain an opposed advance, a large combat power preponderance does not necessarily enable a force to advance more rapidly than is possible if the preponderance is marginal. The historical record indicates that there is a relationship, even though tenuous, between rate of advance and the *combat power* ratio (not the force strength ratio). But, there are so many other considerations affecting or modifying advance rates that combat power ratios taken alone cannot determine advance rates. There is no direct relationship between advance rates and personnel strength or force strength ratios because these ratios do not include the circumstantial factors affecting the forces.

3. *Under comparable conditions, small forces advance faster than larger forces.* One of the best examples of this verity is the pursuit of Darius III by Alexander the Great after the Battle of Arbela. Alexander, accompanied by a handful of his Companion Cavalry, quickly outdistanced even the swift cavalry contingents of his fast-moving army in this famous chase. It is not necessary to go back 2,000 years to demonstrate this verity. The raids of Grierson and Stuart in the Civil War, and the advance of German armor to the English Channel in 1940 are typical examples. We shall see in Chapter 14, that this verity is simply a manifestation of the effect of "friction" in war.

4. *Advance rates vary inversely with the strength of defenders' fortifications.* This refers not only to the trenches and other works that enhance the fighting capability of defenders, but also to the man-made obstacles that defenders use to strengthen those works and to enhance the degrading effects of natural terrain features. Man-made obstacles include such things as minefields, ditches, tank traps, abatis, and destroyed bridges.

5. *Advance rates are greater for a force that achieves surprise.* While perhaps it is not self-evident, it is certainly logical that surprise should have an effect upon advance rates. Surprise works in three ways to increase advance rates. First, surprise increases combat power and this makes it easier to advance and advance faster. Second, surprise enhances mobility, making advance easier and faster. Third, surprise increases the defender's vulnerability, facilitating the advance of the surpriser. Examples of the effect of surprise include Grant's advance in the Vicksburg Campaign; the Megiddo Campaign in 1918; the

German blitzkriegs in Poland, France, the Balkans, and Russia; and the Sinai Campaign in 1967.

6. *Advance rates decline daily in sustained operations.* Comparing three- and four-day advance rates with one hundred-day advance rates in the examples shown earlier suggests that there is a fatigue factor that degrades sustained movement significantly. There has been no systematic analysis of this effect.

7. *Superior relative combat effectiveness increases an attacker's advance rate.* The way in which relative combat effectiveness superiority contributes to combat power, and thus to the ability to advance or to prevent advance, has been discussed. When possessed by the attacker, superior combat effectiveness confers an additional advantage, and in this situation the advance rate will be faster, for the same combat power ratio, than if the combat effectiveness of the two sides were equal.

   The reason for this is that superiority in combat effectiveness reflects a combination of better leadership, better training and higher morale, which will inevitably manifest itself in greater initiative, more imagination and superior skill. The force with greater effectiveness can be expected to make better use of its combat power superiority, of the terrain conditions, and the various other considerations that affect advance rates. This was demonstrated often by the Germans in World War II, as well as by the Israelis against the Arabs in their recent wars.

8. *An "all-out" effort increases advance rates at a cost in higher casualties.* For short periods of time a force with superior combat power can advance somewhat more rapidly against serious opposition than its capabilities would normally indicate, provided the commander is willing (and the troops are able) to sustain considerably greater casualties than would be the case if standard operating procedures were followed. This verity relates to the ability to move against substantial opposition and does not relate to rapid advances against limited opposition.

9. *Advance rates are reduced by difficult terrain.* This seems so obvious it is hardly worth mentioning. Yet, it demonstrates why a strength ratio or force ratio cannot be used alone to determine advance rates.

10. *Advance rates are reduced by rivers and canals.* This is another almost-too-obvious verity. It is listed separately to

assure that the discrete problem of relating river crossings to advance rates is not just lumped together with the quite different problems of coping with other variations in terrain.

11. *Advance rates vary positively with the quality and density of roads.* There will probably be no argument that road marches are facilitated by road quality and road density, but questions may be raised about what these things have to do with the movement of troops who are engaged in battle and, consequently, more likely to shun than to use roads. Two things need to be remembered. First, when opposition is light, there will be considerable use of roads by the spearheads of advancing forces, as well as by the main bodies. Second, when opposition is intense, sustained ability to move will depend in substantial part upon logistical support provided over roads.

12. *Advance rates are reduced by bad weather.* A major effect of bad weather is impaired and reduced mobility of individuals and units moving off roads. Almost as important is the effect of bad weather upon the alacrity with which individuals perform routine and assigned tasks. Clausewitz commented that the frailties and interactions of individuals create the phenomenon he called "friction of war." Friction increases when the weather is bad.

13. *Advance rates are lower at night than in daytime.* This is another verity that is perhaps self-evident. But things that appear self-evident are not necessarily remembered in the planning and simulation processes. The inhibiting and delaying effects of darkness on movement must not be ignored.

14. *Advance rates are reduced by inadequate supply.* This is another verity that is self-evident, yet may be overlooked. It operates in several ways. The first, and most obvious of these is related to fuel for armored, mechanized, or motorized forces. Lack of fuel can bring the movement of such a force to a complete halt, as occurred in western Europe in early September, 1944. It is not only inadequacy of fuel that can slow or even halt a force. If ammunition is short, a commander will have to wait for replenishment. Even a small force not dependent upon vehicles and with adequate ammunition will have to slow down to forage, if adequate food is not delivered.

15. *Advance rates reflect interactions with friendly and enemy missions.* One reason why a force strength ratio, or even the combat power ratio cannot be used as the primary determinant of advance rates is that few commanders have either the authority or the opportunity to press an advance without constraint. Advance rates usually have to be adjusted to conform to some degree to the movements of adjacent commands. Advance rates more often than not are related to geographical objectives, and once such objectives are reached, advance will halt or the pace will slacken until new missions and/or new objectives are set.

The pace of an advance can be affected substantially by the manner in which the opposing force conducts its defense or its retrograde movement. A skillful delay is likely to slow down the attacker's advance rates more than would be expected from a straightforward comparison of the strengths and inherent capabilities of the opposing forces.

There are many examples of forces with substantial combat superiority being compelled to slow down their advance by the very skillful delay of defenders. The manner in which Joe Johnston slowed Sherman's advance on Atlanta is a case in point. When Johnston was replaced by Hood, Sherman was able to pick up speed. There are many, many examples of the Germans slowing down the advance of far superior Allied forces in 1944 and 1945.

Then there are numerous examples of advancing forces, facing negligible opposition, being required to curtail their advance rate to conform to the movement of adjacent commands. One of the best known of such examples was the need in August 1914, by von Kluck's First German Army, to slow its advance toward the Marne River after von Bulow's Second Army was temporarily halted at Guise. In fact, Kluck did not slow down enough, and this was one of the several reasons why the Germans lost the Battle of the Marne.

I am not prepared to assert that these fifteen verities take into consideration every factor or influence that has affected advance rates in the past. I am reasonably satisfied, however, that the list includes *most* such factors and influences. I find nothing in the list that either outrages my sense of logic, or seems likely to be affected in the slightest by the presence on future battlefields of new weapons or new means of movement. The methodology used in the QJM to treat advance rates is based on these verities. The realism of any planning or simulation methodology that is inconsistent with these verities must be suspect.

Advance Rates in the QJM

In the QJM, the advance rates for an engagement are computed according to the following relationship:

Advance Rate = (Standard Advance Rate) (Variable Factors).

The standard advance rate is that rate in kilometers per hour that would be achieved by an attacking military force over flat terrain with other things being equal. The standard advance rate, itself, is not modified by any of the environmental or operational factors affecting movement. The determinant of the value of the standard advance rate to be used in an engagement is the calculated combat power ratio for the engagement. The greater the combat power ratio, the faster the standard advance rate. Different values of the standard advance rate are given for armored mechanized forces and infantry forces.

The variable factors that modify the standard rate are

Terrain (rm). More difficult terrain reduces the rate,

Weather (hm). Inclement weather reduces the rate,

Road Quality and Density (RQ&RD). Poor and sparse roads reduce the standard rate,

Streams (St). A stream crossing reduces the rate,

Day/Night (dn). Movement at night reduces the rate,

Surprise (Su). Attacker surprise increases the rate; defender surprise reduces the rate,

Posture (uar). The greater the degree of resistance indicated by the defender's posture, the slower the advance rate,

Fatigue (ff). The longer the duration of a sustained advance, the greater the fatigue factor and the lower the advance rate,

Mission Effect (me). The missions of both attacker and defender affect the advance rate.

The QJM formula for calculating an advance rate (A) is as follows:

$$A = Sr \times rm \times hm \times RQ \times RD \times St \times uar \times dn \times Su \times ff \times me.$$

Chapter 13

Attrition in Combat

"Fighting's for Killing"

THEY TELL A story about Nathan Bedford Forrest, the self-taught military genius of our Civil War, that illustrates the preeminence of attrition among the various processes of combat. A young Confederate officer, recently assigned to Forrest's cavalry corps, was walking through camp one day, and saw the commanding general in front of his tent, bending over a grinding wheel, putting the sharpest possible edge on his saber. The young man expressed some surprise that a lieutenant general would be doing something like that. Forrest raised his head briefly from his task to look the officer in the eye, then bent down to continue his work. "Fighting's for killing, son," he briefly remarked.

Forrest was simply expressing one of the facts he had learned about warfare. The force with the greatest combat power —whether due to more numbers, better marksmanship, sharper sabers, more imaginative leadership—wins battles, and does so by inflicting more casualties on the opponent, and suffering fewer itself. There is an inextricable relationship between attrition and battle outcome.

Attrition is the loss of force strength through enemy action in combat, or as a result of accidents or disease. In precise terms, attrition is the difference between losses and returns to duty. In this book our focus is on combat losses, as seen in historical perspective. Most attention is given to personnel losses, or casualties. However, some consideration is also given to materiel losses. The convention is to refer to attrition of people as casualties and casualty rates; materiel attrition is usually described in terms of item losses—such as tank losses, truck losses, etc.—and item loss rates.

Attrition can be understood best, and analyzed best, in terms of loss rates. Absolute losses are important for a single combat engagement or battle but they cannot be compared meaningfully with other losses in combat events. An attrition rate is the proportion of the strength of a unit or force lost per time period. There may be several different kinds of rates, and comparisons should be made only among the same kinds of rates. For comparative purposes, the three important dimensions of an attrition rate are duration, unit strength, and level of combat. Thus, there can be a division daily casualty rate, a theater annual casualty rate, or a battalion daily engagement casualty rate. The engagement rate applies to the battalion only when it is engaged in combat, but in practical terms, since most records are kept on a 24-hour basis, the battalion engagement casualty rate is not easily distinguishable from the daily rate. This chapter is intended to provide sufficient information on attrition to allow the reader to understand how this process is treated in the QJM.[1]

Historical Trends in Attrition

It was a survey of historical casualty statistics that originally led HERO to try to find ways of quantifying the effects of forces and weapons on combat outcomes. In the process of relating cause to effect, we at first used highly aggregated figures that, although helpful in showing how outcomes could be related to casualties, did not give more than a very general indication of likely casualty levels in any particular engagement. Casualties varied so greatly in otherwise apparently similar situations that it was necessary to look carefully to identify the correct historical patterns that would permit reasonable and reliable casualty predictions.

Two reasons were found for presuming that the apparently random values of historical casualty rates were not really random. First, it was clear from much past research that casualty rates in historical combat had varied to some extent with differences in terrain and weather, and that both were affected by intensity of combat, which in turn was influenced by mission. Second, there was the substantial evidence that, with large bodies of data, patterns in attrition rates were discernible.

Two very general patterns are evident in the historical casualty data that has been tabulated and analyzed. Casualty rates have declined generally over the past four centuries, but have apparently levelled off at the rates experienced in World War II and the Arab-Israeli Wars. And casualty rates incurred by opposing military forces were almost invariably lower for the successful or victorious force.

Figure 13-1 is a graph showing casualty rate experience from 1600 to the present day. During the seventeenth and eighteenth centuries casualty rates declined for both winners and losers until the period of the French Revolutionary and Napoleonic Wars. At that time, the rates increased for several reasons: the introduction of mass armies, columnar tactics, more effective use of field artillery, and in particular, Napoleon's tactics in his later wars, when his troops were of relatively lower quality. Rates declined again after Napoleon until another sharp increase occurred at the time of the American Civil War. The reason for this increase was the introduction of the conoidal bullet (or "minié-ball"), which greatly increased the range and effectiveness of the rifle-musket. Thereafter, the rates declined again until World War II and thereafter seem to have leveled off.

Casualty rate data from selected battles from the Civil War to the 1982 War in Lebanon are in Table 13-1. These examples provide specific evidence to support the general downward trend shown in Figure 13-1. The Israelis (usually the winners) have lower daily casualty rates than their Arab opponents, and the overall rates in these wars are about the same as for World War II. U.S. daily division casualty rates decline from World War I to World War II to the Korean War.

Although casualty rates have declined rather steadily over the centuries, there is no guarantee that they will not go up again in the future. There are persuasive arguments that casualty rates in a future war will be high, much higher, many believe, than they have been in the past. Weapons are much more lethal and much more accurate than ever before. Means of target acquisition are greatly improved, and the future battlefield is expected to be "target-rich."

Figure 13–1

Average Daily Battle Casualty Rates
1600-1973

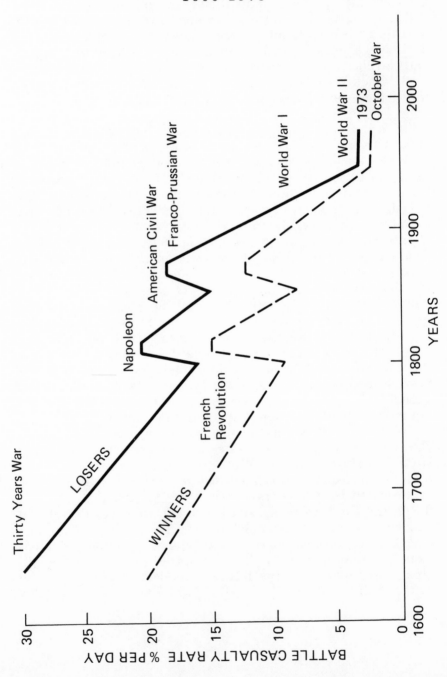

Table 13–1

Selected Daily Battle Casualty Rates, 1861–1982
(in battles or engagements)

	YEAR	AVERAGE STRENGTH	% PER DAY CASUALTIES
American Civil War, 8 Battles,			
Union	1861–65	68,250	11.5
Confederacy	1861–65	50,193	15.0
World War I,			
German Divisions, 9 Engagements	1915	18,133	5.7
British Divisions, 9 Engagements	1915	13,628	8.5
US Divisions, Overall Average	1918	28,000	2.0*
US Bde Slice, Overall Average	1918	14,000	4.0*
World War II,			
US Divisions, Overall Average	1943–45	14,000	0.9*
US Divisions, 82 Engagements	1943–44	14,000	1.2*
German Divisions, 82 Engagements	1943–44	12,000	1.8*
German Divisions, Overall Average	1941–45	12,000	2.0*
German Corps, Kursk, 3 Engagements	1943	58,000	1.1
Soviet Army, Kursk, 3 Engagements	1943	85,000	3.0*
Korean War,			
US Divisions, Overall Average	1950–53	15,000	0.8*
Six-Day War,			
Israeli Units, 20 Engagements	1967	12,232	2.8
Egyptian Units, 11 Engagements	1967	14,245	6.0
Jordanian Units, 5 Engagements	1967	8,750	5.6
Syrian Units, 4 Engagements	1967	11,371	4.0
October War,			
Israeli Units, 33 Engagements	1973	14,593	1.8
Egyptian Units, 16 Engagements	1973	34,321	2.6
Syrian Units, 17 Engagements	1973	16,975	2.9
Lebanon,			
Israelis vs. Syrians, 2 Engagements	1982	31,000	1.2
Syrians vs. Israelis, 2 Engagements	1982	27,500	5.0**
Israelis vs. PLO (4 days)	1982	28,000	0.2
PLO vs. Israelis (4 days)	1982	8,000	13.1**

* Approximate, more research required
** Estimated

Although there may be validity to some of the arguments that higher casualty rates are inevitable in the future, the experience of historical combat does not support a significant reversal of the trend toward lower casualties. In the first place, the declining casualty rates shown in Figure 13-1 occurred during the period when the measurable lethality of weapons was increasing at a prodigious rate. This is shown in Figure 13-2, in which the increasing lethality of weapons is shown on a semi-logarithmic graph.

The major reason that casualty rates have declined despite increasing weapons lethality is that targets have become more dispersed. As weapons have become more lethal, the targets of those weapons—the troops deployed for battle—have spread out in order to lessen the effectiveness of the weapons. The effect of dispersion in relation to weapon lethality is shown graphically, in Figure 13-3.

A key point is that the battlefield of the future is unlikely to be "target-rich" in comparison with the battlefield of the past. As shown in Table 13-2, battlefield density of men, weapons, and other major items of equipment has declined substantially since World War I. Current NATO doctrine calls for still more target dispersion. When this trend is combined with the virtual certainty that means of hiding targets will at least keep pace with means of finding them, a target-rich environment seems unlikely. There is every reason to expect that past trends toward increased target dispersion (to counter increased lethality of weapons) will continue (although logic suggests the trend cannot continue indefinitely).

Personnel and tank loss rates in specific tank operations of World War II and the 1973 Arab-Israeli War are compared in Table 13-3. Despite increased lethality of weapons in the thirty years from 1943 to 1973, the attrition rates of the 1973 October War indicate no rising trend in casualties or tank losses. The October War rates are remarkably close to those of World War II.

This assessment confirms the general nature of casualty rate trends, despite the fluctuations in any set of casualty rates. With sufficient data, it is possible to fit the often contradictory evidence into a systematic methodology for forecasting future casualty rates. There are two reasons for this. First is the consistency of the historical evidence. Despite fluctuations in individual cases, overall division casualty rates of recent wars have averaged a little less than 2% per day during periods of intense combat. The second reason is that the major deviations of these rates from the

Figure 13–2

Increase of Weapon Lethality Over History

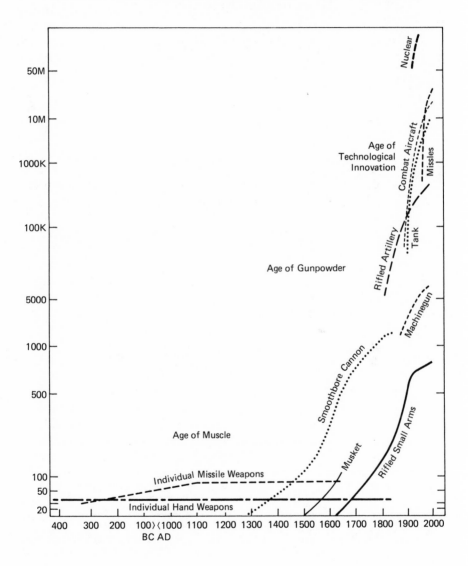

Figure 13–3

Increase of Weapon Lethality and
Dispersion Over History

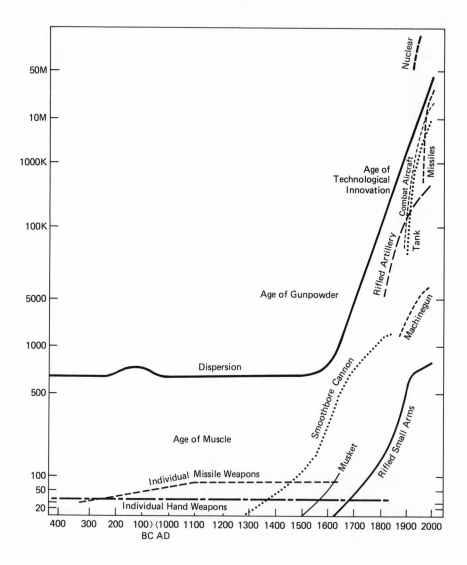

Table 13–2

Twentieth Century Army Disposition Patterns
Average Densities per/Km²

	TROOPS	ARMED VEHICLES	ARTILLERY PIECES	OTHER WEAPONS
World War I	404	0.40	1.62	16.15
World War II	36	0.31	0.20	2.07
1973 October War	25	0.61	0.11	1.38
1980's NATO Doctrine	15	0.60	0.11	1.11

Table 13–3

Selected Tank Operations
(1943–1973)

OPERATION	FORCE	PERSONNEL LOSS RATE PER/DAY %	TANK LOSS RATE DAY %
World War II			
Kursk-Oboyan, 1943	Soviet	3.09	18.75
Kursk-Oboyan, 1943	German	1.07	6.70
Orel, 1943	Soviet	1.24	8.73
Goodwood, 1944	British	1.76	12.96
1973 Arab-Israeli War			
Suez-Sinai	Israeli	1.46	7.84
Suez-Sinai	Egyptian	2.05	14.87
Golan	Israeli	1.34	7.05
Golan	Syrian	2.59	20.46

average can be explained as the result of circumstantial factors, such as terrain, weather, posture, surprise, and relative combat effectiveness. A good example is the rough and bitter fighting that took place in late 1943 in the mountains of Italy between the Volturno and Rapido rivers in miserable, wet and cold weather; in spite of heavy, intense combat, the actual casualty rates were quite low.

Weather and terrain are two environmental factors that influence combat and affect casualty rates. The separate effects of these environmental factors, however, cannot be measured until their impact can be isolated from the effects of surprise and relative combat effectiveness.

In the development of the Quantified Judgment Model, HERO has made substantial progress toward quantifying the effects of surprise and relative combat effectiveness. With these two factors identified and roughly quantified, it has been possible to develop some hypotheses concerning casualty rates, and to test these sufficiently to give them respectability. In fact, the consistency of the historical evidence has led me to dignify these hypotheses by calling them verities.

Combat Attrition Verities

The following list of twenty-eight attrition verities is asserted with confidence that ranges from absolute for most of them, to reasonable certainty for a few. The evidence to support all of them is in the historical record. The first two verities do not deal with attrition directly but are important statements of historical combat experience that have great relevance for attrition. They are circumstantial points of reference for the remaining twenty-six verities.

1. *In the average battle, the attacker's numerical strength is about double the defender's.* This is perhaps surprising in light of general acceptance of the rule of thumb that an attacker needs a three-to-one superiority in order to be confident of success. In fact, however, it appears that an attacking commander who has a two-to-one superiority will risk a battle under such circumstances for one or more of three principal reasons: he has the initiative and thus can expect to initiate combat at a time and place of his choosing; he hopes to be able to surprise the defender, and thus magnify, or multiply, his superiority; and/or if he has confidence in the qualitative superiority of his troops or his leadership (or both), he counts on this to give him the additional margin of superiority he needs for success.

   The defending commander, also, plays some part in a combined decision to bring about a battle under such circumstances. If the odds were three or more to one against him, he would likely try to avoid battle. With odds around two-to-one he can hope that the rule of thumb will work in his favor, that he can avoid being surprised, and that he can also make use of surprise, or superior quality of troops or leadership to achieve success.

2. *In the typical modern battle the attacker is more often successful than the defender.* In a data base of 601 battles between 1600 and 1973, the attacker was successful in 366 battles, or 61%. In the most recent wars—World War II and the Arab Israeli Wars—the attacker has been successful in nearly 75% of the cases. This is logical, of course; since the attacker has the initiative, it would be surprising if he were to attack unless he believed the circumstances were conducive to victory. Further, it makes historical sense that most wars are won by the side that has been on the offensive longer and more successfully, as demonstrated by the American Civil War and World War II.

3. *Casualty rates of winners are lower than those of losers.* The casualty *rates* (not absolute numbers) of successful forces are almost always lower than the rates of unsuccessful opponents. This is true regardless of whom is attacker and whom is defender.

4. *Casualty rates of small forces are higher than those of large forces.* Writing nearly 100 years ago, American military historian Theodore Ayrault Dodge noted that this phenomenon was as evident in the battles of antiquity as it was in the wars of the nineteenth century. Under comparable or equivalent conditions, smaller forces *always* have higher casualty rates than larger forces. This is due in part to the fact that larger forces usually have a lesser proportion of their troops exposed directly to hostile fire than do smaller forces, and in part to the effect of "friction" on larger forces (see Chapter 14).

5. *More effective forces inflict casualties at a higher rate than less effective opponents.* Forces with higher combat effectiveness values have greater casualty-inflicting capability than their less effective opponents. In World Wars I and II, the Germans had higher combat effectiveness than their opponents, and they almost always had higher casualty-inflicting rates under all conditions: when they had air support; when they did not; when they were attacking; when they were defending; when they were successful; and when they were defeated. The same phenomenon is

found in the casualty statistics of the Arab-Israeli Wars, particularly that of 1973, where both sides won victories and suffered defeats in about equal proportion, but the Israelis had a substantially higher casualty-inflicting capability than the Arabs.

6. *There is no direct relationship between force ratios and casualty rates.* Attrition rates depend on many factors, such as weather, terrain, tactical posture, and relative combat effectiveness. Accordingly, the influence of personnel strength ratios or force strength ratios on attrition rates is reduced to a point where no clear relationship exists. Combat power ratios, which take into account the circumstances of combat, do influence attrition rates, but only due to several interacting factors.

7. *In the average modern battle the numerical casualties of attacker and defender are often similar.* This seems to be true when the combat effectiveness of the opponents does not differ markedly and the battle outcome is not an overwhelming catastrophe for the loser.

8. *Casualty rates for defenders vary inversely with strength of fortifications.* There is considerable historical evidence that, if other conditions remain unchanged, the casualty rates of defenders decrease as the strength of their fortifications increases. As Clausewitz wrote, "Defense is the stronger form of combat."

9. *Casualty rates of a surprising force are lower than those of a surprised force.* This is because the organized and determined forces of the surpriser, fully prepared for battle and given greater confidence by the knowledge that the opponent is caught unawares, perform more effectively at the moment of surprise. The forces being surprised, on the other hand, are disorganized, unprepared, and possibly demoralized, and are less effective until they recover from being surprised.

10. *In the average modern battle, attacker casualty rates are somewhat lower than defender casualty rates.* This is in large part because winners have lower casualty rates than losers, and attackers win more often than defenders. Also contributing is the fact that attackers achieve surprise more often than defenders, since attackers have the initiative. There is also a mathematical reason: the attacker is usually more numerous than the defender, though the

numerical casualties of both sides are usually similar.

11. *In bad weather, casualty rates for both sides decline markedly.* This is because soldiers do not use their weapons as effectively in inclement weather as they do in good weather. More time is spent surviving or remaining comfortable than in bringing fire to bear on the enemy.

12. *In difficult terrain, casualty rates for both sides decline markedly.* This, too, is a reflection of the effect of environmental circumstances on the ability of troops to employ their weapons. In difficult terrain, more effort has to be used to move, and thus less effort is available for firing weapons.

13. *The casualty-inflicting capability of a force declines after each successive day in combat.* The reason for this phenomenon is not clear, although fatigue is unquestionably a factor. The reduction in capability occurs steadily while a unit is in combat but capability is recovered fairly rapidly after short periods of rest from combat. The degradation of casualty-inflicting capability is one way in which the effect of casualties incurred on unit effectiveness can be determined and measured. More research needs to be done on this phenomenon.

14. *Casualty rates are lower at night than in daytime.* This is another example of casualty rates being related to opportunities to employ weapons effectively. There is simply less capability to acquire targets and bring fire to bear on them at night than in the daylight.

15. *Casualty rates are higher in summer than in winter.* This applies primarily to temperate climates, where the distinction between summer and winter is marked by substantial differences in the hours of daylight. The increased time for effective employment of weapons seems to be only slightly offset by the inhibiting effects of more luxuriant foliage in summer.

16. *The faster the front line moves, the lower the casualty rates for both sides.* The reason for this phenomenon, which is validated by historical experience in combat in World Wars I and II, is that troops advancing rapidly have less time to use their weapons than troops advancing slowly. When the rate of advance is rapid, more of the soldier's time is spent on the movement itself, and less time is available to fire on targets. At the same time, it is more

difficult to acquire targets during rapid movement, so the defenders as well as the attackers are hit less often.

17. *Casualty rates seem to decline during river crossings.* This relationship, which needs further study, is apparently due to the fact that attackers are very largely occupied with matters other than using their weapons, and the number of exposed targets for defenders to fire at is generally smaller than usual, except at the actual crossing site.

18. *An "all-out" effort by one side raises loss rates for both sides.* This is true whether it be the attacker making an attack *à outrance*, or a defender holding a position at all costs. This verity is simply a result of the fact that a commander willing to take higher losses to accomplish his mission will, in fact, incur higher losses, but will also force his opponent to fight more intensively and be more exposed.

19. *A force with greater overall combat power inflicts casualties at a greater rate than the opponent.* Combat power includes consideration of the environmental, operational, and human factors comprising the circumstances of a particular battle or engagement. A numerically inferior force in well-prepared defenses with highly mobile reserves and good morale and leadership could have greater combat power than a numerically stronger attacker. This can be true even if the attacker has higher combat effectiveness. It is the aggregate of the various factors that determines the ability to inflict casualties on the opponent.

20. *The killed-to-wounded distribution of personnel casualties in twentieth century warfare is consistent.* About 20% of battle casualties are killed immediately. This corresponds to a wounded-to-killed ratio of 4:1. About 65% of battle casualties survive their wounds, even with minimal care. This leaves about 15% of those hit who are seriously wounded and not likely to live without medical care. The proportion of seriously wounded who survive has increased over the past century and a half from less than 5% of those hit to more than 12% due to improvements in medical evacuation and treatment.

21. *Materiel loss rates are related to personnel casualty rates.* People are hit in most cases when tanks, vehicles, and artillery weapons are hit. Thus, personnel casualties are caused by the same impacts that destroy or damage materiel. This means that there are relationships between person-

nel casualties and materiel losses that can be used to estimate the latter, given the former. These relationships vary from item to item, and they depend on battlefield density and distribution of the equipment and its relative vulnerability to damage from hostile fire.

22. *Tank loss rates are five to seven times higher than personnel casualty rates.* This applies to combined arms engagements in which armored forces make up a substantial proportion of the fighting strength on one or both sides.

23. *Attacker tank loss rates are generally higher than defender tank loss rates.* This is in relation to personnel casualty rates on the opposing sides. If the attacker's tank loss rate is about seven times that of the attacking personnel casualty rate, the defender's tank loss rate will probably be closer to five times (or even less) the defender's casualty rate.

24. *Artillery materiel loss rates are generally about one-tenth personnel casualty rates.* For towed guns the relationship is closer to one-twentieth. This is an observed phenomenon that applies to artillery pieces hit by enemy fire. It does not include catastrophic losses of artillery pieces due to overrun or surrender.

25. *Self-propelled artillery loss rates are about three times greater than for towed guns.* This is due to a combination of factors: larger exposed target; presence of fuel and ammunition in the self-propelled guns carriages; and vulnerability of engines to damage even when the weapon is still able to fire effectively. They are also more likely to be committed under more immediately lethal combat circumstances than are towed artillery pieces. It should be noted, however, that crew loss rates are slightly lower for self-propelled guns than for towed guns.

26. *Average World War II division engagement casualty rates were 1–3% a day.* Successful divisions in Western Europe lost about 1–2% casualties a day in intensive combat; losing or unsuccessful divisions lost about 2–3% a day.

27. *Attrition rates in the 1973 October War were comparable to World War II.* In spite of the increased lethality of weapons and the greater sophistication of military technology, personnel casualty rates and tank loss rates for engagements in the October War seem to have been approximately the same as those for both personnel and tanks in intensive battles of World War II in western

Europe; they were slightly less than comparable World War II loss rates on the Eastern Front.

28. *Casualty rates in minor hostilities after 1945 are about half those experienced in World War II*. This has been true for sophisticated forces; accurate records are not available for their opponents. The lower rates are probably due to a combination of higher CEVs, as well as to the absence of sustained artillery fire in many of these kinds of combat engagements.

Significance of the Attrition Verities

Although these twenty-eight attrition verities cannot be tested in a trial run of future combat, they were valid for recent historical combat. It is not unreasonable to conclude that attrition in future combat will be similar in many—or even most —respects with attrition experience in recent historical combat.

The adverse impact of incorrect estimates of attrition in future combat can be great. Consider, for instance, that authoritative predictions of the casualties that U.S. forces in Europe could expect to suffer in the first ten days of a possible war between NATO and the Warsaw Pact vary from more than 50,000 to less than 20,000. For planning purposes this means a difference in hospital requirements of up to 30,000 beds and large numbers of highly trained medical personnel. It is a difference in personnel replacement requirements the equivalent of more than an entire division. And that is only for the first ten days!

Obviously it is impossible to forecast exactly what would happen if war broke out in Europe or elsewhere. There are historical data available, however, that would enable our planners to estimate combat attrition with much more confidence than now possible. Systematic and comprehensive historical analysis of attrition in modern war could correct many of the current misunderstandings about combat attrition.

Unfortunately, there has been no comprehensive study west of Moscow of attrition experience in modern war. The evidence is overwhelming, however, that there have been many such studies by Soviet military scholars. Yet the actual contemporary World War II records of U.S. and British forces in all theaters of war and of German forces on all fronts in Europe and North Africa are available to researchers. There are also relatively reliable records of both sides in the Arab-Israeli Wars of 1967 and 1973. There are as well good records for United States forces in Korea and

Vietnam. Some of this data has been used over the years for a variety of unrelated studies on specific aspects of attrition. Data from both primary and secondary sources could add significantly to information about attrition in earlier wars if it were compiled and organized so as to be useful to analysts.

HERO used these sources to study in detail more than 275 battles and engagements that took place between 1915 and 1982, developing over 500 sets of combat attrition data. While far from complete coverage of modern combat experience, this data base is sufficient to indicate that there are wide variations in attrition rates in modern combat and that there are some very clear patterns. With more data (organized and compiled properly) and more analysis, it would be possible to substantiate the patterns and delineate other features of attrition in combat more clearly than is now the case.

Attrition in the QJM

The QJM calculates losses in an engagement for personnel, tanks, artillery, other weapons and equipment. The basis for the QJM approach to attrition is the experience derived from the analysis of attrition in modern warfare mentioned in the preceding section and summarized qualitatively in the combat attrition verities.

The basic calculation is for personnel losses. Losses for tanks, artillery, and other materiel items are based on their historical relationship to personnel losses. The basic relationship to determine the personnel loss rate is as follows:

Personnel Loss Rate = (standard casualty rate)
(variable factors).

The standard casualty rate (SR) is the average casualty rate experienced for a particular war or historical era. This value may be determined by historical analysis, or assumed for future combat. For modern combat a standard casualty rate of 3% per day is assumed for an exposed force of division strength. Personnel casualties include killed, wounded, and missing in action. (It does not include men or units that surrender or are captured after the engagement or battle.)

The variable factors that influence personnel casualties include:

Terrain (rc). Casualties decrease as the terrain becomes more difficult,

Weather (hc). Casualty rates go down in bad weather,

Season (zc). This factor recognizes the influence of the time of year and the general climate on casualties,

Shoreline (Sh). Attacker casualties are higher and defender casualties are lower at or near the landing sites in major river crossings, or amphibious operations,

Day/Night (dn). Casualties are lower at night than in the daylight,

Surprise (Su). The surpriser suffers fewer casualties and the force being surprised more casualties than the standard rate,

Posture (uc). The defender's posture affects the casualties of the defender,

Strength-Size (tz). The smaller the size of the forces, the greater the casualty rate,

Velocity (vl). After a certain point, faster advance rates cause lower casualty rates for both attacker and defender,

Fatigue (ff). The longer a force is engaged in sustained combat, the lower the casualty rates of its opponent will tend to be,

Opposition (op). This factor is determined by the combat power ratio. The greater the combat power ratio, the greater the casualty rate of the other side.

The QJM formula for the personnel casualty rate is:

$$CR = SR \times rc \times hc \times zc \times dn \times Su \times uc \times tz \times vl \times ff \times op.$$

The casualties suffered in an engagement by a force of strength N are calculated as $C = CR \times N \times$ Duration of Engagement (days).

For equipment and weapons, the QJM attrition calculation includes both losses and recovery. Recovery takes into account the repair and return to units of lost equipment. Losses of equipment are related to the calculated personnel casualty rate, and they are adjusted to take into account special factors relating to the particular kind of equipment. Recovery rates are based on modern experience.

Chapter 14

Friction in Combat

Clausewitz's Concept

LONG BEFORE MURPHY ever voiced his famous law ("Anything that *can* go wrong *will* go wrong"), Clausewitz expressed this same idea in terms of a practical metaphor at least equally famous: friction in war. He described this in the following terms:

> Everything in war is very simple, but the simplest thing is difficult. The difficulties accumulate and end by producing a kind of friction that is inconceivable unless one has experienced war. . . . Countless minor incidents—the kind you can never really foresee—combine to lower the general level of performance, so that one always falls far short of the intended goal. . . . Friction is the only concept that more or less corresponds to the factors that distinguish real war from war on paper. . . . None of [the military machine's] components is of one piece: each part is composed of individuals, every one of whom retains his potential of friction [and] the least important of whom may chance to delay things or somehow make them go wrong. . . .

> This tremendous friction . . . brings about effects that cannot be measured, just because they are largely due to chance . . .

> Action in war is like movement in a resistant element. Just as the simplest and most natural of movements, walking, cannot easily be performed in water, so in war it is difficult for normal efforts to achieve even moderate results.[1]

Clausewitz obviously thought of friction in war as a factor degrading combat performance, then went on to say that it could not be measured. But modern developments in data, computers, and analytical techniques now allow the quantitative definition of relationships that hitherto have defied analysis.

Measuring Friction in Combat

The impetus to apply quantitative analysis to the topic of friction had a rather unusual origin. I was sitting in a lecture on combat simulation one day in 1980 when the lecturer asserted that combat casualty rates were directly proportional to force ratios. As indicated earlier, the historical record shows that the relationship of force ratios and casualty rates is an extremely dubious one. I was prepared to debate this matter with the lecturer, particularly when he attempted to buttress his argument by showing how force ratios are influenced by deployments. He showed a schematic diagram of the standard deployment of a field army somewhat similar to Figure 14-1.

Suddenly a light flashed on in my brain, a light that had little to do with what the lecturer was talking about. The deployments he was showing made very clear the unambiguous fact that the larger the force, the smaller the proportion of the force exposed to aimed hostile fire. This phenomenon is illustrated in Figure 14-1 for a normal deployment of a "type" army group.[2] Table 14-1 connects the diagram into numbers.

I did a bit of mental arithmetic to compare those declining proportions with the declining proportions of casualty rates for larger forces. I remembered quite distinctly that as forces became larger, casualty rates seemed to decline much more rapidly than did the proportion of the force exposed to direct fire. How could that be? Then the light flashed again. Could the Clausewitzean concept of friction be the answer? If so, then perhaps friction could be measured after all. I forgot the lecturer and began making notes and doing calculations.

Deployment Geometry Versus Casualty Rates

As Figure 14-1 shows, the larger the unit, the smaller the proportion of people in front line platoons exposed to hostile direct fire weapons at least up to corps and army group level. This phenomenon is based upon two facts. First, at each higher

Figure 14–1

Standard Deployments Front-Line Forces
(1980's US Doctrine)

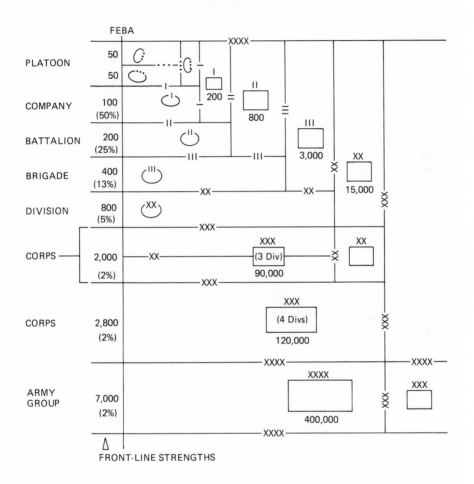

Table 14–1

Approximate Proportion of Personnel in Front Line Platoons For Standard Deployment

Unit	Normal Strength	Personnel in Front Line Platoons	Proportion of Strength in Front Line Platoons
Platoon	50	50	100%
Company	200	100	50%
Battalion	800	200	25%
Brigade	3,000	400	13%
Division	15,000	800	5%
Corps[a]	90,000	2,000	2%
Corps[b]	120,000	2,800	2%
Army Group[c]	400,000	7,000	2%

[a] Three divisions with one in reserve
[b] Four divisions with one in reserve
[c] Three corps with one in reserve

Table 14–2

Deployment of Unit Elements Exposed to Direct Fire (Direct fire exposure)

Unit	Normal Strength	Minimum Standard	Maximum	Percent Range	Median Percent
Company	200	100	200	50–100	75
Battalion	800	200	600	25–75	50
Brigade	3,000	400	1,800	13–67	40
Division	15,000	800	5,400	5–36	21
Corps (4 Div)	120,000	2,800	25,000	2–21	12
Army Group (3 Corps)	400,000	7,000	70,000	2–18	10

echelon of command there is a larger percentage of people charged with administrative, logistic, or support functions. This is the administrative "tail." Second, in standard modern deployment doctrine and procedures (typified by "two up and one back"), the larger the unit, the smaller the proportion of its combat units (the weapons operators) in contact with the enemy. Table 14-1 shows that the percentage of troops in front line platoons in this standard deployment declines from about 50% in an infantry company to about 2% in a type army group of four corps, provided that nearly one-third of each organization is held in reserve.

For a variety of reasons, the average exposure of combat troops to enemy direct fire weapons is actually somewhat higher than shown in Table 14-1. One of the most important of these reasons is that commanders tend to reinforce their front-line units (on offense as well as defense) with elements taken from the portion of their principal fighting force (rarely as much as one-third) that they hold back in reserve under the standard deployment. Commanders also tend to reinforce their front line units with portions of additional attached or assigned combat and combat support units when these are available to them. At least equally important is the fact that in the dynamic process of a battle such activities as maneuver or the commitment of reserves by defenders or attackers will result (at least for a portion of an intensive battle) in most of the available combat units being committed.

In Table 14-2 I have shown not only the sizes of the elements of a command normally deployed at the outset of a battle (as in Table 14-1), but also the approximate maximum number of fighting troops that could be committed and exposed to hostile direct fire weapons at the height of a hard-fought battle. This maximum varies from 100% of authorized personnel strength for a rifle company to around 20% for a corps or army group, with the median percentage of such exposed strength ranging from about 75% for the infantry company to about 10% for an army group of 400,000 men. No wonder smaller units incur casualties at a higher rate than do larger units. But why do we need the concept of friction to explain the phenomenon?

In Table 14-3 I have shown normalized casualty rates according to unit strength. When compared to Table 14-2, the data in Table 14-3 show that the casualty rates for larger units decline much more precipitously than does the proportion of forces exposed to combat.

Daily casualty rates in intensive combat for an infantry company of 200 troops are about 70 times greater than those for an army corps of 100,000 men. Yet, according to Table 14-2, the average exposure of an infantry company's strength to direct fire weapons is only about 7 times as great as that of an army group. A possible

Table 14–3

Average Daily Casualty Rates (%)
In Relation to Unit Strength

Strength Classes	Attacker	Defender	Normalized For 100,000
Fewer than 500	33.0	21.0	70.0
500–1,000	12.0	8.0	26.7
1,000–2,000	8.0	5.0	16.7
2,000–4,000	3.0	2.5	8.3
4,000–6,000	2.2	1.8	6.0
6,000–8,000	1.6	1.4	4.7
8,000–10,000	1.3	1.2	4.0
10,000–12,500	1.2	1.15	3.8
12,500–15,000	1.15	1.1	3.7
15,000–25,000*	1.0	1.0	3.3
25,000–35,000	0.9	0.9	3.0
35,000–45,000	0.8	0.8	2.7
45,000–60,000	0.7	0.7	2.3
60,000–75,000	0.6	0.6	2.0
75,000–80,000	0.5	0.5	1.7
80,000–100,000	0.4	0.4	1.3
Over 100,000 men	0.3	0.3	1

*Unit Strength normalized at division level, approximately 1% per day in intensive combat, World War II.

explanation for this apparent discrepancy is the Clausewitzean concept of friction. Friction seems to have an effect about 10 times as great for an organization of 100,000 men than it has for one of 200 men.

Table 14-4 synthesizes Tables 14-2 and 14-3, with both casualty rates and median direct exposure percentage. The factorial difference between exposure and casualties is attributed to friction. The friction factor is the multiplier needed to equalize the percentages of exposure to the casualty rates. It is assumed that there is no friction (a factor value of 1.0) when casualties are commensurate with exposure, as is the case at the company level. As casualties become disproportionately less than exposure as size increases, friction is present. The formula is as follows:

$$\text{Friction Factor} = \frac{\text{Exposure.}}{\text{Casualties}}$$

Table 14–4

Derivation of Friction Factor Values

Unit	Median Exposure %	Normalized Average Casualty Rate %	Approx. Friction Factor
Company	75	70	1.0
Battalion	50	27	1.9
Brigade	37	8.3	4.5
Division	21	3.3	6.3
Corps	12	1.3	9.2
Army Group	10	1.0	10.0

The relation between the size of a force and the casualties it normally incurs, and the proportion of the force exposed to hostile fire is expressed graphically in Figure 14-2. Superimposed upon the first two curves is another that represents the average friction factor.

As Theodore Ayrault Dodge pointed out nearly a century ago, this relationship has been evident since the dawn of historical warfare.[3] Figure 14-3 presents size-casualty rate relationships for wars in different significant periods of history.

The pre-twentieth century data in Figure 14-3 is based upon figures from Dodge and Livermore,[4] which, even though the Dodge data is not as reliable as modern data, demonstrate that the relation of daily casualty rates to size of force has been similar in all wars from antiquity, through the eighteenth century, the Napoleonic Wars, the American Civil War, up to the present. Figure 14-3 also shows in different form the historical decline in casualty rates discussed in the previous chapter and shown in Figure 13-1.

Explanation of Friction

These curves in Figure 14-3 show that throughout the recorded history of warfare, casualty rates of large units have been lower than the rates of smaller forces. The only apparent explanation for the lower casualty rates of larger forces throughout history is that friction has always been present in war. More study of the relationship of dispersion, deployment, and friction would probably show that the friction curve is similar, if not identical, in all periods of history to that shown in Figure 14-2.

Furthermore, it is quite likely that variations due to differences

Figure 14–2

Relationship Between Casualties, Size of Force, and Exposure to Fire

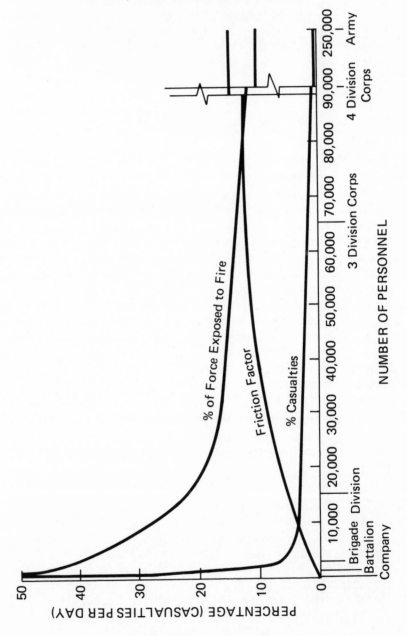

in relative combat effectiveness (CEV) will appear as shown in Figure 14-3. Friction will be less for well-trained, well-led forces than for forces of lower quality.

A critical element in the chain of reasoning that led to these thoughts on the quantification of friction was the set of data summarized in Table 14-3. The data was compiled by HERO in the 1960s and 1970s from some 200 sets of World War II engagement data, about two-thirds of which involved combat between American and German forces, nearly one-third British versus Germans, and a few Russian versus German. The relationships have been confirmed generally by data from the 1973 Middle East War, but this has not been done exhaustively.

Friction in a Single Battle

Analysis of data from a large number of different battles shows that throughout history, regardless of deployment or dispersion, under similar or nearly identical conditions, the casualty rates of large units are invariably disproportionately lower than the casualty rates of small units. Additional support for this finding was later obtained by examining casualty rates for units of different size in the same battle.[5]

Casualty data for three US divisions and their subordinate units in three different high intensity combat operations was analyzed. The divisions and battles are as follows: the 30th Division of Mortain, 6–12 August 1944; the 28th Division at Schmidt, 2–13 November 1944; and the 2d Division in the Ardennes, 13–21 December 1944. None of the data compiled in this study was included in the casualty data summarized in Table 14-3. There is no overlap between the original data from which the friction hypothesis was derived and this more recent set of data used to test the hypothesis.

Of the total of twenty-eight examples of combat data in these three operations, data was found for twenty intensive combat engagements of one to three days duration that permitted comparisons between division daily casualty rates and those of regiments in the same division. Within those twenty engagements, there are fourteen engagements in which the casualty rates of regiments and subordinate battalions could be compared.

Included within this data compilation were seven engagements, of one to three days duration of very intensive combat, in which casualty rates could be compared among division, regiment, and battalion. Four of these were for single days of combat. The results of analysis of this data are shown in Table 14-5, which also includes for comparative purposes the comparable rates for the original 200 World War II data points.

Table 14–5

Comparison of Casualty Rates at Different Unit Levels

	CASUALTY RATES RELATIVE TO DIVISION RATES		
	Division	*Regiment*	*Battalion*
Original WW II Data Points	1.0	2.6	9.5
New Data Points[a] 20–14 intensive, 1–3 days[b]	1.0	2.7	7.3
7 very intensive, 1–3 days	1.0	3.0	9.2
4 very intensive, 1 day	1.0	3.6	10.9

[a] World War II: 2d, 28th, and 30th Infantry Divisions
[b] 20 engagements from division to regiment, 14 from regiment to battalion.

In Table 14-6 I have shown how the results of the new analysis fit into the casualty rates computed from the original set of data shown in Table 14-3. Before proceeding with a comparison of these two independent sets of data, two observations are necessary. First, the data in Table 14-3 came from World War II battles, most of which were at division level. The smallest personnel strength in those 200 sets of data was 3,000 men. Figures for smaller forces are based upon an extrapolation of the graphical curve representing the data. Second, the new data points in Table 14-5 come from operations in which (with the possible exception of the four one-day instances of very intensive combat) there were intermittent lulls in the combat activities of the individual battalions, even though the divisions and regiments might have considered themselves fully engaged.

Figure 14–3

Force Strengths and Average Daily Casualty Rates Wars Through History

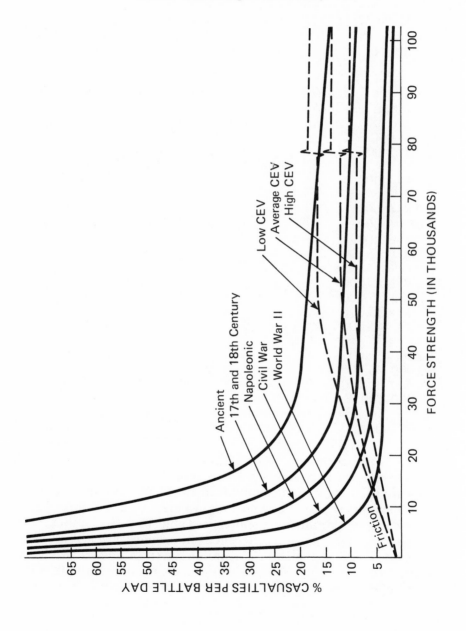

Table 14–6

NEW DATA POINTS FOR AVERAGE CASUALTY RATES PER DAY IN RELATION TO UNIT STRENGTH

ORIGINAL STRENGTH CLASS	NEW STRENGTH DATA	AVERAGE DAILY CASUALTY RATES %			
		Attacker		Defender	
		Old	New	Old	New
Less than 500		33.0		21.0	
	700		14.3		9.5
500–1,000		12.0		8.0	
1,000–2,000		8.0		5.0	
	2,500		3.2		2.6
2,000–4,000		3.0		2.5	
4,000–6,000		2.2		1.8	
6,000–8,000		1.6		1.4	
8,000–10,000		1.3		1.2	
10,000–12,500		1.2		1.15	
	12,500		1.0		1.0
12,500–15,000		1.15		1.1	
15,000–25,000		1.0		1.0	
25,000–35,000		0.9		0.9	
35,000–45,000		0.8		0.8	
45,000–60,000		.07		0.7	
60,000–75,000		0.6		0.6	
75,000–80,000		0.5		0.5	
80,000–100,000		0.4		0.4	
Over 100,000		0.3		0.3	

Even without consideration of these relevant background facts, the correlation between these two sets of data is very good. It appears that in intensive combat in World War II the relation of daily casualty rates of divisions, regiments (brigades), and battalions was approximately as shown in Table 14-7.

How can there be such differences in casualty rates of units at different levels of the same formation for the same battle? This might seem to suggest that the whole is not equal to the sum of its parts, even if we strip out the effects of deployment or friction.

Table 14-7

Intensive Combat Casualty Rates in World War II

ORIGINAL LEVEL (STRENGTH)	PERCENT CASUALTIES PER DAY	NORMALIZED TO DIVISION
Division (12,500)	1.2	1.0
Regiment (2,500)	3.6	3.0
Battalion (700)	11.4	9.5

But this is not so. Casualty rates are compiled, and usually reported, on a daily basis for almost all armies in all wars. At the fighting front casualties are incurred in small combat units during very brief periods of intensive fighting, with lulls between such periods. The figures that we have shown are evidence of the effects of dispersion, deployment, and friction on the daily casualty rates of organizations at all levels.

During the periods of actual combat, the lower the level, the closer the loss rates will approach the theoretical lethalities of the weapons in the hands of the opposing combatants. But there will *never* be a *very* close relationship of such rates with the theoretical lethalities. War does not consist merely of a number of duels. Duels, in fact, are only a very small—though integral—part of combat. Combat is a complex process involving interaction over time of many men and numerous weapons combined in a great number of different, and differently organized, units. This process cannot be understood completely by considering the theoretical interactions of individual men and weapons. Complete understanding requires knowing how to structure such interactions and fit them together. Learning how to structure these interactions must be based on scientific analysis of real combat data.

The Hierarchical Relationships of Models

One value of the quantification of friction is the potential contribution of the concept of friction to the solution of one of the most difficult problems in modeling combat—the problem of hierarchical relationships of models. Early in the process of the development of modern computerized combat models it became evident that it would be desirable to have the results of simulating combat at the company level fit into simulations at the battalion level, which would fit into simulations at the brigade level, and so on up to simulations of combat through the division to the theater and global levels. This would allow the output of a simulation of combat at one level of aggregation to become the input for another level, or vice-versa. Such a hierarchy of consistent models would allow theater models to be based on the presumably more realistic (at least more detailed) company or battalion levels models.

There is one difficulty persisting to this day. It was soon discovered that it was impossible to obtain realistic interfaces between models at different levels of aggregation. The outcomes of simulation of low-level engagements, when incorporated into higher-level models, gave results so unrealistic that they were obviously unacceptable. The first effort to try to deal with this problem was probably undertaken in the Operations Research Office (ORO), the Army's principal think tank from about 1950 to about 1962. Since that early effort, additional attempts to construct believable hierarchies of models have continued, but without success.

It is possible that at least a portion of the hierarchical modelling problem can be resolved by a careful quantification of the element of friction. The concept presented in this chapter is a start. Much more research needs to be done, and more analysis is required as well. For instance, it is clear that the sum *must* equal the total of its parts. The total casualties of a large force is the sum of the losses of its subordinate units, no matter what their different daily casualty rates may be.

It is possible that the different rates can be reconciled by recognizing the fact that, even in the most intensive combat, there are lulls in the activity of smaller units, interspersed between periods in which they are incurring casualties at greater rates than the larger formations. It is probable that these lulls can be related to small unit attrition rates for periods of less than 24 hours, and to the discrepancies in simulated and real advance rates of smaller and larger forces, in models and on the battlefield. This work remains to be done.

Until that research and analysis are performed, however, the friction quantification here indicated will permit reasonable and quite realistic approximations in hierarchical modeling relationships and so facilitate progress in an area of research that thus far has been pursuing various blind alleys.

Clausewitz was both right and wrong. Friction is palpable, and can be visualized; it can also be measured. Friction may even prove to have been a relatively constant factor through history. In any event, it must be taken into account in any theory of combat.

Chapter 15

Technology and Human Behavior in Combat

Relating Capabilities and Effects—Some Dubious Assumptions

MODERN SCIENCE AND technology have done amazing things in increasing the effectiveness of weapons in the last three-quarters of a century. But science and technology have been unable to create combat models that can predict the effects of the marvelous new weapons on the battlefield. This inability to relate weapons' capabilities to their battlefield effects is reminiscent of 1914, except that the dichotomy is probably more acute now than it was then.

There seem to be two major reasons for this distressing state of affairs. In trying to predict weapons effects, military planners and analysts in this country today seem to have made two critical—and erroneous—assumptions. The first of these is that human behavior is random and unpredictable, so that human reactions to combat phenomena are intractable. This attitude, unfortunately, is a self-fulfilling prophecy. While our scientists do well in the purely physical aspects of weapons development, they do not do very well in understanding what they call "the man-machine interface." One reason for this failure is that the comforting assumptions suggest that they needn't try very hard. Despite lip service, we Americans give much, much less attention and devote far fewer resources to understanding the human aspects of combat than we give to the purely physical, hard science aspects. Because, having assumed that we cannot cope with behavioral effects, we tend to ignore them and to push them under the rug.

Our physical scientists' second dubious assumption is that once new technology appears on the battlefield, all prior experience becomes irrelevant. Many operations research analysts, military planners, and scientists insist that they consider historical experience to be a valuable background for military analysis. But few of these people see any benefit in a comprehensive, systematic survey of military historical experience to relate what *has* happened on the battlefield to what in all likelihood *will* happen, because they have assumed that there is no relationship between the two.

Underlying these two assumptions is a third: science must be based upon experimentation. Thus, where it is possible to undertake combat-related experimentation—field tests and laboratory tests for weapons, training exercises and maneuvers for troop units—our operations research analysts uncritically accept the results as valid for war. Since they assume that experimentation is essential to scientific progress, that which cannot be tested, anything not amenable to an approximation of laboratory experimentation, cannot be important and thus can be ignored.

There is, however, a fundamental fallacy to this assumption, a fallacy that applies equally to the two derivative assumptions. In peacetime it is not possible to create the laboratory conditions of war. All peacetime tests and experiments lack the most fundamental and pervasive aspect of war: fear in a lethal environment. The science of war cannot be an experimental science, like physics. It is an observational science, like astronomy.

Military history is the laboratory of the soldier. Fortunately or unfortunately, no other laboratory is available. When human behavior is involved, as it always is in combat, neither test data nor field exercise results can be surrogates for combat data.[1] Reactive tests and field exercises can never establish an environment of fear. Let us see how military history can be useful as the soldier's laboratory.

Historical Eras and Innovations in Weapons

I divide military history into the following periods:

The Era of Muscle, generally up to the mid-thirteenth century; it overlapped with;

The Era of Gunpowder, from between 1250 and 1350 to about 1800; and

The Era of Technological Change, in which we now find ourselves. Muscle and gunpowder remain very much a part of warfare, but more has been added.

Within the Era of Technological Change there have been several sub-periods, for instance:

Early Industrial Revolution, 1800 to 1850;
Ferment in Weaponry, 1850 to 1915;
Electronic Revolution, 1915 to ?.

Table 15-1 lists what I consider to be the most important innovations in weapons since the dawn of history. Listed are twenty-eight classes of weapons, with the fifty-six most significant weapons types. Twelve of them were introduced over the period of the first 1600 years, about 400 B.C. to 1200 A.D. Twelve more were introduced in the next 600 years. And thirty-two of them were introduced over the last 230 years.

The first half-century of the Industrial Revolution had a largely indirect effect upon war. There were some improvements in weapons, such as the introduction of the percussion cap for small arms. However, the major military effects of the Industrial Revolution at that time were on transport and supply through the steam engine (in rail locomotives on land and steamships at sea) and through mass production.

An important and dramatic change in the waging of war occurred in the decade between 1850 and 1860. This was the result of the introduction of an apparently minor improvement in small arms: the conoidal bullet for the infantryman's rifled musket. No other technological change in weaponry, before or *since*, has had a comparable, directly discernible, immediate effect on the battlefield. Table 15-2 shows the effect of this technology on battlefield casualties.

During the French Revolutionary and Napoleonic Wars, and through the last wars of the old era, such as the Crimean War and the Mexican War, artillery was responsible for 50% or more of battle casualties. However, as shown in Table 15-2, in the principal nineteenth century wars after 1860 (the American Civil War, the Austro-Prussian War, and the Franco-Prussian War), artillery was responsible for barely 10% of the casualties. Small

Table 15–1

Major Weapons Development

1. Sword, prehistory
1.1. Roman short sword, ca. 250 B.C.
2. Pike, prehistory
2.1. Javelin, prehistory
2.2. Macedonian sarissa, ca. 359 B.C.
3. Bow, prehistory
3.1. Mongol composite bow, ca. 1100 A.D.
3.2. Crossbow, ca. 1100 A.D.
3.3. English longbow, ca. 1150 A.D.
4. Sling, prehistory
5. Catapult and ballista, ca. 500 B.C.
6. Greek Fire, 673 A.D.
6.1. Flamethrower, 1915
7. Gunpowder, ca. 1200
7.1. Stable gunpowder, ca. 1450
7.2. Smokeless powder, 1885
8. Cannon, ca. 1325
8.1. Breechloading cannon, ca. 1860
9. Explosive shell, ca. 1400
9.1. Canister, ca. 1410
9.2. Shrapnel, 1803
9.3. High explosive shell, 1886
9.4. Improved conventional munitions (ICM), ca. 1960
10. Arquebus, ca. 1400
10.1. Musket, ca. 1550
10.2. Flintlock musket and bayonet, ca. 1690
10.3. Rifle, ca. 1700
10.4. Rifle with conoidal bullet, ca. 1850
10.5. Breech loading rifle, ca. 1855
10.6. Bolt-operated magazine rifle, ca. 1895
11. Pistol, ca. 1425
12. Submarine, 1775
13. Naval mine, 1776
14. Congreve rocket, 1806
14.1. V-2 rocket, 1944
14.2. Intercontinental ballistic missile, 1958
15. Percussion cap, ca. 1815
16. Armored warship, 1859
17. Land mine, 1862
17.1. Scatterable mine, ca. 1970
18. Gatling machine gun, 1862
18.1. Maxim machine gun, 1883

Table 15–1 (cont'd)

Major Weapons Development

19.	Torpedo, 1866
20.	Dreadnought, 1906
21.	Poison gas, 1915
21.1.	Bacteriological and toxin agents, 1916
22.	Combat (bombardment) aircraft, 1915
22.1.	Fighter aircraft, 1915
22.2.	Fighter-bomber aircraft, 1917
22.3.	Combat helicopter, ca. 1950
23.	Aerial bomb, 1915
23.1.	Guided bomb and electronic-guided munitions, 1943
24.	Tank, 1916
25.	Aircraft carrier, 1921
26.	Atom bomb, 1945
26.1.	Hydrogen bomb, 1952
27.	Laser, ca. 1985

arms (rifled muskets) were responsible for nearly 90% of the casualties inflicted. This was because the conoidal bullet so vastly increased the range and accuracy of the rifle that infantry-men could fire effectively as far and as accurately as could artillery. For all practical purposes both could fire to the next ridge line. Thus, hostile artillerymen, as well as hostile infantry-men, were logical targets for riflemen, with results severely damaging to the performance of artillery and the health of artillerymen.

Other new developments during the latter part of the nine-teenth century affected warfare significantly. There were, for instance, the introduction of the breechloading rifle, smokeless powder, more sophistication in artillery weapons, and increasing use of the railroad and the telegraph.

Table 15–2

Causes of Battlefield Casualties in the Nineteenth Century

	BEFORE 1850	AFTER 1860
Artillery	40 – 50%	8 – 10%
Infantry Small Arms	30 – 40%	85 – 90%
Saber and Bayonet	15 – 20%	4 – 6%

Ancillary Technical Developments

At this point it is useful to survey the ancillary technical developments affecting weapons lethality. Table 15-3 lists what I consider to be the twenty-eight to thirty most important ancillary technical developments since the dawn of history. Some of these are simple, but of great significance. Take, for instance, the stirrup, a simple, non-lethal artifact. By providing horsemen with a solid base for wielding lance, sword, or bow, the stirrup made cavalry supreme on the battlefield for one thousand years.

The telegraph, is an important ancillary development that contributed to two trends since the beginning of the Industrial Revolution: (1) the increasing dispersion of troops (a reaction to steady increases in the lethality of new weapons), and (2) the ability of nations to field larger armies as agricultural technology freed an increasing proportion of the population from the farms. The telegraph permitted an army commander to control greater numbers of troops in numerous corps and divisions, more widely dispersed than in the past. It also permitted national commanders in chief to exercise control—whether for good or ill—over larger armies spread out over one or more theaters of operation. This was the beginning of the Electronic Revolution in warfare.

The next important development in the Electronic Revolution was the field telephone. It had a number of effects, but principally it began to redress the imbalance of artillery and infantry effectiveness caused by the introduction of the conoidal bullet in the rifled musket. Without the field telephone none of the many improvements in cannon, such as smokeless powder, recoil mechanisms, extended ranges, and high explosive shells, would have been very useful. The field telephone permitted the artillery to disappear from the sights of hostile riflemen, through the technique of indirect fire.

In order to understand the impact of the field telephone on combat it is necessary to appreciate the meaning of the technical military term: "indirect fire." It is a term not always well understood, even by military analysts and writers on military affairs who should know better. Indirect fire is accomplished when the gunner or gun crew of a weapon (usually an artillery piece) are able to place effective fire on a target that they cannot see. It is *usually* accomplished by means of a communications link between the gun crew and an observer who is so placed that he *can* see the target. Through one of a variety of "observed fire" techniques, the observer adjusts the fire of the gun on the target,

Table 15–3

Major Ancillary Developments in Military Technology

1.	Armor and shield, prehistory
1.1.	Lightweight body armor, ca. 1950
2.	Stirrup, ca. 100 A.D.
3.	Matchlock mechanism, ca. 1450
3.1.	Flintlock mechanism, ca. 1615
4.	Signal flags, ca. 1550
5.	Iron ramrod, ca. 1730
6.	Steam engine, 1769
7.	Semaphore, ca. 1790
8.	Observation balloon, ca. 1792
9.	Steamship, 1803
10.	Railroad, 1825
11.	Telegraph, 1837
12.	Naval gun turret, 1862
13.	Barbed wire, 1874
14.	Field telephone, ca. 1880
15.	Internal combustion engine, 1887
16.	Artillery recoil mechanism, 1888
17.	Wireless radio, 1896
18.	Observation aircraft, 1907
19.	Cryptographic machine, ca. 1910
20.	Naval aircraft flight deck, 1911
21.	Sonar (Asdic), 1917
22.	Radar, 1938
23.	Computer, automatic data processing, ca. 1940
24.	Inertial and electronic guidance, ca. 1950
25.	Electronic sensors, ca. 1950
26.	Nuclear power, 1955
27.	Earth satellite in space, 1956
28.	Laser, 1960

providing corrections for range and direction through the communication link, usually a field telephone or (increasingly since 1940) a radio. The term "direct fire" means fire brought to bear on a target by a gunner or gun crew who *do* see the target, and who can adjust the fire directly on it without the need for an intermediate observer.

There is a form of indirect fire, called "unobserved fire," by which the shells from the guns are fired at a target on the basis of the plotted positions of guns and targets on a map or firing chart. Measurements made on the map or chart are converted to range and direction instructions to the gun crew. Even under the best of circumstances, unobserved fire, which is *always* indirect fire, is not so accurate as observed fire, which can be either direct or indirect.

These methods of placing fire on a target should not be confused with distinctions in which fire is described in terms of the nature of the target, such as "area" targets or "point" targets. In area fire, the projectiles of a number of guns are directed (usually by indirect fire, which can be observed or unobserved) at a target spread out over an area, such as a force of enemy infantry deployed for battle. When a point target (such as a pill box, or a tank, or a house) is engaged, the fire of an individual gun is placed on the target by a technique that, in the artillery, is called "precision fire."

This lengthy explanation will be of benefit to those who have been influenced by the Lanchester equations when they try to contrast "aimed fire" and "area fire," when they really are trying to contrast "observed" and "unobserved" fire. This error leads often to a misinterpretation of the distinction between Lanchester's square law and linear law (see Chapter 2). It should also be of benefit to writers on military affairs who think mistakenly that firing a weapon at a high angle above a level plane—in order to increase range—is indirect fire. It *may* be, but need not be. The high angle fire of the English archers at Agincourt, for instance, was *not* indirect fire.

In the early days of indirect fire, communications links other than the field telephone were employed. For instance, an observer could be located in a church steeple, or a tree, or on a hill near the gun position, but high enough to see targets beyond the mask that concealed the guns from enemy observation. In such a situation the observer could shout observations or commands to the gun crews. Rarely, however, would the terrain and the circumstances of battle permit observer and guns to be close enough to each other for this kind of arrangement, and even if they were close, the noise of battle usually made shouting impracticable. An alternative means of communication was for the observer to use a messenger to send commands to the guns, but this was so cumbersome and time-consuming that it was rarely worth the effort. However, signal flags could often be used, communicating by semaphore or Morse code.

It was the field telephone that made indirect artillery fire really practical, and practical indirect fire made artillery much more effective than before. After a half-century of development of weapons and doctrine, by the end of World War I artillery was again responsible for more than 50% of battle casualties, despite the introduction of the machine gun and other automatic and semi-automatic small arms.

Technological Change and the World Wars

World War I saw the military fruition of a number of new technological developments, most of which had been germinating since the latter part of the nineteenth century. In a little more than four years of combat there were probably more technological innovations in weapons and ancillary war equipment introduced than ever before or since in a comparable period of time. Most of the new weapons of World War II were developed from prototypes that first appeared in World War I. Among the innovations of World War I were the tank, the combat aircraft, poison gas, sonar, and the field radio, to mention just a few. In the case of only one of these new weapons did the side that introduced it retain a clear-cut advantage for a substantial period of time.

That one case is significant. It was the tank, developed by the Allies, and never seriously challenged during the war by the Germans. The tank was the product of a mechanical, technological effort to solve the "riddle of the trenches," which was the inability of either side to break through the opposing barriers of entrenchments and barbed wire from the North Sea to Switzerland. The Germans had almost simultaneously developed a conceptual answer to that riddle (infiltration tactics, often called "Hutier Tactics" by the Allies) and were content to confine their efforts to refining that technique. Near the end of the war the Germans realized that they had made a mistake, but by then it was too late. In retrospect, it is clear that the tank was no better an answer to trench warfare than were infiltration tactics. In World War II the Germans were to demonstrate that a combination of the two—blitzkrieg: technological innovation used in a conceptually innovative method of fighting—was far better than either alone.

In the quarter century from the end of the First World War to the end of the Second, a few new lethal weapons were introduced. The most significant of these were the ballistic missile (really an improved form of the rocket, first introduced into Western warfare by the British about 1800) and the guided missile, which was an application of electronic controls to conventional bombs or newer rockets. The Germans pioneered in both of these developments.

Between 1918 and 1945 there were a number of new developments in ancillary equipment, most of them electronic in nature, such as radar, proximity fuzes, inertial and electronic methods of guidance, and the first crude prototypes of computers, used initially by the British for processing intelligence data.

Technological Change Since 1945

In the forty years since World War II the unprecedented pace of technological development has sparked incessant changes in weapons design and characteristics, as well as in the burgeoning, and increasingly sophisticated, non-lethal materiel items that have become incorporated into complex weapon systems. Yet, there have been no startling new developments in weaponry comparable to the introduction of the machine gun, the tank, and the combat aircraft earlier in the century. Change has been evolutionary rather than revolutionary. This is a situation that cannot be ignored, even though it could conceivably change at any time with the introduction of some startling new weapon. There may, in fact, be one or more such new weapons waiting in the wings.

The most important development, or set of developments, of course, has been in the field of nuclear weapons. While the first such weapons were introduced in the closing days of World War II—and helped to hasten the end of that war—they have never been used since and particularly have never been used in tactical combat.

The fact that there have been no instances of employment of tactical nuclear weapons in these past forty years supports the argument that such employment is not likely in the proximate future, but no commander can meet his responsibilities to his superiors or to his men unless his combat decisions reflect the ever-present possibility that nuclear weapons *might* be used against him. The nuclear-related context of his decisions need not necessarily be spelled out at all times; but that context must, at the very least, be deeply rooted in his subconscious as he deals with the dispositions and deployment of subordinate units and individuals. He must not allow himself to be deluded—as some would suggest—that nuclear weapons are not significantly different from other weapons, only somewhat more powerful. Nor should he be similarly self-deluded by the apparent narrowing of the gap between increasingly smaller yields of nuclear narrowing and the progressive increase in power of so-called conventional weapons.

Nuclear weapons differ from conventional weapons not just in power, but in kind. If their use in tactical battle could be assuredly limited to the fractional kiloton variety, then there might be some validity to the easy assumption that they are merely bigger and better weapons. But any use of even the smallest tactical nuke carries with it the possibility of escalation. Escalation with conventional weapons is relatively finite. Escalation with nuclear weapons has potentialities as close to infinity as the human mind can imagine. Such an eventuality is so far from likely that we can *almost* ignore it, but since it *is* possible, it should not be ignored completely.

Far less cataclysmic are the impacts of other new technologies. Possibly the single most pervasive military development of the past forty years is the impact of the computer on the conduct of war. Administration, logistics, and control of firepower, are all keyed to the computer and the various means of electronic communication. It is possible that military operations have become too dependent upon the computer and upon electronic communication. But are there alternatives? There is serious question whether this issue is being addressed adequately in the United States and NATO. There is evidence that the Soviets are giving the matter critical attention—with results we do not know.

I do not have the qualifications to discuss authoritatively the other electronic developments in military affairs, such as the many and varied means of communications, weapons control and guidance, intelligence, surveillance; almost all of which are related in some way or another to the ubiquitous computer. This is, indeed, the Age of Electronics.

Hardly less pervasive, although somewhat more obvious, has been the incorporation of the helicopter into the force structure as a means of mobility and as a weapons platform. The helicopter is obviously here to stay. Yet, there must be a question about whether the new tactics that have been built up around the helicopter will survive intact in a war in which the United States does not have assured air superiority. The challenge of hostile high-performance fixed-wing aircraft will not drive the helicopter from the skies, but it may inhibit employment of the helicopter to a far greater extent than the new doctrine appears to envisage.

It is too early to evaluate the long-term significance of such new technological developments as the following: missiles and rockets, guided munitions, improved conventional munitions, sensors and target acquisition; scatterable mines, lightweight armor, and decoys and deception. Many are related to and dependent on electronics and electronic communications. Some of these work to make the battlefield more lethal. Others tend to enhance the survivability of weapons systems and people. It is far from certain in which direction—toward greater or lesser lethality—is the thrust of the combined effect of these.

The laser is the most recent technological development—both as ancillary equipment and a lethal weapon. The laser has already demonstrated its non-lethal military value in a variety of ways, including particularly target designation for other weapons. Recently it has been proposed as a major destructive component of the weapons systems projected for President Reagan's Strategic Defensive Initiative (popularly known as "Star Wars"). Whether, when, or how the laser will eventually be an employable and deployable weapon is not now clear.

Although they aren't new developments, increasing attention has been given in recent years to chemical and biological weapons. These have not been used extensively or overtly since World War I. Yet there seems to be increasing possibility of their use in future war. If so, what will be their effects on the battlefield? However effective these weapons may be—or however horrible may their specific effects—chemical and biological weapons cannot possibly have the cataclysmic potential of nuclear weapons.

In fact, the experience of World War I suggests that the greatest potential of these weapons will be to make war much more uncomfortable, but without significant effect on attrition or combat outcomes. If these weapons are used, they may well have the overall effect of making the battlefield *less* lethal, and combat activity in general slower, because of the constraints that will result from the various protective measures both sides will have to take, even when only one side employs the weapons.

The Target-Rich Environment

It has been suggested that the combined impact of all of the developments of recent years are likely to reverse the attrition trends discussed in Chapter 13. This is because the increased number of large, high-value targets, combined with improvements in weapons, and with improved means of target acquisition, will result in what has been called a "target-rich environment."

A glance at Figure 13-2 will suggest that the "target-rich environment" is a myth. Indeed, the discrepancy between the numbers of major weapons per square kilometer for World Wars I and II, in comparison with current anticipated deployments in Europe, is probably greater than shown, since these figures do not allow for limbers and caissons for the artillery in World War I, or the prime movers for towed artillery in World War II. However, it might be argued that these comparisons are offset both by the greater lethality and the higher rates of fire for artillery and other major weapons today.

As to the first point, the greater lethality and improved means of target acquisition are to a considerable degree offset by better armor protection and by improved decoys and means of deception, in addition to the offset inherent in greater dispersion.

As to rates of fire, it is very doubtful if these will be higher than in World War II. Artillery rates of fire are going to be determined in large part by the capabilities of the gun crews, and soldiers of the 1980s and 1990s will not be bigger or stronger than those of the 1940s. Perhaps more important, artillery rates of fire will be constrained by the availability of ammunition. While I know of no definitive study of artillery ammunition supply in World War II, it is fairly clear that ammunition was pushed to the front as rapidly as the availability of trucks and the capacity of the roads would permit. Even under ideal conditions, it is doubtful if the availability of trucks and the capacity of the road nets in Europe today will permit any significant increase in the availability of ammunition per gun tube over that achieved in 1944 and 1945. Furthermore, the accumulation of stocks of ammunition in World War II was in a benign Allied air superiority environment

—virtually a condition of air supremacy. Long range air and missile interdiction by Pact forces in the 1980s or 1990s is almost certain to be more effective than the negligible German interference in that earlier war. If it is assumed that the U.S. and NATO will have effectiveness at long range interdiction, it is inconsistent to assume a significantly less capability for the Soviets and the Warsaw Pact.

The Interaction of Military Technology and Military Men

This brings us up to 1985. In an earlier book, I drew a number of conclusions from the first century and a half of interaction between technology and war waged by men using the products of technology.[2] I wish to re-emphasize two of these.

First, it should be noted that after the introduction of a new weapon prototype, and the subsequent adoption of the weapon into the armaments inventory, there has always been a substantial period before the weapon has been assimilated fully into the tactics and doctrine of the forces employing that weapon. In the last two or three centuries, this period of assimilation has been approximately twenty to twenty-five years, or about one generation. Second, the history of combat between 1800 and 1945 confirmed earlier historical evidence that no technology, no weapon, however great its actual or potential lethality, has been as important for the winning of battles or wars as the men who controlled the weapons. There have been no developments in the years since the end of World War II requiring a change in this assessment.

Assimilation of Weapons

It is useful to elaborate a bit on these two points: assimilation of new weapons, and the primacy of men over weapons. The preconditions for the assimilation of new weapons seem to be the following:

Imaginative, competent, knowledgeable, flexible leadership
Effective coordination of national resources
Effective, flexible coordination of military resources
Opportunity to evaluate and analyze combat experience

The word "flexible" is particularly important, and within that word is the reason for the generation gap in assimilation.

The people who rise to the top during a war, particularly a protracted war, are imaginative, competent, knowledgeable, and effective. They have been through the crucible of battle, and they *know* from their experience what is best in the way of doctrine and tactics. Therefore, when new weapons appear, they tend to try to fit these into tried-and-true concepts. It is not until these veterans die off, retire, or otherwise fade away, that a new and still flexible generation has a chance to fit new and old weapons together with a new amalgam of doctrine and tactics.

The experience of the last 500 years indicates that the three principal characteristics in the process of assimilation on the battlefield of increasingly lethal weapons are: greater dispersion; more decentralization, and; improvements in the interactions of the different combat arms. There are a number of ways to ascertain whether or not assimilation has taken place. The principal indications are as follows:

1. Doctrine integrating the weapon into inventories of operational units
2. Confident employment within the integrating doctrine
3. Consistently effective, flexible use
4. Doctrinal capability to deal with anticipated and unanticipated countermeasures
5. Decline in casualties for the user, usually combined with increased lethality capability

It takes combat experience to prove this.

Relative Importance of Technology and Troops

Technology wins battles. It would be a dim-witted historian indeed who would suggest that the echeloned, refused flank, formation of Alexander the Great at Arbela could have fought on equal terms with the echeloned, refused flank formation of Frederick the Great at Leuthen. The important thing is the extent to which the technology of new weapons can bring success in battle between two *contemporary* military forces. History suggests that there have been three kinds of circumstances in which superior technology is the dominant factor:

1. When used against a more numerous, less developed enemy, such as Cortez's employment of gunpowder weapons in Mexico around 1520, and the British machine guns at Omdurman in 1898
2. When the opposing forces are otherwise approximately equal. Examples that come to mind are the German use of poison gas at Ypres in 1915, and the British use of tanks at Cambrai in 1917
3. When the new weapon cancels or greatly reduces an opponent's superiority, such as the German use of submarines against British surface seapower in 1917, and the Arab use of ground-air defense weapons against the Israeli Air Force in 1973

There is, however, a broader historical perspective than that perceived by focusing on these selected examples. Technology can upset, restore, or perpetuate a combat power balance or imbalance. But, the advantage is fleeting, rarely decisive, and *never* as decisive as promised or expected.

There are important implications to be drawn today from this observation about the limits of the effectiveness of technology on the battlefield. One of these has to do with the assessment of how technology could help the United States in the event of a conventional war with the Soviet Union. The United States must be very cautious in basing its survival and NATO's upon doctrinal concepts that assume a capability to capitalize decisively upon Western technological superiority over that of the Warsaw Pact.

Obviously, it is necessary to avoid overrating the enemy. Even more important is the necessity to avoid underrating him. The Russians have shown that they understand technology. They have also demonstrated an understanding of modern war. Again, a historical survey will provide perspective.

Prior to the Age of Technological Change one need only consider Alexander, Hannibal, Caesar, Genghis Khan, Gustavus Adolphus and Frederick the Great as examples of how ideas, rather than weapons, often permitted numerically inferior military forces to overcome forces that were larger and/or better equipped. Napoleon introduced neither a new weapon nor a new tactical system. He was a tactician of genius, but his principal impact on warfare was the injection of new and imaginative ideas into strategy and what we now call operational art.

Twice within the lifetimes of men now living the German Army has offset great numerical odds by scoring stunning tactical successes over its opponents: in 1918 and again in 1940. In neither case did the Germans use new weapons. Every item in their arsenals was familiar. It was the revolutionary *use* of these weapons that surprised Germany's enemies in World Wars I and II.

How did the Germans achieve this? I believe that the Germans did it by emphasizing professionalism in their army from the top to the bottom. In this way, they produced forces that were —without any superiority in quality of weapons or equipment —more combat effective than their enemies' armies.[3] Professionalism, achieved through education of officers and training of officers and men, gave them a combat effectiveness superiority over the Western Allies in both World Wars of about 1.20 to 1.00, and over the Russians of over 2.00 to 1.00. In other words, with comparable equipment, 100 Germans could fight on equal terms with about 120 British or French or American troops, and with 200 or more Russians.

The fact that the Germans were able to use the products of technology more efficiently than their enemies was not the result of any inherent German superiority; it was the result of training, education, and professionalism. The Germans were eventually defeated in both wars because the Western Allies outnumbered them by *more* than 1.20 to 1.00, and the Russians outnumbered them by *more* than 2.00 to 1.00.

The same phenomenon has occurred since 1945, in the consistent superiority of the Israelis over their Arab enemies. My research has shown that, on the average, the combat effectiveness superiority of Israelis over Arabs has been more than 2.00 to 1.00.[4]

The 1982 war in Lebanon provides a particularly sharp picture of the relationship of technology and human performance. After that war I had a chance to ask a retired Syrian General, the most objective Arab military man I know, if the Israeli victory in Lebanon was a reflection of the superiority of American weapons (with which the Israelis were mainly equipped) over the Soviet weapons in the hands of the Syrians. He replied: "Soviet weapons are very good. They are not much different from American weapons, and they are probably better for our soldiers; they tend to be simpler, and easier to use and maintain. The Israeli success was not due to weapons."

About the same time the Chief of Staff of the Israeli Army,

General Rafael Eitan, was asked almost the same question by a group of American visitors.[5] Eitan's response was: "If we had had their weapons, and they had had ours, the result would have been exactly the same."

Soon after that I had a chance to tell the story of these two conversations to General David Ivry, who commanded the Israeli Air Force in June 1982.[6] I then asked him the same question. He responded that the margin of technological superiority of American combat aircraft in the hands of Israelis, over Soviet aircraft manned by the Syrians, may have been somewhat greater than was true of the ground weapons in 1982. However, he concluded: "I agree with the Chief of Staff [General Eitan]. If we had had the Syrian MIGs, and they had had our F-16s, the outcome would have been the same, although the loss ratios might have differed a bit." Ivry then went on to say that this was because the Israelis were able to exploit their weapons to the maximum of the weapon's potential, while the Arabs could not do this.

I draw two important conclusions from this. First, despite United States' superiority in technology, American weapons currently have at best only a marginal superiority over Soviet weapons. Second, what still counts most is not weapons, but the ability of people to use them effectively.

Congruence of Weapons, Tactics, and Doctrine

Another concept that is closely related to the idea of assimilating new weapons and new technology is the concept of congruence and incongruence in the relationship of weapons and tactics.[7] Congruence between weapons of war and methods of war has historically been rare. I nominate only six military systems over the course of history in which there has been real congruence:

1. the Macedonian system of Alexander the Great (ca. 340 B.C.)
2. the Roman system of Scipio and Flamininus (ca. 200 B.C.)
3. the Mongol system of Genghis Khan (ca. 1200 A.D.)
4. the English system of Edward I, Edward III, and Henry V (ca. 1350)
5. the French system of Napoleon (ca. 1800)
6. the German blitzkrieg system (ca. 1940)

With these examples in mind, let us consider what is meant by congruence. The principal characteristics of congruent systems are as follows:

High relative combat effectiveness
Decisive battlefield success
Relatively low casualties for the congruent system
Relatively high casualties for the opposing systems

Incongruence between weapons and tactics and doctrine can result from one or more of several causes. The most important, at least in modern history, has been the introduction of new weapons into military systems, which—no matter how brilliant their military leadership might have been—were unable to adjust to them. Up until the end of World War II, the major incongruities were caused by the introduction of gunpowder, the introduction of the rifle musket with conoidal bullet, and the interaction of high explosives and automatic weapons on the bloody battlefields of World War I. The principal reason World War I, like the American Civil War before it, was so bloody and marked by so many indecisive battles, was that the lethality of weapons had outstripped the capability of generals and soldiers to employ them.

Two of the most brilliant generals in the history of war were Ulysses S. Grant and Robert E. Lee, but they had to cope with a totally unprecedented technology on the battlefield in the form of the conoidal bullet fired from the rifled musket. Without the field telephone, which would have enabled them to provide adequate artillery support to their advancing infantry, they were doomed to failure in their efforts at such places as Gettysburg and Cold Harbor. It is evident that technology was very important in the Civil War. While there was much that these brilliant military intellects could, and did, do to make use of that technology, they were trapped in a situation in which congruence was impossible because their infantrymen had conoidal bullets for their rifles, and their artillery did not have field telephones.

I do not subscribe to the idea that the generals of World War I were stupid blunderers, or "donkeys," as one author describes them. The leaders on both sides were soldiers as competent, on the average, as those of the generation that followed them. They were trying to cope with a situation impossible to resolve without the availability of rapid means of transportation (to move reserves rapidly) or mobile firepower (to exploit initial success).

These things *were* available, however, by the time of World War II, and the Germans put them together in a way that brought congruence between weapons and tactics in the form of blitz-krieg.

Behavior, Technology, and History

Let me summarize why I believe we can learn about the interaction of new technology and human behavior in combat from history. First, I re-emphasize my assertion that up until the present no conventional weapon has been as important to battle success as have been the troops employing the weapons. Second, there is not a lot of evidence or logic to suggest that technology will become more important than the troops in future warfare.

That being the case, I assert further that this country has not put sufficient emphasis on the study of human behavior in combat. The relatively small effort that has been made in the study of human factors has been, in my opinion, largely misdirected. In an earlier book, I suggested a blueprint for a study of how military history can be used to contribute to the analysis of current military problems.[8]

So far there has been no reaction to my recommendations. Let me, therefore, try a new and different approach.

Listed in Table 15-4 is my summary of human behavioral considerations in combat. Other than the efforts that my colleagues and I at HERO in our work on the QJM and other research, I know of no systematic effort to understand these considerations on the basis of historical combat. In our work we have developed some hypotheses (as indicated by the asterisks), but these only scratch the surface of the problems.

The United States' armed forces need to know more about all of the factors listed in the figure. The historical data are available, but there is little attention to or interest in this potentially rich analytical pay dirt. I am forced to conclude, therefore, that —despite considerable lip-service—no one in authority in military circles in the United States really is concerned about using historical experience to gain improved understanding of current military problems.

In the light of what a few of us have accomplished in scratching the surface of this pay dirt, this national failure to undertake a comprehensive and systematic effort to analyze historical combat is disgraceful.

Nothing can be more obscure than future war. Nevertheless, there is a base of certainty for military planning and analysis. That base is known human behavior in combat as described in the extensive records of human experience in past battles. Much can be done to dissipate the obscurities of future combat by examining the new technologies in light of the general eternal verities of combat that have persisted through prior technological change.

Table 15–4

Human Behavior Consideration in Combat

Leadership
    Application of Combat Multipliers*
    Set-Piece Battle Preparations*
    Training/Experience
Disruption
    Surprise*
    Suppression*
    Unit Breakpoints
    Unit Panic
Manpower Quality
    Relative Combat Effectiveness*
    Trends Over Time*
    Morale
Relationship of Moral and Physical Factors*
    Interaction of Firepower, Mobility, Dispersion*
    Combat Intensity*
    Friction*

* Quantification hypotheses exist, but have not been tested thoroughly.

Chapter 16

A New Square Law

The Lanchester Equations and History

THE LANCHESTER EQUATIONS were introduced in Chapter 2. These equations, particularly the Square Law, have appealed strongly to mathematically minded OR analysts and have been used (often with variations or elaboration) as the basis for calculating attrition rates in most combat models in the United States and Western Europe. But there is a problem. Efforts to relate either or both of the Lanchester Laws to historical attrition results have almost always failed.[1]

As Lanchester himself recognized explicitly when he first published his equations, there will probably never be a close and easily recognizable relationship between real world attrition rates and those produced by his use of equations. This is because the combat power relationships in a battle are much more complex than the simple ratio of personnel strengths used by Lanchester.

Lanchester stated that his equations were valid only in situations in which the opposing forces are of equal quality, and are affected equally by the circumstances of the battle. He made it clear that he would expect that the mathematical prediction of casualties and the actual casualties would coincide only when all other things are equal, and then he added, "superior morale or better tactics, or a hundred and one other extraneous issues may intervene in practice."[2] No one should expect that the application of the Lanchester equations to historical battle data should give attrition results similar to those that actually occurred, except in instances in which the quality of the opposing troops is identical and the circumstances of the battle are such that neither side has any advantage through terrain, weather, defensive posture, leadership, or luck.

I know of *no* battle in history in which such equality of circumstances existed, and thus I would expect that historical casualty rates would *never* agree with casualties calculated by the Lanchester equations. Agreement would be possible only if one could normalize the situations of the opposing forces and strip out the effects of differences in weapons, environment, and operational circumstances. Such a comparison of normalized combat power ratios has been done for a substantial body of historical combat data using the QJM, and it has been found that the aggregated attrition results were very close to what would have been attained by the applications of the Lanchester equations to the adjusted data represented by the normalized ratios.[3]

Thus, the theoretically derived Lanchester equations seem to give results consistent with average historical casualty rates only if the input numbers have been normalized in the manner Clausewitz suggests in his Law of Numbers by "stripping out the circumstances of the battle . . . and the value of the troops." In other words, this suggests that the Lanchester equations may be historically sound, *but not as used by most analysts and modelers.*

Thus, one can accept the theoretical validity of the Lanchester equations—as this author does—and still assert that in the real world it is highly unlikely that there will ever be a direct relationship between force ratios, however calculated, and casualty rates. This author and his colleagues have described the absence of such a relationship in a number of publications.[4] Given this, one cannot help wondering how analysts can continue to assume the direct applicability of the Lanchester equations to casualty rates without assuring themselves that they have a methodology that provides results consistent with real-world, historical data.

Combat Effectiveness and Battle Outcomes

Analysis of historical data does reveal, however, a mathematical relationship more easily discernible than that of Lanchester's equations. Whether casualties are high or low, there appears to be a consistent relation between the ratio of the rates at which two opposing forces inflict casualties on each other on the one hand, and the ratio of their relative combat effectiveness values, or CEVs, on the other.

The relationship between casualty-inflicting rates (lethality) and the CEV is directly relatable to the differential equation relationships postulated by Lanchester. The starting point in developing a hypothesis to explain this new relationship is historical evidence on casualties incurred and casualties inflicted.

A Rare Instance of Things Being Almost Equal

The effects of weapons, environment, tactics, and troop quality on combat are such that it is not easy to observe the direct relationship between relative combat effectiveness, and battle outcomes. The 1973 October War in the Middle East provides a rare instance in which it is possible to discern a consistent relationship of calculated values of relative combat effectiveness (CEV) with actual operational statistics from an actual war. In this war, with the exception of CEVs, the relationships approached Lanchester's idea of "all other things equal."

It is generally agreed that on both the Suez front in the south and the Golan front in the north, the opponents in the 1973 war fought each other to a standstill. The Arabs, on the offensive initially, had much the better of the first phases of these campaigns. The Israelis, after they assumed the offensive, had much the better of the later phases. At the end of the war the opponents were in a condition of relatively stable military balance. The opposing armies had overall combat *capabilities* that were approximately equal, irrespective of their differences in types of weapons, numbers of personnel, and quality of units. This situation permits a direct estimate to be made of the combat effectiveness value of each force from the actual statistics.

A comparison of the numbers of fully mobilized personnel facing each other on these fronts is shown in Table 16-1. The ratios of personnel in the opposing forces on these fronts are almost identical to the averages of the relative combat effectiveness ratios (CEVs) calculated by means of the QJM for individual engagements on these fronts: an Israeli average combat effectiveness superiority of about 2.50 compared with the Syrians, and about 2.00 compared with the Egyptians.

In Table 16-2 I show the combat effectiveness values that I have calculated for the opposing forces in a number of campaigns and battles in World Wars I and II and in the Middle East Wars of 1967 and 1973. CEVs for pairs of opponents are shown in Table 16-2. Particularly interesting is a comparison of the CEV of the Germans with respect to the British in World War I, and with

Table 16–1

Personnel Strengths in the 1973 Arab-Israeli War

Front	Israeli Strength	Arab Strength	Personnel Strength Ratio
Golan	60,000	150,000 Syrians	1.0:2.5
Suez	120,000	240,000 Egyptians	1.0:2.0

Table 16–2

Combat Effectiveness of Armies in Four Wars

Combat Effectiveness Values of Opposing Forces

World War I	Germans vs. British	1.27
	British vs. Turks	1.98
World War II	Germans vs. Western Allies	1.26
	Germans vs. Russians	2.00
	Russians vs. Japanese	1.04
1967 ME War	Israelis vs.	
	Jordanians	1.54
	Egyptians	1.75
	Syrians	2.63
	Palestinians	3.50
1973 ME War	Israelis vs.	
	Jordanians	1.88
	Egyptians	1.98
	Syrians	2.54
	Iraqis	3.43

respect to the Western Allies (including the British) in World War II. This suggests that ratios of combat effectiveness of different national forces tended to remain stable during the first half of the twentieth century.

The Lethality-Casualty Relationship

The data in Tables 16-1 and 16-2 provide a basis for deriving a mathematical relationship representing troop quality. In Table 16-3 some other historical data are summarized, showing average CEVs and casualties for 140 battles or engagements during World War I, World War II, and the Middle East October War.

The third column of Table 16-3 presents average CEVs, similar to those in Table 16-2. The fourth column shows the average percent casualties per day *suffered* by each of the opposing forces. (Or, expressed another way, number of men hit per day *in* 100 men.) The right-hand column shows the average casualties per day inflicted by one hundred men under the circumstances of these operations. (Or, in a parallel expression, number hit *by* 100 men.) This historical casualty-inflicting performance rate (given the symbol K) is defined as the average daily casualties of a force, divided by 1/100th of the strength of the opposing side. Although these figures are computed to two decimal places, they are probably accurate to, for the most part, no better than 10%, and the highly aggregated casualty figures on which they are based are probably accurate to within ±20%. Nevertheless, they provide a generally consistent measure of the ability of a force to cause casualties in the opposing force.

In Table 16-4 I show some computed refinements of the historical data in Table 16-3. A new term, lethality, is shown in the center column of Table 16-2. Lethality (L) is defined as the inherent casualty-inflicting *capability* of a force. Lethality values are computed by applying a posture factor to the historical casualty inflicting rate (K) of the actual battle.

An integral element of the QJM concept is that the combat power of a force is affected directly by circumstantial factors. One of the most important of these factors, and the only one that is applied consistently to defender or attacker, is the posture factor. The variations among the other factors are such that, in averaged statistics of battle outcomes, it is possible that only the

Table 16-3

Historical Data About Combat
Effectiveness and Casualties

War, Campaign, Year (Number of Battles)	Opponents	CEV	% Casualties/Day Incurred	Casualties per Day Inflicted by 100 (K)
World War I				
1. Western Front 1914–1917 (5)	Germans vs. French	1.30	2.02	2.53
			1.59	1.37
2. Western Front 1916–1918 (5)	Germans vs. British	1.27	1.90	2.18
			1.46	1.35
3. Eastern Front 1914–1916 (5)	Germans vs. Russians	3.10	1.83	13.26
			10.73	1.47
4. Palestine (Megiddo) 1918 (1)	British vs. Turks	1.88	0.98	4.40
			12.33	2.75
World War II				
5. Italy, Salerno 1943 (9)	Germans vs. W. Allies	1.45	1.44	2.96
			2.25	1.10
6. Italy, Volturno 1943 (20)	Germans vs. W. Allies	1.45	0.46	1.22
			0.63	1.24
7. Italy, Anzio 1944 (11)	Germans vs. W. Allies	1.25	1.34	1.48
			2.01	1.81
8. Italy, Rome (Diadem) 1944 (24)	Germans vs. W. Allies	1.20	3.12	2.42
			1.13	1.46
9. NW Europe, Lorraine,	Germans vs.	1.25	1.98	2.02

Table 16–3 (cont'd)

Historical Data About Combat Effectiveness and Casualties

WAR, CAMPAIGN, YEAR (NUMBER OF BATTLES)	OPPONENTS	CEV	% CASUAL-TIES/DAY INCURRED	CASUALTIES PER DAY INFLICTED BY 100 (K)
World War II				
1944 (18)	W. Allies	1.18	1.08	1.05
10. NW Europe, Ardennes (Bulge) 1944 (1)	Germans vs. W. Allies		1.34	0.67
			0.78	1.55
11. E. Europe, Ukraine 1941 (5)	Germans vs. Russians	3.10	0.73	4.58
			4.03	0.65
12. E. Europe, Kursk 1943 (3)	Germans vs. Russians	2.58	1.07	4.72
			3.09	0.70
13. E. Europe 1944*	Germans vs. Russians	2.00	1.05	6.22
			2.34	0.80
October War				
14. Suez-Sinai 1973 (16)	Israelis vs. Egyptians	1.98	1.67	4.21
			2.05	0.81
15. Golan 1973 (17)	Israelis vs. Syrians	2.54	1.34	4.52
			2.59	0.76

*Based on annual statistics, not on one or more battles.

posture factor will have a consistent and significant effect. If an average value of the posture factor is stripped away from the casualty-inflicting experience, there should be a close approximation of the relative inherent casualty-inflicting capability of the two sides. This is done by the following calculation:

$$L = K/u. \quad (1)$$

> Where   L is lethality
>   K is historical casualty-inflicting rate
>   u is posture factor.

The posture factor (u) is always 1.0 for the attacker and ranges from 1.2 to 1.6 for the defender, depending on the strength of the defender's position. While posture is the principal modifier of lethality, other factors obviously had some influence. However, these other influences tend to be offsetting, so the resultant value of L is an approximation of the overall effect of variables on the historical casualty-inflicting rate.

The fourth column of Table 16-4 is the ratio of the calculated lethalities of the opponents as shown in column 3. The right-hand column of the table is the square of the CEVs from Table 16-3. There is a close correlation between the values for the lethality ratios and the values of the CEV squared. This is confirmed by the graphical presentation in Figure 16-1, where the lethality ratio and the CEV squared values have been plotted. If the relation were exact, all the points would lie on the equal value line, which they do not. However, the fit is generally good. This less-than-perfect fit is due to less-than-precise data, as well as to the use only of the posture factor in converting casualty-inflicting rates to lethality rates. Under the circumstances the closeness of the fit is remarkable. This is possible, I suggest, only if the computed CEV values represent an approximation of what actually happened on the battlefields.

Although CEVs are derived from comparisons of combat power ratios to results ratios based on actual battle outcomes, and casualties are one of the outcome measures used in calculating the result ratio, this comparison between CEVs and casualty-inflicting capability is not circular reasoning. The casualty rate contributes less than 20% to the result ratios and consequently less than 10% to the CEV calculation. Moreover, the calculation of CEVs is a measurement of the effects of intangible factors upon the outcomes of one or more battles. The casualty-inflicting

Figure 16–1

Relation Between Effectiveness and Lethality in the Historical Data

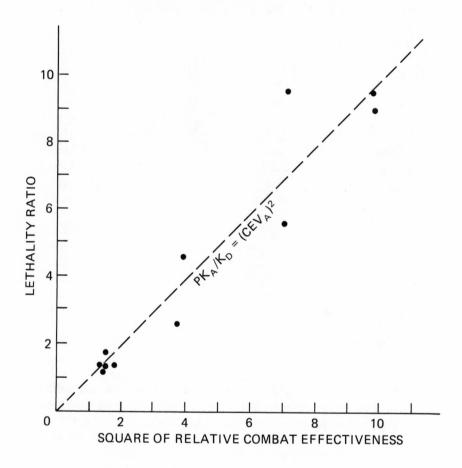

Table 16–4

Key Values Related to Lethality and Effectiveness in the Historical Data

War or Campaign, Year (Number of Battles)	Opponents	Lethality (L)	Ratio of Lethalities	Square of Combat Effectiveness Value (CEV²)
World War I				
1. West Front, 1914–1971 (5)	Germans vs. French	2.11 1.24	1.70	1.69
2. West Front, 1916–1918 (5)	Germans vs. British	1.68 1.23	1.37	1.54
3. East Front, 1914–1916 (5)	Germans vs. Russians	12.05 1.34	8.99	9.61
4. Palestine (Megiddo), 1918 (1)	British vs. Turks	4.40 1.72	2.56	3.53
World War II				
5. Italy, Salerno, 1943 (9)	Germans vs. W. Allies	2.28 1.00	2.28	2.10
6. Italy, Volturno, 1943 (20)	Germans vs. W. Allies	0.76 0.26	2.85	2.10
7. Italy, Anzio, 1944 (11)	Germans vs. W. Allies	1.35 1.21	1.16	1.56
8. Italy, Rome (Diadem), 1944 (24)	Germans vs. W. Allies	1.61 1.45	1.11	1.44
9. NW Europe, Lorraine, 1944 (18)	Germans vs. W. Allies	1.39 1.05	1.32	1.56
10. NW Europe, Ardennes (Bulge), 1944 (1)	Germans vs. W. Allies	0.67 0.54	1.24	1.39
11. E. Europe, Ukraine, 1941 (5)	Germans vs. Russians	4.58 0.48	9.54	9.61
12. E. Europe, Kursk, 1943 (3)	Germans vs. Russians	4.72 0.50	9.44	6.66
13. E. Europe, 1944[a]	Germans vs. Russians	4.78 0.80	5.98	4.00
October 1973 War				
14. Suez-Sinai, 1973 (16)	Israelis vs. Egyptians	3.23 0.68	4.76	3.92
15. Golan, 1973 (17)	Israelis vs. Syrians	3.20 0.61	5.25	6.45

[a]Based on annual statistics, not on one or more battles.

capability of a force, on the other hand, is based entirely on the relation between that force's numerical strength and the casualties incurred by the opposing side. The extent to which the CEV and the casualty-inflicting capability of a force are based on similar or overlapping casualty data is very small indeed, and certainly too tenuous to cause the kind of consistent relationship between these values such as we have seen.

The New Square Law Equations

From the above discussion we may express the observed relationships as follows:

$$\frac{L_a}{L_d} = \frac{K_a}{K_d/u} = \frac{uK_a}{K_d} = (CEV_a)^2. \quad (1)$$

$$\frac{L_d}{L_a} = \frac{K_d/u}{K_a} = \frac{K_d}{uK_a} = (CEV_d)^2. \quad (2)$$

Where: CEV_i = combat effectiveness value of a force.

K_i = casualty-inflicting *performance* rate per one hundred men in a force either attacking (a) or defending (d) in historical combat.

L_i = casualty-inflicting *capability* of one hundred men in a force, attacker or defender, "all other things being equal."

u = posture factor for the defender: 1.3 for hasty defense; 1.5 for prepared defense; 1.6 for fortified defense. (The posture factor for the attacker is 1.0, and is not included in the equations.)

Transposing terms in a standard algebraic fashion produces:

$$K_a = \frac{(CEV_a)^2 K_d}{u}. \quad (3)$$

$$K_d = \frac{u K_a}{(CEV_a)^2}. \quad (4)$$

Since K_a and K_d are expressed in terms of casualty rates per day, they are analogous to $\frac{dD}{dt}$ and $\frac{dA}{dt}$ in the Lanchester equations. K_a and K_d, respectively, represent the casualty-inflicting performance rate of one hundred men of forces A and D, and $\frac{dD}{dt}$ and $\frac{dA}{dt}$ represent the casualties incurred by the opposing sides,[5] then:

$$K_a = \frac{dD}{dt} \times \frac{100}{A} \text{ or } \frac{dD}{dt} = {}^-.01 K_a A. \quad (5)$$

$$K_d = \frac{dA}{dt} \times \frac{100}{D} \text{ or } \frac{dA}{dt} = {}^-.01 K_d D. \quad (6)$$

Substituting the value of K_a in equation 3 for that in Equation 5, and the value of K_d in equation 4 for that in equation 6, results in the following equations:

$$\frac{dD}{dt} = \frac{(.01 K_d)}{u} (CEV_a)^2 A. \quad (7)$$

$$\frac{dA}{dt} = \frac{(.01 u K_a)}{(CEV_a)^2} D. \quad (8)$$

The Lanchester square law equations, in the same notation, are as follows:

$$\frac{dD}{dt} = -cA. \quad (9)$$

$$\frac{dA}{dt} = -CD. \quad (10)$$

The coefficients, c and C, are constant for a given battle or engagement. They represent the combined effect of all environmental, operational, and human factors affecting the combat. It is possible to derive a more general expression by combining equations 7 and 8 with equations 9 and 10. In effect, equations 7 and 8 define the Lanchester coefficients more strictly, as follows:

$$c = c' (CEV_a)^2 \frac{Kd}{u}.$$

$$C = C' (CEV_a)^2 u K_a.$$

The next step is taken by substituting force strength (S) for A and D, the respective personnel strengths. The constants will assume new values to take into account the environmental and operational factors that influence attrition. The human factors are recognized explicitly with the CEV term. The revised equations are as follows:

$$\frac{dD}{dt} = -c'' \, (CEV_a)^2 \, S_a. \quad (11)$$

$$\frac{dA}{dt} = -C'' \, (CEV_a)^2 \, S_d. \quad (12)$$

Equations 11 and 12 are the New Square Law equations. The Lanchester equations have been modified to replace personnel strength with force strength (as was done earlier with the Clausewitz's law of numbers), and the behavioral factors act to the second power.

Interpretation of the New Square Law

It is interesting to note the differences between equations 7 and 8 and the classical expressions of Lanchester's Square Law in equations 9 and 10. Both sets of equations express attrition rates, but equations 7 and 8 describe actual, historical attrition rates in terms of the relative quality of the two forces and the lethality of the opposing force. Equations 7 and 8 have been estimated from experiential data, suggesting that casualties in history appear to be influenced far more strongly by a change in relative combat effectiveness than by a change in firepower or numerical strengths. The results of this historical analysis provide empirical corroboration of the validity of the basic form of the Lanchester Square Law equations.

Another possible conclusion that could be drawn from equations 7 and 8 is that the attrition rate of a force will increase as its hitting rate increases. In equation 7, dD/dt is directly proportional to K_d, for any given values of CEV and u, and the same relationship holds in equation 8 for dA/dt and K_a. This is not so counterintuitive as it might appear. Since the CEV postulates a given relationship in the combat effectiveness of the two forces, if the hitting rate for one side goes up for whatever reason, and u and CEV are unchanged, then the hitting rate for the other side and casualty rates for *both* sides will go up.

Possibly immodestly, I suggest that equations 11 and 12 be designated the Dupuy equations, and equations 7 and 8, the Lanchester Square Law equations with Dupuy coefficients. When dealing with historical data, equations 3 and 4 provide a substitute for the Lanchester equations. When relevant historical data is not available, there is at least an historically valid basis for estimating the coefficients in the Lanchester square law equations. Finally, the New Square Law equations provide an improved yet general expression for attrition in combat consistent with the basic concept of the QJM as derived from Clausewitz.

The significant thing is that casualty rates vary directly as the square of the combat effectiveness value.

On the basis of the above discussion, I shall venture even to refine one of Napoleon's favorite ideas on relationships in war:

The moral is the equivalent of the physical squared.

Implications of the New Square Law

What are the implications of the New Square Law? There are two major implications of immediate practical value. In the first place, it is now possible to use battle casualty data to calculate an approximate CEV, even when there is insufficient data for a complete QJM calculation. This may be very important in providing a basis for estimating CEVs for future warfare. In the second place, the New Square Law provides a basis for analyzing defense policy and priorities.

People and weapons are the two basic elements that make up armed forces and military strength. U.S. defense policy generally puts weapons first and people second. This has been true at least since the end of World War II, and it is certainly true today. Probably no official would make such a blunt statement, and many probably do not even think this is so, but the decisions they make show that it is. This country is working hard to produce the most advanced weapons possible, while hoping, with whatever optimism it can muster, that, despite austere funding for training, education, and personnel support, our military men and women will be able to use these weapons effectively.

One reason for this emphasis on weapons is the political reality of the manpower policies of the United States and our NATO allies. For more than thirty years NATO has been faced by Soviet and Warsaw Pact forces approximately double the size of those available to NATO. Despite warnings and appeals from successive SACEURS (Supreme Allied Commander, Europe), the NATO countries have not been willing to make the political and economic sacrifices to increase their forces to narrow or eliminate this gap.

Western politicians and military leaders have been able to reconcile themselves to this political fact of life in large part because of two questionable assumptions: first, our scientific/technical/technological superiority can assure us of keeping far ahead of our potential foes in weapons quality; and second, if we have to choose (as we seem to have done) between weapons quality and manpower quality, the one is readily substitutable for the other.

The Arab-Israeli wars provide a useful basis for examining these assumptions. The 1967 and 1973 wars confirmed that American weapons used by the Israelis were qualitatively superior to those of the USSR used by the Arabs. However, that qualitative superiority was only marginal. After the 1973 war I was told by Maj. Gen. "Bren" Adan, probably the most successful tank commander in the history of the Israeli Defense Forces (IDF), that there was not much difference between the best American tanks and the best Soviet tanks. Brig. Gen. Uzi Eilam, the IDF's former chief of Defense Research and Development, stated in a symposium about the 1973 war that was held in Jerusalem in 1975:

> We have noticed an Eastern [i.e., Soviet] lead as far as system philosophy and design is concerned. We have found crude, robust and not-so-sophisticated, but highly reliable subsystems in the East. Technologies are more advanced in the West [i.e., United States], yet it takes less effort to be second in a new technological area. It would be wise for the West to make a real effort to assess the lessons of the Yom Kippur War, to try to apply them to a better system approach, and to base the engineering effort on the highly advanced technologies which are already at hand.[6]

The 1982 war in Lebanon provided further evidence that the quality of Soviet weapons in comparison to American weapons has not changed substantially since 1975. As reported in Chapter 15, there was agreement among a Syrian general and Israeli Generals Eitan and Ivry that the difference in quality of weapons had little to do with the outcome of that war. They agreed that the comparative values of Western weapons and Eastern weapons, as seen by General Eilam just after 1973, had not changed substantially by 1982. American weapons may still be somewhat more advanced technologically than those of the Soviets, but the difference is not significant. In both wars the margin of Israeli superiority was the better quality of their soldiers, not of their weapons.

A basic problem for U.S. defense policy is how to overcome the fact that the armies of the Warsaw Pact outnumber those of NATO in troops, tanks, and guns by a factor of two-to-one or more. The political leadership of the NATO countries, including the U.S., will not double the size of their conventional forces. So matching the Warsaw Pact forces quantitatively is not feasible. Numerous combat encounters between American weapons and Soviet weapons in three wars in the Middle East have demonstrated quite conclusively that, despite a slender technological advantage, Western nations apparently cannot make weapons that are twice as good as those of our potential opponent. So matching the Warsaw Pact Forces with a two-to-one edge in technology is also ruled out.

The only way for NATO to match the Warsaw Pact is by increasing the effectiveness of NATO troops. In this respect, the Arab-Israeli war experience confirms a lesson learned from World War II. By use of high standards of professionalism and training, it *is* possible for NATO to produce soldiers that are qualitatively better than the soldiers of the Warsaw Pact. Some of the most important instances of qualitative superiority of troops trained and led in accordance with the highest professional standards are as follows:

Germans vs. Western Allies, 1940–1945: superiority of 1.20.
Germans vs. Russians, 1941–1945: superiority of more than 2.00.
Israelis vs. Arabs, 1967–1982: superiority of more than 2.00.

As we saw in Chapter 10, General John Sloan showed with his 88th Division that, with training and professionalism, he could raise the quality of his troops by a factor of about 1.43 above the average quality of Allied divisions. That would be good enough. It is not necessary to make the NATO troops twice as good as those of the Warsaw Pact to gain equality with them on the battlefield. According to the New Square Law a factor of 1.41 will do. Because $1.41 \times 1.41 = 2.00$. Q.E.D.!

Chapter 17

Application: The Bekaa Valley, June 1982

Practical Analytic Application

THE UTILITY OF the QJM as a theory of combat was demonstrated in Chapter 9 by showing how it could clarify and explain a well-known modern battle (Flanders, 1940) for which the data is readily available. Subsequent chapters have shown how the theory can reveal the fundamental relationships of battlefield phenomena that would otherwise remain inexplicable: relative combat effectiveness; diminishing returns; advance and attrition rates; friction; and the New Square Law.

Now I would like to turn to some practical applications of the QJM, and show how it can be applied to the analysis of recent events for which data is scarce or to the analysis of problems we can expect to face in the future. Let's look first at an example of recent military history about which knowledgeable and reliable analysts produce conflicting assessments.

The 1982 War in Lebanon

On 6 June 1982, Israeli forces advanced across their border with Lebanon to attack PLO forces distributed throughout southern Lebanon, and had initially destroyed those forces by June 11. At the same time the Israelis inflicted a crushing defeat upon a substantial portion of the Syrian Army in southeastern and east-central Lebanon. Politically this was a very controversial move by Israel. Militarily, however, it was at first acclaimed as another demonstration of the skill and prowess of the Israeli Defense Force (IDF). Later, however, some military critics had second thoughts. They suggested that the Israeli performance was sloppy and indicative of a decline in Israeli military capability from the previous high points of 1967 and 1973.[1] What is the truth? Are the Israelis really in a military decline? Is the gap between the military capability of Israel and that of its Arab neighbors narrowing?

After the 1973 October War there were similar comments by many foreign (and Israeli) military observers and analysts. In the 1967 Six Day War, said those critics, the Israelis had overwhelmed Egypt, Jordan, and Syria in three brief, brilliant campaigns to establish clear military supremacy in the Middle East. In the October War, however, the Israelis had been surprised, defeated in opening battles in the Sinai Desert and the Golan Heights, and despite some subsequent victories over the Egyptians and Syrians, had been forced to accept virtual stalemates on both fronts.

I have used QJM analyses to demonstrate that the gap in military capability between the Arabs and Israelis had actually widened between 1967 and 1973. The average Israeli-Arab CEV increased from about 1.9:1.0 in 1967 to more than 2.1:1.0. in 1973.[2] I was able to do that, however, only after several years of research and extensive compilation of statistical data in five Middle East countries.

Unfortunately, it is not possible to undertake that kind of QJM analysis of the Lebanon operations, because the requisite data is still not available. In fact, examination of the nature of the operation indicates that there were no really significant battles between the IDF and the PLO. The Israelis overwhelmed the Palestinians in all field operations and in the assault of a few PLO strongholds, like Beaufort Castle, and were held up only briefly in their advance on Beirut by siege operations against PLO fortified camps in Tyre and Sidon. The PLO part of the war provided no real contest to which a QJM analysis could be applied.

This was not true, however, of the Israeli operations against the Syrians in the Bekaa Valley of Eastern Lebanon, where the IDF encountered substantial and sometimes difficult opposition. Even though we do not have adequate data about that fighting to perform a full QJM analysis, there is quite a bit of general information about the forces engaged, the losses incurred, and the movement rates of the Israeli forces. There is enough data, in fact, to allow a quite useful analysis of the combat of Israeli and Syrian forces, using a modified QJM approach similar to that used to analyze the Battle of Flanders in Chapter 9.

The Bekaa Valley Operation

Approximately 70,000 Israeli troops, in four divisions plus miscellaneous forces, invaded Lebanon on 6 June 1982. About half of these forces focused their attention on PLO forces in southwestern and western Lebanon. The remainder, after a short advance, halted when they came in contact with scattered Syrian units in southeastern Lebanon. These Israeli troops, were organized into a corps-type formation of two divisions plus other units, about 35,000 men in strength. This force was designated the Bekaa Forces Group (BFG) and was commanded by Major General Avigdor Ben Gal. Save for some patrol activity and some exchanges of artillery fire with the Syrians to their front, the BFG had little activity on the 7th and 8th of June. This was consistent with the Israeli announcement that they would not attack the Syrians if the Syrians did not interfere with the Israelis fighting against the PLO. As the BFG and the Syrians faced each other warily in the southeast, the Israeli troops in western Lebanon were smashing the PLO, and driving the remnants back toward Beirut.

Late on the 8th, however, near Jezzine and in the mountains just west of General Ben Gal's command, an Israeli brigade (that would come under his command the next day) had a severe fight with a Syrian brigade. The Israeli brigade defeated the Syrians and drove them north toward the Beirut-Damascus highway. (See Figure 17-1.)

Late on the 8th and early on the 9th, the Israelis in the BFG came under heavy Syrian artillery fire. It is not clear whether this was because the Israelis provoked the Syrians into an artillery exchange. In any event, early on the 9th of June, Syrian aircraft attacked elements of the Bekaa Forces Group. The Israelis seem to have concluded that the Syrians were not heeding their warning and decided to attack the Syrians in the Bekaa Valley. It is quite possible that, having destroyed the PLO military organization, the Israelis were simply looking for an excuse for attacking the Syrians. In any event, about mid-morning on

Figure 17–1

The Bekaa Valley

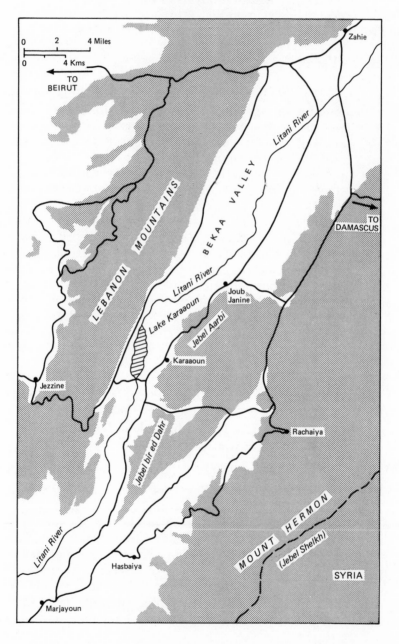

the 9th the Bekaa Forces Group initiated a powerful offensive northward into the Bekaa Valley.

The Syrians had established a prepared defensive line across the southern Bekaa Valley, taking advantage of rugged Jebel Aarbi, which fits like a bottle stopper in the southern valley. This position continued up the slopes of the even more rugged mountains east and west of the valley. In these positions were the bulk of a Syrian armored division and several commando battalions. The total Syrian force was about 22,000 men and 300 to 350 tanks. It was the right flank brigade of this force that the Israelis had driven back north of Jezzine late on the 8th of June.

There were three main thrusts to General Ben Gal's BFG offensive. On the left, one reinforced brigade advanced through the rugged Lebanon mountains, its axis the road north from Jezzine to the Beirut-Damascus highway. On the right, a division of two brigades advanced astride the Hasbiyah-Rachaeya road through the equally rugged Anti-Lebanon mountains. In the center, another division drove up the Bekaa Valley, its flanks advancing also along mountain roads on the slopes east and west of the Valley.

Soon after the ground troops began to smash their way through the Syrian positions, the Israeli Air Force attacked Syrian air defense missiles along the Beirut-Damascus highway. In one of the most dramatic successes ever achieved in air-land combat, the Israelis destroyed seventeen missile batteries without the loss of a single aircraft. When challenged by Syrian fighters, the Israelis turned against these and shot down at least 40, again without any losses themselves. The Israeli aircraft then provided close air support to the attacking ground troops.

During the 9th the Israelis advanced steadily, driving through the Syrian positions in the mountains on both flanks as well as in the valley, and—despite stubborn resistance—forced a general Syrian withdrawal. By the end of the day Israeli spearheads had advanced nearly 20 kilometers on the left and more than 10 kilometers on the right.

The Syrians had already moved elements of their 3d Tank Division into Lebanon to take up positions in another previously prepared defensive line just south of the Beirut-Damascus highway. Now they rushed the remainder of that division from the vicinity of Homs toward the front. One brigade of the division was badly damaged when it was hit on the road by the Israeli Air Force near Zahle shortly after daylight on the 10th of June.

The fighting on the 10th was little different from that on the 9th. The Syrians, despite their reinforcements, fell back to new positions south of the highway, and dug in there. During the day the average Israeli advance was again more than 10 kilometers, although some spearheads went farther and faster. Cease-fire negotiations were begun, and a cease-fire went into effect at noon on the 11th of June.

Modified QJM Analysis

The total forces deployed by Israel and Syria in the three days of fighting in and around the Bekaa Valley are shown in Table 17-1. It must be realized, however, that the Syrians added forces piecemeal during the battle.

In Table 17-2 I show the opposing force strengths late on June 8, when the first serious fighting broke out between Israeli and Syrian forces.

The opposing strengths early on the 10th, after the Syrians rushed reinforcements to the Bekaa Valley, allowing for losses on both sides in the previous 36 hours are shown in Table 17-3.

Finally, Table 17-4 is an estimate of casualties and major materiel losses of the opposing sides.

Table 17–1

Estimated Syrian and Israeli Force Strengths Bekaa Valley Battle, 8–11 June, 1982

	ISRAELI	SYRIAN
Troops	35,000	30,000
Tanks	800	600
Aircraft Available for Close Support	275	225
Non-Organic Air Defense Missiles (SAMs)	—	120[a]

[a]There were 76 launcher units, some with single launchers (SA2), some with double launchers (SA3) and some with triple launchers (SA6).

Table 17–2

Estimated Opposing Syrian and Israeli Force Strengths Late, 8 June 1982 Bekaa Valley Battle, Phase I

	ISRAELI	SYRIAN
Troops	35,000	22,000
Tanks	800	300
Aircraft Available for Close Support	275	225[a]
Non-Organic Air Defense Missiles (SAMs)	—	120[b]

[a]Reduced to less than 200 by mid-afternoon, June 9.
[b]Reduced to about 12 (8 launcher units) by mid-afternoon, June 9.

Table 17–3

Estimated Opposing Syrian and Israeli Force Strengths Early 10 June 1982 Bekaa Valley Battle, Phase II

	ISRAELI	SYRIAN
Troops	34,000	28,000
Tanks	750	400
Aircraft Available for Close Support	225	130
Non-Organic Air Defense Missiles (SAMs)	—	12

In order to undertake a meaningful analysis without detailed order of battle information, some assumptions have to be made. Principal among these are:

1. Relationships between force inputs and battlefield results which have been consistent for World War II and the earlier Arab-Israeli Wars, are assumed to apply to Lebanon in 1982.
2. For the circumstances of operations in and around the Bekaa

Valley in June 1982, the Israeli CEV relative to the Syrians is assumed to be similar to that calculated for the 1967 and 1973 wars: 2.50.

3. The applicable QJM advance rate and defense factors for terrain and posture are assumed to be those in Table 17-5. The advance rate factor, when applied to standard rates for types and relative strengths of opposing forces, provides a basis for estimating expected advance rates of the attacking force. The defense factors are the multipliers that yield a value for the defender's combat power when applied to the force strength of the defender.

Table 17–4

Estimated Israeli and Syrian Losses
Bekaa Valley Battle, 8–11 June 1982

		ISRAELI	SYRIAN
Personnel	Killed	195	800
	Wounded	872	3200
	Missing	15	150
	Total	1082	4150
Tanks		30	400
Aircraft		0	90
Non-Organic Air Defense Missiles (SAMs)		0	120
% Casualties/day		1.05	5.53
Casualties inflicted by 100/day		4.01	1.44

Table 17–5

QJM Factors for Bekaa Valley Analysis

	ADVANCE RATE FACTOR	DEFENSE FACTOR
Terrain (mostly rugged, with some flat)	.6	1.5
Posture (for Syrians, mixture of hasty & prepared defense)	.7	1.4

4. Modern main battle tanks, of the sort with which both Israelis and Syrians were equipped, are assumed to be the equivalent of a 100-man "slice" of the non-armor and non-air support components of a modern army. Such a slice would include infantry weapons, artillery, anti-armor weapons, and air defense weapons. This assumption is based upon QJM analyses of the 1973 October War, and, very generally, reflects the integrated firepower relationships of the QJM.
5. The average value of one Israeli close support aircraft, calculated upon a similar basis, is assumed to be the equivalent of a 250-man slice of Israeli troops. The average value of one Syrian close support aircraft, also calculated in the same way, is assumed to be the equivalent of a 200-man slice of troops. And the average value of one Syrian SAM air defense missile is assumed to be the same as for one Syrian fighter aircraft.

After application of the above assumptions, we can calculate the force strengths and combat power of Israeli and Syrian forces for the period 8–11 June as shown in Table 17-6. This permits the calculation of the following Israeli to Syrian ratios:

Force strength ratio: 1.16
Combat power ratio (without CEV):   0.55
Combat power ratio (with 2.50 Israeli CEV):   1.38

Table 17–6

QJM Computations
Bekaa Valley Battle: June 1982

	ISRAEL FORCE STRENGTH	SYRIA FORCE STRENGTH	
Troops 35,000 × 1	= 35,000	30,000 × 1 =	30,000
Tanks 800 × 100	= 80,000	600 × 100 =	60,000
Aircraft 275 × 250	= 68,750	225 × 200 =	45,000
Air Defense Missiles	—	120 × 200 =	24,000
Force Strength	183,750		159,000
Terrain Factor	—		× 1.5
Posture Factor	—		× 1.4
Combat Power (without CEV)	183,750		333,900

The force strength ratio indicates that there should be a stand-off between the Israelis and Syrians in Lebanon. The data is not sufficiently precise for us to evaluate the slight calculated Israeli preponderance. The combat power ratio without the CEV is hardly more useful, since it tells us that the Syrians will decisively repulse the Israeli offensive. A meaningful comparison of the opposing forces is possible only when the combat power comparison includes consideration of the CEV. The combat power ratio of 1.38, however, would not indicate an Israeli superiority as overwhelming as was actually demonstrated on the battlefield between the evening of June 8 and the morning of June 11.

The next step is to divide the three days of serious fighting into two phases, each of about 36 hours, and analyze each phase separately. Table 17-7 shows the computation of the force strength and combat power of the opposing forces late on June 8. This permits the calculation of the following Israeli to Syrian ratios:

Table 17–7

QJM Computations: Phase I
Bekaa Valley Battle: 8 June 1982

	ISRAELI MANPOWER EQUIVALENTS		SYRIA MANPOWER EQUIVALENTS	
Troops 35,000 × 1	= 35,000	22,000 × 1 =		22,000
Tanks 800 × 100	= 80,000	200 × 100 =		20,000
Aircraft 275 × 250	= 68,750	100 × 200[a] =		20,000
Air Defense Missiles	—	12 × 200[b] =		2,400
Force Strength	183,750			64,400
Terrain	—			× 1.5
Posture	—			× 1.4
Combat Power (without CEV)	183,750			135,240

[a] An estimate of one hundred Syrian close support sorties is generous.
[b] Israeli aircraft did not begin close support until they had destroyed or neutralized most of the Syrian SAMs.

Force strength ratio: 2.85
Combat power ratio (without CEV): 1.36
Combat power ratio (with 2.50 Israeli CEV): 3.40

The Israeli to Syrian combat power ratio of 3.40 is based on the historical combat power effectiveness value of Israeli troops over Syrians of about 2.50. This combat power ratio suggests that an overwhelming Israeli success was to be expected; and that is the way it was.

Analysis of Advance Rates

An examination of the Israeli advance rates in Phase I indicates that the Israeli CEV may have been greater than the assumed value of 2.50. The Israeli armored force advanced an average of about 12 kilometers on the 8th of June through the extremely rugged terrain on both sides of the Bekaa Valley. By applying the advance rate factors in Table 17-5 for posture (.7) and terrain (.6), this Israeli advance rate is the equivalent of a standard advance rate of 28 kilometers per day. According to the QJM Rule Book, the standard advance rate of 28 kilometers per day can be expected when the combat power ratio of the attacker to defender is about 4.00. We can calculate the Israeli CEV to achieve an effective combat power ratio of 4.00 by dividing this by the combat power ratio without CEV (1.36), as follows: 4.00/1.36 = 2.94. In other words, in this situation, to advance as well as they did the Israeli CEV would have had to have been about 2.90.

Now for Phase II, beginning early on June 10th. The results of this day's fighting led the Syrians to request a cease-fire, which went into effect at noon on the 11th. Table 17-8 reflects both Syrian reinforcements and estimated force erosion due to estimated combat and non-combat losses. The resulting Israeli to Syrian rates are as follows:

Force strength ratio: 2.19
Combat power ratio (without CEV): 1.16
Combat power ratio (with 2.5 Israeli CEV): 2.90

Again, when the Israeli CEV is taken into consideration, an overwhelming Israeli success was to be expected.

Table 17–8

QJM Computations: Phase II
Bekaa Valley Battle: 10 June 1982

	Israeli Manpower Equivalents	Syrian Manpower Equivalents	
Troops 34,000 × 1	= 34,000	28,000 × 1 =	28,000
Tanks 750 × 100	= 75,000	400 × 100 =	40,000
Aircraft 225 × 250	= 56,250	12 × 200	2,400
Force Strength	165,250		75,400
Terrain	—		× 1.5
Posture	—		× 1.4
Morale[a]	—		0.9
Combat Power (without CEV)	165,250		142,506

[a]Syrian morale had been shaken badly on June 9th.

This time the Israelis advanced an average of about 10 kilometers during the day. Again applying the advance rate factors, (0.7 and 0.6) this translates to a standard advance rate of about 24 kilometers a day. Using the same procedure as for Phase I, the combat power ratio to achieve a standard advance rate of 24 kilometers per day is about 3.60. We can calculate the Israeli CEV by dividing 3.60 by 1.16, which gives a calculated Israeli CEV of about 3.10. The Israeli CEV would have been even higher if degraded Syrian morale had not been taken into consideration. In both phases of the battle, therefore, the advance rates achieved by the Israelis are indicative of an Israeli CEV of about 3.00, which is higher than the assumed value of 2.50, based on the results of combat in earlier wars.

Analysis of Casualty Rate

There is insufficient data to assess the daily casualties or casualty rates for either the Israelis or the Syrians. However, the overall casualty rates for the Israelis, compared with the estimated losses for the Syrians, provide another way of checking the validity of the QJM comparison.

As demonstrated in Chapter 16, the casualty experience of World War II and the prior Arab-Israeli Wars suggests that the ratio of the casualty-inflicting capabilities of two opposing forces is generally about equal to the square of the relative combat effectiveness value (CEV). From Table 17-4, the total Israeli casualties against the Syrians were about 1082; the total Syrian casualties were about 4150. The Israeli figures are close to accurate. The Syrian figures are estimates only.

On the basis of these figures, the Israeli daily casualty rate was about 1.05%; the estimated Syrian casualty rate was about 5.53% per day. The casualty-inflicting *rate* for the Israelis (average strength 34,500) was 4.01 Syrian casualties per day per one hundred Israeli soldiers. The casualty-inflicting rate for the Syrians (average strength 25,000) was 1.41 Israeli casualties inflicted per day per one hundred Syrian soldiers. However, as shown in Table 17-5, the Syrian capability on the defense was multiplied by a factor of 1.4 for posture and 1.5 for terrain. Without those advantages the normalized casualty-inflicting *capability* of the Syrians was about 0.67 Israelis per one hundred Syrians per day $(1.44/(1.5 \times 1.4))$. The ratio of Israeli casualty-inflicting capability to that of the Syrians, therefore, was $4.01/0.67$, or 5.98. The New Square Law tells us that the square root of this ratio is roughly equivalent to the CEV value for the Israelis. This value is 2.45.

Thus, even though we do not have enough detailed data to permit a comprehensive QJM analysis, we have been able to use two historically validated methods to calculate an approximate Israeli-Syrian CEV during their three-day battle in the Bekaa Valley. On the basis of the rate of the Israeli advance, the CEV was calculated as being approximately 3.00. Using the ratio of estimated casualty inflicting capabilities, the calculation is a CEV of 2.45. Given the paucity of the data, and the approximations that were necessary, the results of the different methodologies are sufficiently close as to inspire confidence that the true CEV actually lay somewhere between these values.

Implications of the QJM Analysis

Now, what does all of this number-crunching tell us about the 1982 Battle of the Bekaa Valley and about the opposing Syrian and Israeli troops that fought the battle? Certainly much more than would have been possible without the analytical framework supplied by the QJM.

The analysis demonstrates that the usual static comparisons of weapons and numbers of troops are useless. Static comparisons are useful only if there is some basis for assuming that the opponents are reasonably equal in combat effectiveness. This means an assessment of the relative capabilities of the weapons without any consideration of troop quality. (Not that a comparison of relative weapon capability is unimportant; it is just different, and *less* important than comparison of troop quality.) The analysis also shows that the Israeli performance in the Bekaa Valley Battle was just as brilliant as the Israeli performance had been in the 1967 and 1973 Wars.

The Israelis, who apparently are very capable of making their own assessments of relative combat effectiveness, had prepared meticulously for this operation. They have a war planning advantage, of course, not shared by the United States. The Israelis can plan in advance for operations in a known, nearby area, against a known foe, under relatively predictable circumstances. This comment is not intended to diminish or disparage their accomplishment. The fact is that they *did* plan with a brilliance at least comparable to that of the Egyptians before their Suez Canal crossing triumph of 1973.

The record is very clear that the average relative combat effectiveness superiority factor (CEV) of Israelis with respect to Syrians was about 2.50 in the 1967 and 1973 Wars.[3] With less assurance, because of less confidence in more aggregated data, the modified QJM analysis above has just demonstrated that the Israeli CEV with respect to the Syrians is 1982 was between about 2.45 and about 3.00. The consistency of the results from two different sets of calculations, strongly suggests that the Israeli CEV in 1982 with respect to the Syrians was at least 2.50, and probably more. Thus, the gap in combat capability between the Israelis and their foes is certainly not closing, and may still be widening.

It matters not what one's sympathies may be in the Arab-Israeli conflict. Facts are facts. It is as important for the Arabs to understand these facts and take them into consideration in their military and political decisions relating to war as it was for the Soviet leadership to understand and take into consideration the comparable differential between their combat effectiveness and that of the much more efficient Germans in World War II.

Chapter 18

Application: Suppression

The Urgency of the Problem

THERE IS PROBABLY no obscurity of combat requiring clarification and understanding more urgently than that of suppression. While many people in our army, mostly artillerymen, are aware of this, the investigation is not proceeding with the insistent vigor that the urgency of the requirement demands. Furthermore, the possibility of determining the answer from historical research appears to be unappealing to our military authorities.

Suppression usually is defined as the effect of fire (primarily artillery fire) upon the behavior of hostile personnel, reducing, limiting, or inhibiting their performance of combat duties. Suppression lasts as long as the fires continue and for some brief, indeterminate period thereafter. Suppression is the most important effect of artillery fire, contributing directly to the ability of the supported maneuver units to accomplish their missions while preventing the enemy units from accomplishing theirs. It is, therefore, an essential element in the modeling of artillery fire.

I believe now that suppression is related to and probably a component of disruption caused by combat processes other than surprise, such as a communications failure. Further research may reveal, however, that suppression is a very distinct form of disruption that can be measured or estimated quite independently of disruption caused by any other phenomenon.

Suppression and Neutralization

Official US Army field artillery doctrine makes a distinction between "suppression" and "neutralization." Suppression is defined to be instantaneous and fleeting; neutralization, while also temporary, is relatively longer-lasting. Neutralization, the doctrine says, results when suppressive effects are so severe and long-lasting that a target is put out of action for a period of time after the suppressive fire is halted. Neutralization combines the psychological effects of suppressive gunfire with a certain amount of damage. The general concept of neutralization, as distinct from the more fleeting suppression, is a reasonable one. The specifics, however, seem less reasonable.

The doctrine asserts that if a unit suffers 10% or more in casualties it is neutralized, until the casualties are replaced and the damage is repaired. This is almost certainly the wrong way to approach quantification of neutralization. Not only is there no historical evidence that 10% casualties are enough to achieve this effect, there is no evidence that any level of losses is required to achieve the psycho-physiological effects of suppression or neutralization. Furthermore, the time period in which casualties are incurred is probably more important than any arbitrary percentage of loss, and the replacement of casualties and repair of damage are probably irrelevant.

Attempts to derive a methodology for measuring or quantifying either suppression or neutralization have not been successful. There is not even a way of drawing a clearcut line to establish when suppression turns into neutralization. The most serious consequence of this inability to measure these phenomena is that they generally are ignored both in combat models and in field exercises. That is, the outputs of combat models and the results of exercises fail to consider the most important effect of artillery fire: suppression (and neutralization).

Because of the current inability to make a definite distinction between neutralization and suppression, I prefer to deal with them both under the general heading of suppression. My definition, which is not conceptually different from the official definition, is as follows:

Suppression is the degradation of hostile operational capabilities through the employment of military action that has psychological and/or physical effects temporarily impairing the combat performance of enemy forces and personnel who have not themselves been killed or wounded.

But until it is possible to measure or estimate the amount of degradation, relate it to a specific level of military action, measure the effects, and specify the duration of "temporarily," the definition does not have practical utility.

An Elusive Topic

How can the experience of military history help to come to grips with this elusive topic, which has thus far defied efforts at quantification or simulation in models and exercises? Analysis of historical battle outcomes made it possible to develop consistent factor values for the effects on the battlefield of surprise and relative combat effectiveness. By using large samples of data from military history, it has been possible to quantify the effects of these essentially behavioral phenomena. And it should also be possible to arrive at factor values for the effects of suppression by resorting again to the laboratory of the soldier—military history.

An After-Dinner Speech

Armed with this conviction, I gave an after-dinner speech on the subject at a 1977 symposium on suppression. Here, in part, is what I said:

Let me demonstrate why I believe something can be done about this matter of suppression and at the same time demonstrate why it is important that it be done. I'll deal with this latter point first.

It is important that we be able to deal with the phenomenon of suppression because it undoubtedly affects battle outcomes. If we cannot find some way of representing it in our models, we cannot expect our models to give us results in which we can have confidence. I hope that this is self-evident. I hope that no one here thinks that if we cannot measure it or represent it, that suppression can be ignored.

Yet, that is what we are doing in most of our models, and particularly in our more aggregated models.

Take the Concepts Evaluation Model (CEM), for instance. I mention CEM only because I know enough about it to use it as an example for a very specific and very important point, not because it is any less reliable than other models in this or any other respect.

In CEM the effect of artillery fire is represented in ammunition tonnages. In some uses of CEM, this artillery tonnage is converted to "155mm equivalents."

Now then, let me tell you about a British operations research report of a post-combat analysis of several World War II engagements in which suppressive effects of artillery fire were assessed. By careful study of the data—opposing strengths, casualties, amount of artillery ammunition expended, rates of artillery fire, nature of defensive protection, and the like—the British OR analysts were able to determine, in a very general way, a number of critical considerations relevant to the suppressive effect of artillery fire. This included such things as the duration and intensity of fire required to achieve a given suppressive effect.

One of the things that emerged clearly from the British analysis was the following, and I quote:

"There is the question of numbers of shells as opposed to sheer weight—the age-old argument in another form of field versus medium artillery. There are a lot of jobs where the heavier shells are essential, either because of their greater range or greater penetration and explosive powers. But where lighter stuff can reach, and is capable of hurting the enemy, the evidence . . . seems to be that the thing that counts most of all is the number of bangs. Clearly one 100 pound shell is better than one 25 pounder one. It is on the other hand very questionable whether it is four times better."[1]

This British finding from historical combat analysis is relevant to the CEM method of measuring artillery effect. If CEM were to show some 100 tons of artillery ammunition fired in a target area in a given period, that could be about 400 rounds of 8″ ammunition; it could be approximately 2,000 rounds of 155mm ammunition; or it could be some 5,700 rounds of 105mm ammunition. With or without the British report, can anyone believe that the same suppressive effect can be achieved with 400 8-inch rounds in a given period of time as by 5,700 105mm rounds in the same amount of time?

Dinner talks should not be long. They should be provocative. I hope I have provoked some of you into exploring how combat historical data can help us understand, measure, and represent the phenomenon of suppression.

I received polite applause as I sat down. No one was in the slightest provoked to follow my admonition to seek the answer to suppression in historical data.

In the following years I thought often and seriously about this matter. But, despite developing a number of concept papers, and two or three complex formulae, I was unable to resolve the problem until suddenly, one day, an answer—maybe *the* answer —revealed itself to me. This answer came from combat historical data, and the analytical tool that led to the answer was the QJM.

Some Answers from History

The revelation was the result of QJM analyses of the battles of Tarawa and Iwo Jima in World War II. In those analyses the firepower potentials of the many supporting air, naval and ground weapons were calculated and considered. Having no basis for calculation of the suppressive effect of the intensive pre-assault bombardments, the analyses began with the landings. The only consideration given to artillery fire was that related directly to the assault and subsequent fighting. The pre-assault bombardments were thus, in effect, ignored—albeit reluctantly.

The preliminary results of the QJM analyses suggested that the combat effectiveness value (CEV) of the U.S. troops with respect to the Japanese was about 2.50 for Tarawa, November 1943, and about 5.00 for Iwo Jima, February 1945. In other words, 100 Americans in combat units, at Iwo Jima were the combat effectiveness equivalent of 500 Japanese soldiers. Earlier at Tarawa, they had been the equivalent of 250 Japanese.

A combat effectiveness superiority of Americans over Japanese had been expected, both for intuitive reasons based upon personal combat experience,[2] and because of previous QJM analyses involving Japanese combat effectiveness with respect to Russian and British forces. On the basis of comparisons of German-Soviet CEVs, Soviet-Japanese CEVs, and British-Japanese CEVs, the estimated U.S.-Japanese CEV was about 1.50. The value of the U.S. CEV for Tarawa was nearly double what would have been expected, and that for Iwo Jima was more than three times greater.

It seemed unlikely that these larger CEVs were typical of the true U.S.-Japanese relations combat effectiveness. Thus, they reflected some kind of degradation of Japanese combat power. It was impossible to avoid the conclusion that this degradation was due primarily or entirely to the effects of pre-assault bombardment and the suppression, neutralization, and disruption resulting therefrom. The bombardment at Iwo Jima, we knew, had been much greater and more effective than at Tarawa. Combined with known effects of suppression reported in a few British OR analyses from World War II, and with available data with respect to the volume and intensity of the pre-assault bombardments at Tarawa and Iwo Jima, this led to hypotheses that would explain the known historical facts.

Research has not yet begun on the conversion of this finding into a reliable suppression methodology; however, the general hypotheses are relatively simple and straightforward:

1. Suppression is a function of the volume, quantity, and intensity of suppressive firepower:
   a. volume is the amount of high explosive firepower per unit of surface area in terms of some logical measure, as tons of high explosive (HE).
   b. quantity is the number of firepower impacts per unit of surface area (or, in the British terms, "the number of bangs");
   c. intensity is the combination of volume and quantity of firepower per unit of time.
2. Suppression is an instantaneous (or near-instantaneous) phenomenon until some threshold of volume, quantity, and intensity of firepower is reached, at which point it becomes "neutralization" and is residual, but the residual effects are temporary, lasting for some measurable period of time.

Human Behavior, Combat Outcomes, and Suppression

Over the past several years I have been devoting a substantial proportion of my time to consideration of variables of combat, considering not only those that are physical, tangible, and measurable, but also those relating to what Clausewitz called the fighting value of the forces. In other words, I have been seeking to identify and quantify the effects of behavioral considerations on military performance and battle outcomes. Some results of this consideration are presented in earlier chapters of this book.

As discussed earlier, one of the most important things to emerge from that research has been the development of a methodology to measure consistently the composite effects of all of the variable factors that I call the qualitative intangibles—those that are related to that fighting value or quality of the troops, and to their leadership and control systems. This composite measure is the Combat Effectiveness Value (CEV). The CEV, as we have seen, provides the explanation for the vast majority of cases in which a numerically inferior force defeated a large force.

Other behavioral factors also affect combat outcomes. There is, for instance, surprise. Presumably there is some bonus accruing to the side that possesses the initiative, but this is still to be proven. There is certainly a behavioral effect, which we can call disruption, and unquestionably related to disruption, is suppression.

The U.S. Army generally ignores the phenomenon of suppression in planning and preparation for war. Troops are sent to the National Training Center at Fort Irwin, California, to participate in field training exercises that are designed to be as realistic as possible in peacetime training. During that training, however, they are not subjected to anything that could simulate the effect of suppression nor are their own weapons given credit for suppressive effects. The reason is understandable; we don't know enough about the subject to know how to represent it. More serious, however, is the fact that these troops are apparently not warned about how significantly this lack of suppression simulation distorts the realism of the training they are undergoing.

Yet—as our top military leadership knows and is constantly reminded by our military intelligence agencies—possibly the most significant aspect of Soviet military doctrine is its reliance upon the suppressive effects of firepower. If U.S. Army training is to be realistic, there is no aspect of Soviet doctrine about which the troops need more exposure and understanding. At the same time they should also be trained to recognize the paramount importance which American artillery doctrine also places upon suppression in both the offense and defense.

It is clear that when models are used to simulate combat for training or analytical purposes, it is necessary to be able to represent the suppression effects of firepower. This is at least as important as the highly theoretical individual "kill probabilities" of the weapons. However, in the "bottom-up" approach adopted for the development of models in the United States, if an effect cannot be measured, the effect is not represented. A very useful application of the QJM would be to identify, measure, and represent suppression in combat.

Chapter 19

Application: Force Multipliers

"Flight Outnumbered and Win"

FOR CENTURIES, MILITARY men have recognized that the circumstances of combat can enhance or degrade the fighting capability of military forces. Originally, such enhancement or degradation was thought of in terms of an additive bonus of some sort, but more recently it has been assumed that the effect is more probably multiplicative.

In the past decade much has been written in both official and unofficial American military literature about the availability of force multipliers such as leadership, terrain, weather, surprise, morale, and training. This concept of force multipliers has become the basis of an Army doctrinal assertion that, despite the numerical superiority of the potential foes of the Warsaw Pact, the U.S. Army will be able to "fight outnumbered and win."

The Army doctrine of force multipliers is based upon a simple mathematical concept, but it is mathematics without numbers or scale. The doctrine does not define, list, or quantify these multipliers, and it does not suggest the quantity or value of the multiplicand, nor the size or the nature of the product. A major reason for this lapse between doctrinal concept and doctrinal reality is that most combat models are unable to represent the multipliers. The models in intensive use do not provide even approximate values for most of these force multipliers.

The concept of multipliers is basically sound. It is the essence of Clausewitz's Law of Numbers. It is accepted without question by the Soviets as the basis for their concept of Correlation of Forces. It is what the QJM is all about. There are masses of empirical data that demonstrate the effects of force multipliers in combat for a century or more.

HERO has done two analyses that are particularly relevant to the question of combat multipliers. One of these was done several years ago, when the QJM was just beginning to be used for analytical purposes. It shows how the concept of combat multipliers can be useful to planners and analysts. The other was done more recently. It suggests how the multiplier concept can be useful to a commander in a particular battlefield situation. In both cases historical analysis has permitted the definition of values for factors that in actual combat can be seen to have augmented—probably multiplied—the combat power of a military force. These examples show that the QJM lends itself readily to understanding and using force multipliers. It can do in concrete fashion what the Army has only been able wistfully to talk about.

Analysis of Breakthrough Operations

Several years ago HERO did a study of "breakthrough operations" for the Defense Nuclear Agency. We examined fourteen operations that took place between 1918 and 1967 in which attacking forces, varying in size from a small field army to a reinforced brigade, attacked and achieved significant breakthroughs. In all except one of these examples, the initial breakthrough success of the attacker led to a decisive victory. In one instance (Kursk, 1943), the arrival of substantial defending reinforcements prevented exploitation of an incipient breakthrough and drove back the attacking forces.

The basic QJM ratios for these successful breakthrough operations are shown in Table 19-1. Additional information on these, including the rates of advance, are in Tables 12-3 and 12-4. Inspection of Table 19-1 reveals that the attacker was numerically smaller than the defender in five operations, that the attacker and defender were about even in strength in another three operations, and that the attacker was larger than the defender in only six of these operations. Of the six operations in which the

Table 19–1

Data on Breakthrough Operations

OPERATION	ATTACKING FORCE	ATTACKER TO DEFENDER RATIOS		
		PERSONNEL STRENGTH RATIO	FORCE STRENGTH RATIO	COMBAT POWER RATIO
Megiddo, 1918	Allies	2.81	2.99	5.20
Flanders, 1940	Germans	1.07	2.42	2.70
Ukraine, 1941	Germans	0.88	1.17	3.36
Malaya, 1941	Japanese	0.58	2.06	2.52
Leningrad, 1943	Soviets	4.00	4.83	1.51
Kursk-Oboyan, 1943	Germans	0.69	0.79	1.31
Belgorod-Kharkov, 1943	Soviets	4.67	5.03	1.57
Normandy, 1940	Allies	4.20	7.34	2.99
Manchuria, 1945	Soviets	1.96	4.00	3.16
North Korea, 1950	North Koreans	1.58	1.73	3.20
Sinai-Rafa, 1967	Israelis	1.00	1.45	4.19
Sinai-Abu Ageila, 1967	Israelis	1.04	0.94	3.12
Syria-Qala, 1967	Israelis	0.91	2.27	4.47
Syria-Tel Fahar, 1967	Israelis	0.90	1.79	4.47

attacker was stronger in personnel, there were only three in which the attacker had an overwhelming strength advantage of four-to-one or more. Yet all of these operations (except Kursk) were successful, even decisive. In eleven of fourteen cases, the attacker had to rely on some kind of force multipliers to achieve the decisive combat power superiority that led to victory. In the other three cases, the attacker achieved breakthrough with the overwhelming numerical strength of four-to-one or more despite defensive force multipliers that reduced the attackers' combat power ratio.

This is shown by inspection of the combat power ratio for the operations. In all but one case, the attackers combat power ratio was over 1.5 to 1.0, and in the one exception (Kursk), the breakthrough was not achieved. The composite force multiplier factor is the combat power ratio divided by the personnel strength ratio. In Table 19-2 I show the force multiplier effects for each of three classes of operations grouped according to relative strengths.

Table 19–2

Impact of Force Multipliers on Breakthrough Operations

RELATIVE NUMERICAL STRENGTH ATTACKER/DEFENDER	AVERAGE STRENGTH RATIO	AVERAGE COMBAT POWER RATIO	FORCE MULTIPLIER FACTOR
< 1.0 (5 cases)	.79	3.23	4.09
1.0 to 3.0 (6 cases)	1.58	3.60	2.53
> 3.0 (3 cases)	4.29	2.02	0.48
Total (Average)	1.88	3.13	1.66

This clearly shows the significant impact of force multipliers. For the five operations in which the attacker was numerically smaller than the defender, the effect of the force multipliers was to increase the combat power by an average factor of 4.0. For the six operations in which the strength ratios were between 1.0 and 3.0, the force multiplier effect averaged about 2.5. However, in those three cases for which the attacker had a strength advantage greater than 3.0, the defender's force multipliers reduced the combat power ratios of the attackers by a factor of about 0.5. The attackers who were successful although numerically smaller made the best use of force multipliers, perhaps because they had to. Those who had the greatest preponderance of numbers won through brute strength, even though the defenders made better use of the force multipliers. It is noteworthy that two of those three victories by brute strength were won by Soviet forces, and one by U.S. forces.

What are these force multipliers? Examination of Tables 19-3 and 19-4 provides some answers. These two tables show the results of a qualitative assessment of each of the breakthrough operations to determine which factors influenced the outcome by giving an advantage or disadvantage to attacker and defender. The attacker advantages (and some disadvantages) are shown in Table 19-3 and the defender advantages and disadvantages are shown in Table 19-4.

The successful attacker had the advantage on the average of about three different force multipliers. The most important attacker force multipliers in these breakthrough operations were relative combat effectiveness, battlefield mobility, air superiority, and surprise. The extent to which the major attacker force multipliers were advantageous and decisively advantageous are shown in Table 19-5.

The qualitative assessment of the defender force multipliers is shown in Table 19-4. When compared to the attacker force, the defender usually had the advantage of fortifications and availability of reserves; however, these were also usually insufficient to overcome the attacker force multipliers. In addition, the propensity of the defenders to have poor leadership undoubtedly contributed to the success of the attackers.

The Kursk-Oboyan operation in 1943 is instructive because it was the only one of the breakthrough operations studied that did not result in a breakthrough and decisive victory for the attacker. In this case, the Germans were attacking the Soviets. The Germans did have the advantage of superior combat effectiveness and superior battlefield mobility, but these were insufficient to overcome the decisive Soviet advantages of large reserves and well-fortified positions. Despite rapid advances in the early stages of the operation, the Germans simply ran out of effective troops and were forced to halt for lack of reinforcements. The Soviets, on the other hand, were readily able to put fresh troops into the

Table 19–3

Attacking Force Multipliers in Breakthrough Operations

OPERATION	WEATHER AND TERRAIN	RELATIVE COMBAT EFFECTIVENESS	BATTLEFIELD MOBILITY	AIR SUPERIORITY	SURPRISE	AVAILABILITY OF RESOURCES
Megiddo	A	A	A	–	A+	A
Flanders	A	A+	A+	A+	A	–
Ukraine	A	A+	A	A	A+	A
Malaya	D	–	A+	A	A	–
Leningrad	D	–	–	–	–	A
Kursk-Oboyan	–	A	A	–	–	D–
Belgorod-Kharkov	–	–	–	–	–	A+
Normandy	A	–	–	A+	–	A
Manchuria North	D	A	A	A	A+	A
Korea	D	A+	A	A	A+	–
Sinai-Rafa	A	A+	A+	A	A	A
Sinai-Abu Ageila	A	A+	A	A	A+	A
Syria-Qala	–	A+	A	A+	–	A
Syria-Tel Fahar	–	A+	A	A+	–	A

A = Advantage; A+ = Decisive Advantage D = Disadvantage; D– = Decisive Disadvantage

Table 19–4

Defending Force Multipliers in Breakthrough Operations

BATTLE/ CAMPAIGN	FORTIFICATIONS	RESERVES	LEADERSHIP
Meggido	A	D	–
Flanders	–	–	D–
Ukraine	–	A	D
Malaya	–	D	D–
Leningrad	A	–	–
Kursk	A+	A+	–
Belgorod- Kharkov	A	–	–
Normandy	A	D	–
Manchuria	A	D	–
North Korea	–	–	D–
Sinai-Rafa	A	A	D
Sinai-Abu Ageila	A	A	D
Syria-Qala	A	A	D–
Syria-Tel Fahar	A	A	–

A = Advantage;   A+ = Decisive Advantage.   D = Disadvantage;
D– = Decisive Disadvantage.

Table 19–5

Attacker Force Multipliers Summarized

FORCE MULTIPLIER	ADVANTAGE	DECISIVE ADVANTAGE
Relative Combat Effectiveness	10	7
Battlefield Mobility	11	3
Air Superiority	10	4
Surprise	8	5

battle. The Germans were able to use their force multipliers to raise their strength ratio of 0.69 to a combat power ratio of 1.31, but this was not enough to provide breakthrough and victory.

Based upon the QJM analyses summarized in Table 19-1 and the qualitative assessment in Table 19-3, the estimated average values of these four major force multipliers are as follows: combat effectiveness superiority was about 1.9; mobility superiority was about 1.3; air superiority (where present) roughly 1.2; and surprise (where present) in the range of 1.1 to 2.0, averaging approximately 1.3.

This analysis of fourteen breakthrough operations demonstrated the validity of a consistent, logical concept of force multipliers. It also permitted the establishment of reasonable, approximate values for several important force multipliers. This, in turn, permitted the derivation of reasonably accurate estimates of values for the factors required to achieve the preponderance of combat power necessary for successful breakthrough operations, regardless of the relative size of the opposing forces.

The QJM and Historical Force Multipliers

QJM analyses of more than 200 engagements between 1915 and 1973 have revealed patterns that permit establishing ranges of values for more than forty factors. These are probably accurate within ± 20%. While this is not rigorous precision, it is better than educated guesses, which are probably accurate to within ± 100%.

QJM analyses have produced a good deal of specific information about the effects of force multipliers. This information can be applied in a practical way to allow commanders and staffs to estimate in advance what could be done to increase combat power by applying force multipliers.

The starting value (multiplicand) is the force strength (S) of the unit or force in combat. Values for QJM force effects factors are applied to the force strength to convert it to combat power (P). The principal force multipliers used in this set of examples are the factor values that represent the effects of terrain (r), weather (h), season (z), posture (u), mobility (m), vulnerability (v), surprise (su), and relative combat effectiveness (CEV). All are important, all have varying but predictable effects depending on the circumstances, and all can be used advantageously by a skilled commander.

Surprise and combat effectiveness are force multipliers that potentially can yield the most return in response to command skill, for they are controllable by the commander to a considerable degree. Surprise may not always be achievable, because the enemy will play a part in either the success or failure of efforts to achieve surprise. Combat effectiveness, however, is something about which a commander can do a great deal, particularly in training of troops and in the honing of subordinate leadership skills.

I analyzed six historical battles in each of which the successful force was outnumbered by its opponent; in other words, a force that was able to "fight outnumbered and win." These battles are as follows: Austerlitz (1805), Antietam (1862), Montdidier (1918), Sedan (1940), Lanuvio (1943), and Chinese Farm (1973). In each of these six instances the victory for the outnumbered side was due essentially to the application of the force multipliers available to the successful commander of the outnumbered force.

Battle of Austerlitz

In this battle Napoleon won one of the most decisive victories of history against a more numerous allied army of Austrians and Russians. The principal factor in the scale of the victory was the relative combat effectiveness of the French. I estimate that at least three-fourths of this superiority was the generalship of Napoleon. Other multipliers were the tactical surprise achieved by the French, and their slightly superior tactical mobility. Table 19-6 shows the way in which the French numerical inferiority was converted into an exceptional four-to-one superiority in combat power.

Battle of Antietam

After the battle of Antietam, or Sharpsburg, Union Major General George B. McClellan was able to claim a strategic victory because he had stopped the Confederate invasion of the north. On the battlefield, however, his poorly coordinated efforts were repulsed by General Robert E. Lee and the Army of Northern Virginia, who won a tactical victory with the help of defensive posture and good use of terrain. The decisive factor was the superior combat effectiveness of General Lee's army. If one assumes that the quality of troops was roughly equal on both sides (as one must after study of Thomas L. Livermore *Numbers and Losses in the Civil War*[1]) the differential was solely that of generalship. If General Lee was a 10.0, then it seems historically reasonable that General McClellan was a 6.0.

The Battle of Montdidier

A World War I example was selected from the second phase of the German Somme Offensive. During the Peronne phase of the offensive (March 21–26), the Germans had overwhelmed the British Fifth Army in a surprise offensive that broke through the Allied lines. By March 27, however, the Allies had sealed the gap and, although still outnumbered and still being driven back, had at least rejoined the battle. British air power substantially reduced the German strength superiority to achieve near equality in force strength. That was insufficient to offset the 30% German qualitative superiority. Nevertheless, the advantages of defensive posture and terrain multiplied force enough for the British to repulse the Germans.

Battle of Sedan (1940)

The following examples are World War II battles, in both of which the Germans were outnumbered and successful.

The first of these battles was the crossing of the Meuse River at Sedan in 1940 by General Heinz Guderian's panzer corps. Even though Guderian was outnumbered, he had massive air support. This gave him a substantial force strength superiority. He also had the benefit of the disruptive effects of surprise upon the French. It was this surprise multiplier and his relative combat effectiveness multiplier that more than offset the French advantages of numerical superiority, defensive posture, and terrain.

Battle of Lanuvio

The second World War II example is the attack by the American 34th Infantry Division on the badly battered German 3d Panzer Grenadier Division during the Allied advance upon Rome in "Operation Diadem," May 1943. The Americans had a three-to-one numerical advantage. Yet the Germans, despite low morale and the devastating effects of Allied air interdiction upon their logistical system, were able to use the defensive strength of the Caesar Line and their residual combat effectiveness superiority to stop the Americans in a bitter four-day battle.

Table 19-6

Battle of Austerlitz: Force Multipliers

	Personnel Strength N	Force Strength S	Terrain r	Posture u	Mobility m	Surprise Su	CEV	Combat Power P
French	75,000	140,823	1.20	1.15	1.10	1.60	2.48	846,761
Allies	89,000	163,310	1.20	1.15	1.00	1.00	1.00	225,368
Ratio	0.84	0.86	—	—	—	—	—	3.76

Table 19-7

Battle of Antietam: Force Multipliers

	Personnel Strength N	Force Strength S	Terrain r	Posture u	Mobility m	Surprise Su	CEV	Other Factors	Combat Power P
Confederates	45,000	171,547	1.30	1.30	1.00	1.00	1.67	1.00	483,552
Union	80,000	305,140	1.00	1.00	1.00	1.00	1.00	1.10	335,654
Ratio	0.56	0.56	—	—	—	—	—	—	1.44

Table 19-8

Battle of Montdidier: Force Multipliers

	Personnel Strength N	Force Strength S	Terrain r	Posture u	Mobility m	Surprise Su	CEV	Combat Power P
Allies	500,000	9,911,475	1.20	1.40	1.00	1.00	1.00	16,651,278
Germans	600,000	10,257,550	1.00	1.00	0.94	1.00	1.30	12,534,726
Ratio	0.83	0.97	—	—	—	—	—	1.33

Table 19-9

Battle of Sedan: Force Multipliers

	Personnel Strength N	Force Strength S	Terrain r	Posture u	Mobility m	Surprise Su	CEV	Other Factors	Combat Power P
Germans	48,000	209,564	1.00	1.00	1.16	1.46	1.37	0.85	413,302
French	60,000	115,754	1.45	1.30	1.00	1.00	1.00	0.70	152,737
Ratio	0.80	1.81	—	—	—	—	—	—	2.71

Table 19-10

Battle of Lanuvio: Force Multipliers

	Personnel Strength N	Force Strength S	Ter- Rain r	Pos- Ture u	Mobil- ity m	Sur- Prise Su	CEV	Other Factors	Combat Power P
Germans	6,108	30,605	1.30	1.60	1.19	1.00	1.20	0.66	59,997
Americans	17,300	46,327	1.00	1.00	1.00	1.00	1.00	0.80	37,062
Ratio	0.35	0.66	—	—	—	—	—	—	1.61

Table 19-11

Battle of the Chinese Farm: Force Multipliers

	Personnel Strength N	Force Strength S	Ter- Rain r	Pos- Ture u	Mobil- ity m	Sur- Prise Su	CEV	Other Factors	Combat Power P
Israelis	28,700	520,996	1.00	1.00	1.17	2.19	1.66	0.94	2,083,053
Egyptians	36,840	607,550	1.00	1.40	1.00	1.00	1.00	0.97	990,063
Ratio	0.78	0.86	—	—	—	—	—	—	2.10

The Battle of the Chinese Farm

Next is a battle from the 1973 Middle East War. This was the attack of General "Bren" Adan's division to restore communications with General "Arik" Sharon's division, which had been cut off by an Egyptian counterattack after crossing the Suez Canal. Although the attacking Israelis were outnumbered about five-to-four, they had a substantial advantage in air support, which reduced their inferiority in force strength. Even that would have been insufficient to overcome the Egyptian multiplier advantages of terrain and defensive posture, however, had it not been for the continuing disruptive effects of the Israeli surprise counteroffensive upon the Egyptians, plus a substantial Israeli combat effectiveness superiority.

Battle of the Suez Canal

It is perhaps instructive to note that in at least one instance in that 1973 war the Israelis fought outnumbered and did *not* win. Table 19-12 shows the application of multipliers to the initial crossing of the Suez Canal by the Egyptian Second Army on 6 October 1973. The Israelis had a slight terrain advantage and a substantial posture advantage, and they had an even more substantial combat effectiveness advantage. But the Egyptians, thanks to surprise, and thanks to their careful plans and rehearsals for the set-piece battle, had multipliers that—applied to their substantially greater numerical and firepower advantages —assured a major Arab success. Multipliers can and do work for *both* sides and, as Clausewitz told us, numbers (multipliers considered) win battles.

Force Multipliers and Future Battlefields

What is the practical value of having been able to calculate, after the fact, the multipliers that enabled successful commanders to win some historical battles? Can this approach to force multipliers be useful on the modern battlefield?

Indeed it can!

The reader should try to imagine being the commander of an American division stationed in Germany, who must contemplate a possible attack by a numerically superior Warsaw Pact force, such as a Soviet combined-arms army. You, as the division commander, must now do the same kind of correlation of forces assessment that you can be sure is being done by your potential opponent, the Soviet army commander.

With a total manpower strength of 20,200 men, you can expect to be attacked by a force of about 58,000, thus giving the enemy nearly a three-to-one numerical strength superiority. Considering the likely levels of air support for both sides and the weather and terrain, you calculate the force strength of the firepower that you can bring to bear as 266,957 for your division, and 1,312,273 for the anticipated attacker. That gives the enemy a raw firepower preponderance over you of 4.92. In other words, the Soviets will enter the battle with nearly a five-to-one force strength superiority.

The odds are pretty grim, but you know that you have some advantages accruing from your defensive posture, which will outweigh at least some additional advantages the enemy is likely to have. You have a terrain multiplier advantage of about 1.45. In the likely weather conditions, the enemy strength may be degraded by a factor of 0.9, but this will be offset by his seasonal advantage in the best fighting months of the year.

You can hope for plenty of warning, but you cannot be sure of it. You have prepared plans for digging field fortifications, installing obstacles, and laying mines, once NATO orders mobilization, but—for political reasons—you are not allowed to start work on these in peacetime. If you do not have warning, you may not have time for these planned defensive preparations and may be forced to fight in a hasty defense posture, which has a multiplier value of 1.30. A systematic calculation of the relative mobility characteristics of your forces and theirs indicates that the Warsaw Pact will have a 1.20 mobility multiplier advantage over you. A similar calculation of vulnerability shows that, despite your defensive posture, under the anticipated circumstances of the battle the enemy's vulnerability will be slightly less than yours.

You apply all of these factors to the initial opposing firepower strengths and you find that the odds are reduced substantially. The calculations are shown in Table 19-13. The enemy still has a combat power superiority over your forces of 3.16. Thus, in practical terms, his superiority is still three-to-one. If you had to fight under these conditions, you would be defeated.

Table 19-12

Battle of the Suez Canal: Force Multipliers

	Personnel Strength N	Force Strength S	Terrain r	Posture u	Mobility m	Surprise Su	CEV	Other Factors	Combat Power P
Israelis	4,455	129,424	1.13	1.55	1.54	1.00	1.72	0.93	558,415
Egyptians	29,490	361,216	1.00	1.00	1.00	3.84[a]	1.00	0.95	1,317,716
Ratio	0.15	0.36	—	—	—	—	—	—	0.42

[a] Includes set-piece advantage.

Table 19-13

Battle of Fulda A: Force Multipliers

	Personnel Strength, N	Force Strength, S	Terrain & Posture	Weather, Season, Mobility & Vulnerability	CEV	Combat Power, P
US Div.	20,000	266,957	1.89	0.93	1.00	469,230
Sov. Army	58,285	1,312,273	1.00	1.13	1.00	1,482,868
Ratio	0.34	0.20	—	—	—	0.32

What can you do about it?

You should be able to improve your defensive position. There probably are a number of additional preparations you can make so that it will be easier for your division to have the advantage of prepared defenses at the outset, even with scanty warning. Whether or not you can get your corps commander to allow you to do all of the pre-hostilities preparations you would like to do is questionable, but let's assume that there are things you can do with his permission and without arousing too much antagonism among the local German farmers. The multiplier factor for prepared defense is 1.45 instead of 1.30. Thus, you probably can achieve a multiplier enhancement of 1.15. This will in turn provide a slight enhancement to your vulnerability multiplier.

These two multiplier enhancements are peanuts. You have only chipped at the surface of the three-to-one odds against you. You must resort to the two means that historically have been most important in enabling outnumbered commanders to defeat more powerful foes. You must figure out some way to *surprise* the enemy, and you must devote every possible thought and effort to improving the *quality* and readiness of your troops.

I am not about to suggest the specifics by which an outnumbered defender can achieve surprise. Beginning with Hannibal at the Battles of Lake Trasimene and Cannae there is a rich historical record that can be reviewed for inspiration, and you and your staff and your subordinate commanders can concoct a really unexpected welcome for the potential attackers. You might even be justified in estimating that your surprise will double your combat power. The multiplier arithmetic tells you this is still not enough, although it might be if your surprise works better than you dare hope.

You would be wise to assume that the enemy will still have a 1.20 advantage over your division, even if he is surprised. To have reasonable confidence in success you will have to count on the intensive efforts you have been making to improve troop quality. This factor is easy to discuss but hard to accomplish. There is no royal road, but in this example we assume you have been working on it.

There is another historical example that could inspire you. As we saw in Chapter 10, in 1943 and 1944 US Army Major General John Sloan was able to raise the combat effectiveness of his 88th Infantry Division to a level approximately 1.43 times superior to the average effectiveness of other U.S. divisions formed at about the same time. He did this with an imaginative, intensive training program and other measures within his grasp as a division commander. High standards of combat effectiveness have been achieved with average American troops, and it may be done again!

If you have been as successful in your training and readiness program as General Sloan was, you can assume that you have raised your division's combat effectiveness by a factor of about 1.43. The result is a comfortable overall combat power margin of superiority over your potential enemy of 1.20:1.00.

By using force multipliers to calculate the nature and effects of the other measures you need to take, you can "fight outnumbered and win." Force multipliers will not do the work for you as a battle leader, but they can provide essential guidelines for what you can do, and what you must do. If you do it, Clausewitz and John Sloan will look down at you approvingly from their heavenly abode.

Table 19–14

Hypothetical Battle of Fulda B: Force Multipliers

	Personnel Strength, N	Force Strength, S	Terrain & Posture	Surprise	CEV	Other Factors	Combat Power, P
US Div.	20,000	266,957	2.12	2.00	1.43	0.93	1,505,311
Sov. Army	58,285	1,312,273	1.00	1.00	1.00	1.13	1,482,868
Ratio	0.34	0.20	—	—	—	—	1.20

Chapter 20

The QJM as a Theory of Combat

Clausewitz's Amanuensis

I GAVE CONSIDERABLE attention in Chapter 6 to a concept of inductive theory development and its relevance to the search for a theory of combat that has been ongoing for more than a century and a half. I elaborated on the development of the theory of gravitation—in which the names of Copernicus and Newton were prominent—because I believe the history of that theory is of more than incidental relevance to our own search. Not the least important aspect of that relevance is the fact that neither astronomy nor military science can be based upon laboratory research, and both sciences are dependent upon repeated observations of a very large number of observations of individual, fleeting phenomena.

In Chapter 1, I quoted J.F.C. Fuller comparing Clausewitz to both Copernicus and Newton, and I pointed out that the comparison is exceptionally apt. Clausewitz (like Copernicus) not only initiated a revolution in theory, but also (like Newton) enunciated a specific mathematical formulation (in words, not symbols), which would emerge from that revolution. It matters not that the formulation was not recognized for more than a century. It was there, waiting to be elaborated. So, in that respect, I consider myself not only Clausewitz's disciple, but also his amanuensis.[1]

I took on the role only after I had independently built on the ideas and approach of Clausewitz and his various successors—of whom Fuller was probably the most noteworthy—and used my own historical research to develop the Quantified Judgement model to represent real-world combat. Having done that, I was struck not only by the similarity of my own independently derived concept to Clausewitz's Law of Numbers, but also by its similarity to another independently derived theoretical concept—the Soviet Correlation of Forces and Means. This led me to recognize that the Law of Numbers was a statement of a very simple mathematical formula, which was almost identical with the simplified formula of the QJM. Later came the discovery that the Clausewitz formula allows the inherent (but hidden) historical validity of the Lanchester Equations to be confirmed by historical data. The independent derivation of practically identical concepts by Soviet military scholars is a clear indication of the universality of Clausewitz's theory. There is no doubt in my mind that the QJM is a faithful elaboration of the fundamental mathematical formula of Clausewitz's theory of combat: his Law of Numbers.

The QJM as a Model: A Summary

The QJM is both a model and a theory of combat. Let's examine its nature and function in each of these roles. First, I summarize the QJM as a model of combat.

The QJM provides a basis for comparing the relative combat power of two opposing forces in historical combat by determining the influence of variable factors upon the opponents. Two kinds of variables are considered in this process: those affecting weapons effectiveness, and those affecting the employment of the force as a whole. Data from more than 200 selected historical engagements between 1915 and 1973 has been analyzed to obtain factor values of many of these variables under a variety of different battlefield circumstances. For some intangible variable factors, such as leadership (or the more general Relative Combat Effectiveness Value (CEV), which includes leadership), it is necessary to estimate values or to assume equality if there is no basis for such an estimate. Once these variables have been applied to the numerical strengths of each of the opposing forces under the circumstances of the engagement, a combat power ratio is produced. This combat power ratio indicates which of the opponents should theoretically have been successful in the engagement, and by what margin.

Note that in arriving at this combat power ratio, the relative combat effectiveness of the troops is either estimated or assumed to be equal. In the analysis of historical combat, it is possible to test such estimates and assumptions.

The first step is to compare the combat power ratio to the result ratio, which is a quantification of the actual outcome of the battle. This outcome value, also derived from historical records, represents the comparative performance of the opposing forces in terms of their (1) accomplishment of their respective missions, (2) ability to gain or hold ground, and (3) efficiency in terms of casualties incurred. If the combat power ratio of force A with respect to force B is greater than 1.0, the result ratio of force A with respect to force B should also be greater than 1.0. In the event the value of the combat power ratio is not consistent with that of the result ratio, further exploration is necessary to explain the discrepancy. Such discrepancies are usually due to the effects of surprise, and/or to a difference in the relative combat effectiveness of the two sides. The effects of surprise are quantifiable and can be stripped out. Then the residual difference between the combat power ratio and the result ratio is a reflection of the relative combat effectiveness of the opponents.

QJM analyses have shown patterns of relative combat effectiveness values (CEVs) in different historical forces. In World Wars I and II the Germans—on the average—had a CEV of about 1.20 with respect to the Western Allies and about 2.50 with respect to the Russians. In other words, 100 Germans in combat units were the equivalent of about 120 British or American troops in combat units, and equivalent to about 250 Russians in combat units. In the recent Arab-Israeli Wars the Israeli CEV has been over 2.00; i.e. 100 Israelis in combat units were the equivalent of more than 200 Arabs in combat units.

Note my emphasis on "in combat units." I do not believe the qualitative differences represented quantitatively in the CEV reflect any greater strength, intelligence, motivation or individual skill on the part of the individual soldiers of opposing units or national forces. The CEV represents the quantitative differences in *force* quality resulting from a number of factors affecting unit performances, of which leadership, training, and experience—in other words, professionalism—are probably the most important.

The basic operation of the QJM is a two-step mathematical process. In the first step, force strength (S), is the sum of the firepower of weapons (categorized as infantry, anti-tank, artillery, air defense, armor, and air support), after the effects of each of these weapons have been modified by all applicable variable factors affecting their effectiveness, such as weather, terrain, and season. The formula for this is expressed as follows:

$$S = (W_n \times V_n) + (W_{gi} \times V_{gi}) + (W_g \times V_g) + (W_{gy} \times V_{gy}) + (W_i \times V_i) + (W_g \times V_g). \quad (1)$$

In the second step, force strength (S) is modified by force effectiveness variable factors to yield a value for combat power potential (P). The most important of these variable factors are as follows: surprise (su), mobility (m), posture (u), vulnerability (v), terrain (r), weather (h), and season (z); and such intangible, behavioral factors as leadership (le), training/experience (t), morale (o), and logistical capability(b). This is expressed in the basic QJM formula as follows:

$$P = S \times su \times m \times u \times v \times r \times h \times z \times \frac{(le \times t \times o \times b)}{(CEV)} \quad (2)$$

The basic QJM formula is further simplified by consolidating the intangible or behavioral variables as a relative combat effectiveness value (CEV), and aggregating all of the other operational variables together as V_{fe}, or more simply, V. The general model, then, is expressible as follows:

$$\text{Combat Power} = \text{Force Strength} \times \text{Variable Factors} \times \text{CEV}. \quad (3)$$

The QJM as a Theory

As noted earlier, the above general formula is identical in concept, structure and content to the formula representing Clausewitz's Law of Numbers, or his theory of combat. When Clausewitz referred to numbers in *On War*, and particularly in his Law of Numbers, he was undoubtedly thinking of the composite strengths of infantrymen, cavalrymen, and cannon. And so the symbol N, which appears in the above formula is in reality the same kind of entity which—in dealing with more complex modern weaponry—is called force strength in the QJM. In other words, Clausewitz's N and the S of the QJM are virtually identical. It is equally clear that CEV in the QJM is conceptually identical with Q in the Clausewitz formula.

I believe that Clausewitz would agree with the asserted identity of the formula reprsenting his theory and that of the QJM. The conceptual and practical similarity of the theory statements of Clausewitz and the QJM, and of their basic mathematical renditions, is evident. Just as Clausewitz viewed Napoleon as "the god of war", and just as Clausewitz was his doctrinal prophet, so the QJM can be seen as the modern dogma of that doctrine. It is demonstrable not only that Clausewitz did have a coherent theory of combat, but that that theory has been elaborated, and is now available in the United States as the QJM.

Testing the Theory

How and why is the QJM a theory of combat? Let me refer the reader back to the discussion of theory development in Chapter 6 and the definition of a theory of combat in Chapter 7.

I have defined a theory of combat as the embodiment of a set of fundamental principles governing or explaining military combat, whose purpose is to provide a basis for the formulation of doctrine, and to assist military commanders and planners to engage successfully in combat at any level. Such a theory includes the following elements:

(1) Identifying the major elements of combat, the combat processes through which they operate, and patterns in the interactions and relationships among them;

(2) Describing combat structures and patterns of interactions, and relationships of variable factors that constantly shape or determine the outcome of combat;

(3) Expressing in quantitative terms the patterns so identified and described.

The discussions in Chapters 8, 9, 10, and 11 show that the QJM is indeed an embodiment of a set of fundamental principles explaining military combat. The QJM was developed by the identification of the major elements of combat, the processes through which the elements operate, and by structuring and quantifying the patterns, relationships, and interactions among these elements and processes, and among the variable factors shaping or determining the outcome of combat.

The reader must decide, from the previous chapters of this book, and from what follows below, whether this developmental process and its product—the QJM—has validity. If so, then the QJM provides a basis for the formulation of doctrine and for assisting military commanders and planners to engage in combat at any level.

How does the QJM fit the process of theory development? Let's look at this, step by step.

1. *Observation.* The QJM is to a substantial extent based upon the many years that my colleagues and I have spent in studying military history. Our study has focused on observation and detailed description of the phenomena of combat over the centuries of recorded history. More specifically, it is based upon the patterns and relationships observed in some 200 combat engagements in modern warfare between 1915 and 1973.

2. *Identification of Measurables.* The QJM has disaggregated Clausewitz's three basic measurables (N, V, and Q) into a larger group of systematically related measurables, of which weapons' lethality, weather, terrain, posture, casualty rate, and opposed movement rate parameters are possibly the most important.

3. *Data Collection.* In the development of the QJM my colleagues and I have assembled a substantially greater data base than was available either to Clauzewitz or to Fuller. This facilitates the work of those who wish to challenge, modify, confirm, or amplify the theory development work to date.

4. *Data Analysis.* This book, along with various other books, articles, and papers produced by me and HERO over the past 20 years, provides ample evidence of the nature of the analysis that is ongoing and that has been done. Empirical relationships among the measurables have been derived to include means of quantifying the elements, processes, and variables in their relationships to each other.

5. *Definition of Derivative Concepts.* Amongst the various derivative concepts that have emerged from the analysis of Step 4, the following are worth noting:

   Relative combat effectiveness

   The New Square Law

   Quantification of surprise

Quantification of friction

Quantification of force multipliers

Suppression hypothesis

6. *Formulation of General Principles or Hypotheses*. The general principles have been enunciated by the elaboration of the Clausewitz Law of Numbers into the QJM Formula, and the derivation of supporting formulae such as those for advance rates and attrition rates.
7. *Testing*. Unlike the generalizations of the Principles of War, the formula $P = S \times V_f \times (CEV)$ can be, and has been, tested extensively against real world combat data. A very significant aspect of the testing described in this book is the coincidence that is found between the theoretically derived Lanchester equations and the empirically derived Quantified Judgment Model.

The QJM clearly fits the definition of a theory of combat, and it is fully consistent with a responsible statement of the process of theory development.

Implications

Does this then mean that there is no need to search further for a theory of combat? Can The Military Conflict Institute gracefully declare its job done and disband?

Of course not!

Even if the derived formula for the QJM theory of combat is as useful as Einstein's $E = MC^2$, this is no more the end of scientific military research than the work of Newton or of Einstein was the end of research in astronomy and physics. As strongly as I believe that the QJM version of the Clausewitz formula is definitive for the year 1987, it is not necessarily either the only way, or even the best way, to understand or represent combat. Nor is the QJM version necessarily the only way that the basic Clausewitz formula can be elaborated into a more comprehensive and modern theory.

All that I say, and what I believe, is that the concept of the QJM is virtually identical with *a* theory of combat, described by Clausewitz. It may not be *the* theory of combat, which I am sure cannot be found any more readily than the Holy Grail. But it is a step forward in the search for that theory. The quest must and shall continue, and I trust that, as Clausewitz's disciple, I have helped point the way.

Notes

Introduction

1. As quoted in *U.S. Naval Academy Catalog*, 1984–1985 (Annapolis, MD, 1984).
2. Napoleon, "Military Maxims of Napoleon," (78), in *Roots of Strategy*, ed. Thomas R. Phillips (Harrisburg PA: Military Service Publishing Co., 1941), 432.
3. J.F.C. Fuller, *British Light Infantry in the Eighteenth Century* (London: Hutchinson, 1925), 242.
4. J.F.C. Fuller, *Sir John Moore's Systems of Training* (London: Hutchinson, 1925) 222–223.
5. J.F.C. Fuller attributed the Waterloo victory to the Wellington-Blucher 3–2 numerical superiority over Napolean. The numbers were 129,000 allies to 72,000 French; thus the ratio was really about 9–5.

Chapter 2

1. Important among the military members of this illustrious group were Karl von Grolmann and Hermann von Boyen. In some ways Prime Minister Baron Karl vom und zum Stein could be considered a member of this group.
2. See, for instance, *Makers of Modern Strategy*, ed. Edward Meade Earle, Princeton: 1943. Earle and his collaborators had a slightly different focus and objective in selecting their protagonists. They include eight of the twelve names on my list.

3. Possibly the best discussion of Mahan is to be found in R. E. Dupuy, *Where They Have Trod*, (New York: Stokes, 1940).
4. See T. N. Dupuy, *A Genius for War: The German Army and General Staff, 1807–1945*, (Fairfax, VA: HERO Books, 1984) passim, particularly Chapter 7.
5. See Gerhardt Ritter, *The Schlieffen Plan*. See also my discussion of this book, its foreword, and its prejudices, in T. N. Dupuy, *A Genius for War*, op. cit., 140–144. Perhaps the best known work in German was by a worthy successor, Wilhelm Groener, *Das Testament des Grafen Schlieffen* (The Legacy of Count Schlieffen) (Berlin: 1927).
6. The standard work on Fuller and his writings is Anthony John Trythall, *"Boney" Fuller, the Intellectual General* (London: Cassell, 1977).
7. Trythall, op. cit., 31
8. Ibid., 38.
9. Ibid., 209–210.
10. J.F.C. Fuller, "The Principles of War with Reference to the Campaigns of 1914–1915," *Royal United Services Institution Journal* Vol. LXI: 1.
11. The article is reprinted in its entirety in *History, Numbers and War*, I (3), (Fall 1977): 142.
12. See T. N. Dupuy, "History and the Validity of the Lanchester Hypotheses," *History, Numbers, and War*, I (3) (Fall 1977): 146–150.
13. Ibid. Also see T. N. Dupuy, *Numbers, Predictions, and War* (Fairfax, VA: HERO Books, 1985), 148–149.

Chapter 3

1. Trythall, op. cit., 251. This was the comment of a mature Fuller, after he had studied and written about military theory for many years. In his earlier years he had not understood Clausewitz and had been critical of him.
2. *Jomini, Clausewitz and Schlieffen* (West Point, NY: USMA, 1951), 37.
3. See chapter 4; the letter from Lincoln to Hallek.
4. Carl von Clausewitz, *On War*, Book One, Chapter 7, 119–120. Edited and translated by Michael Howard and Peter Paret (Princeton, NJ: Princeton University Press, 1984).
5. Carl von Clausewitz, *On War*, Book Three, Chapter 8, 194–195.

Chapter 4

1. See T. N. Dupuy, *The Military Life of Abraham Lincoln* (New York: Franklin Watts, 1969).

2. See T. N. Dupuy and Arnold C. Dupuy, "Understanding War From a Historical Perspective," *Marine Corps Gazette* (June 1985), 53.

Chapter 5

1. Grigorenko was later the most senior Soviet military man to defect to the West.
2. Emphasis added.
3. Some of the thoughts expressed in this section have been adapted with permission from an article by Maj. Gen. Edward Atkeson, USA, Retired, "In Pursuit of the Essence of War," *Army* (January 1984), 18.
4. Adapted from an article by V.I. Belyakov in the *Soviet Military Encyclopedia* (1979).

Chapter 6

1. T.N. Dupuy, *Numbers, Predictions, and War* (Fairfax, VA: HERO Books, 1985).

Chapter 7

1. These definitions are based upon results of discussions in The Military Conflict Institute, and upon T. N. Dupuy, Curtiss C. Johnson and Grace P. Hayes, *Dictionary of Military Terms* (New York: H. W. Wilson, 1986).
2. Clausewitz, Carl von, *On War*. Translated by Howard and Paret. (Princeton, 1976), 128.
3. Jomini, Baron Antoine, *Tableau Analytique des Principales Combinaisions de la Guerre*, Paris, 1830, 58–60.
4. Herman Foertsch, *The Art of Modern Warfare*, (New York: Veritas Press, 1940), 20.
5. For a more detailed rendition, see R. E. Dupuy and T. N. Dupuy, *The Encyclopedia of Military History*, (revised edition New York: Harper and Row, 1986), 1203.
6. An important new book on naval tactics should, however, be noted: Wayne Hughes, *Fleet Tactics: Theory and Practice* (Annapolis, MD: Naval Institute Press, 1986).

Chapter 8

1. By this author in 1956, as part of a study for the US Army: *Historical Trends Related to Weapons Lethality* (McLean, VA: 1966).
2. Readers interested in obtaining more detailed information about the QJM and its Factor Values should consult *Numbers, Predictions, and*

War (Fairfax, VA: HERO Books, 1985). It should be noted, however, that the application of the Result Value (R) as described in that earlier book has been modified by the procedure discussed in Chapter 8 of this book.

Chapter 9

1. T.N. Dupuy, *Options of Command* (New York: Hippocrene Press, 1984). This chapter is adapted from the Appendix to that book.

Chapter 10

1. Dupuy, *A Genius for War: The German Army and General Staff, 1807–1945* (Fairfax, VA: HERO Books, 1984).
2. As an old 1st (Infantry) Division man, I must emphasize that the 1st Division was not in the data base.

Chapter 11

1. Brian Holden Reid, "Colonel J.F.C. Fuller and the Revival of Classical Military Thinking in Britain, 1918–1926," *Military Affairs* (October 1985), 192.

Chapter 12

1. See for instance, HERO Study no. 36, "Opposed Rates of Advance of Large Forces in Europe" (ORALFORE), 1972.

Chapter 13

1. A more detailed treatment is in the HERO Report: *Handbook on Ground Forces Attrition in Modern Warfare,* January 1986.

Chapter 14

1. Clausewitz, op. cit. 119–120.
2. Current US Army doctrine does not envisage the use of field armies, and corps will be the main elements of army groups.
3. Theodore Ayrault Dodge, *Alexander,* (Boston, 1890), Appendix B, 680. He expanded on this in later works.
4. T. L. Livermore, *Numbers and Losses in the Civil War* (Bloomington, IN, 1957).
5. HERO Report no. 97, *Historical Survey of Casualties in Different Sized Units in Modern Combat,* prepared for the US Army TRADOC Systems Analysis Activity (TRASANA), 1982.

Chapter 15

1. Since these words were written, but before publication, the results of a significant (possibly monumental) study have been published in the June 1986 issue of *The Journal of the Royal United Services Institution:* "Assessments of Combat Degradation," by David Rowland of the British Defence Operational Analysis Establishment (DOAE). The DOAE study was based upon a comparison of historical experience and field test experience. It determined that the effectiveness of small arms in inflicting casualties in real combat is degraded by a factor of from 7.0 to 10.0 from the casualty-inflicting rates to be found in modern British field tests. This degradation, by an order of magnitude, is a dramatic corroboration of the casualty rate patterns in historical combat which my colleagues and I have determined from examining a very large body of other historical experience.
2. T. N. Dupuy, *The Evolution of Weapons and Warfare,* (Fairfax, VA: HERO Books, 1984).
3. See T. N. Dupuy, *A Genius for War; The German Army and General Staff, 1807–1943* (Fairfax, VA: 2d edition: HERO Books, 1984).
4. T. N. Dupuy, *Elusive Victory, the Arab-Israeli War, 1947–1974* (Fairfax, VA: HERO Books, 1984).
5. Conversation with General George S. Blanchard, USA, Retired.
6. Conversation with Maj. Gen. David Ivry, Israeli Air Force, Retired.
7. See *Evolution of Weapons and Warfare,* op. cit., 341.
8. *Ibid.*, pp. 337–343.

Chapter 16

1. The one effort that claims success, for the Battle of Iwo Jima, has been criticized as imperfectly describing the historical data.
2. F. W. Lanchester, "The Principle of Concentration," *Engineering,* October 2, 1914, as reproduced in *History, Numbers and War,* Fall 1977, p. 142.
3. See T. N. Dupuy, *Numbers, Predictions and War* (Fairfax, VA: HERO Books, 1985), 148–150.
4. Ibid. also HERO, *Effects of Combat Losses and Fatigue on Operational Performance* (Virginia: Dunn Loring, 1978), and HERO, *The Impact of Nuclear Weapons Employment on the Factors of Combat* (Dunn Loring, VA, 1981), etc.
5. I am indebted to Dr. Janice B. Fain, Dr. Joseph Fearey, Capt. Wayne Hughes, (USN, Ret), and Brig. Gen. Dr. Adrian Freiherr von Oer (West German Army) for having assisted me in presenting the mathematical relationships shown in equations (3) and (4), and for properly including these relationships in equations (5) and (6).

6. Williams, Louis (ed), *Military Aspects of the Israeli-Arab Conflict,* University Publishing Projects (Tel Aviv, 1975), 27.

Chapter 17

1. See, for instance, Martin van Creveld, "The War; A Questioning Look," *Jerusalem Post,* 12–18 December 1982; also, Richard A. Gabriel, *Operation Peace for Galilee; The Israeli-PLO War in Lebanon* (New York:, 1984), 193–194 and passim; also Carlton Sherwood "Israeli 'Ineptitude' blamed for 'friendly fire' casualties," *Washington Times,* 27 August 1984.
2. T. N. Dupuy, *Elusive Victory, the Arab-Israeli Wars, 1947–1974* (Fairfax, VA: HERO Books, 1984), Appendices A, B.
3. See, for instance, T. N. Dupuy, *Numbers,* op. cit., 133–137 and T. N. Dupuy, *Elusive Victory,* op. cit., Appendices A, B.

Chapter 18

1. Number 2 Operational Research Section Report (Army Council), *Operational Research in NW Europe,* (London: ca. 1946), 185.
2. I had been involved in about 18 months of continuous combat against the Japanese in Burma in 1943–1945.

Chapter 19

1. Op. cit., passim.

Chapter 20

1. Amanuensis: One who copies or records what another has written.

Appendix A

Summary of Data for 93 World War II Engagements:
Combat Power and Result Ratios*

Selected World War II Battles
Allies (f) vs. Germans (e)
Attackers (a) vs. Defenders (d)

	A	**D**	**P_f/P_e**	**R_f/R_e**	**P_a/P_d**	**R_a/R_d**
1. Port of Salerno	Br	G	1.09	.98	1.09	.98
2. Amphitheater	Br	G	1.22	.64	1.22	.64
3. Sele Calore Corridor	US	G	1.29	.86	1.29	.86
4. Vietri I	G	Br	1.90	1.48	.59	.67
5. Battipaglia I	G	Br	4.50	1.57	.22	.64
6. Tobacco Factory	G	US	2.64	1.40	.38	.71
7. Vietri II	G	Br	2.49	1.65	.40	.61
8. Battipaglia II	Br	G	1.23	1.30	1.23	1.30
9. Eboli	US	G	1.08	1.01	1.08	1.01
10. Grazzanise	Br	G	1.74	1.08	1.74	1.08
11. Capua	Br	G	.83	.40	.83	.40
12. Triflisco	US	G	1.44	1.26	1.44	1.26
13. Monte Acero	US	G	1.34	1.17	1.34	1.17
14. Carazzo	US	G	1.33	1.07	1.33	1.07
15. Castel Volturno	Br	G	1.09	.80	1.09	.80
16. Dragoni	US	G	1.12	1.24	1.12	1.24
17. Canal I	Br	G	1.05	1.11	1.05	1.11

*P/P is the ratio of combat POWER
R/R is the ratio of relative performance in battle RESULTS

	A	D	P_f/P_e	R_f/R_e	P_a/P_d	R_a/R_d
18. Monte Grande I	Br	G	.63	.65	.63	.65
19. Canal II	Br	G	1.48	1.01	1.48	1.01
20. Francolise	Br	G	1.26	.71	1.26	.71
21. Santa Maria Oliveto	US	G	1.21	1.16	1.21	1.16
22. Monte Camino I	Br	G	.59	.51	.59	.51
23. Monte Lungo	US	G	.49	.83	.49	.83
24. Pozzilli	US	G	.37	.52	.37	.52
25. Monte Camino II	G	Br	4.69	.50	.29	2.00
26. Monte Rotundo	US	G	.52	.63	.52	.63
27. Calabritto	Br	G	.70	.80	.70	.80
28. Monte Camino III	Br	G	.72	.79	.72	.79
29. Monte Maggiore	US	G	1.70	1.59	1.70	1.59
30. Aprilia I	Br	G	1.35	1.14	1.35	1.14
31. The Factory	G	Br	2.60	1.60	.39	.64
32. Campoleone I	Br	G	.58	.84	.58	.84
33. Campoleone C. Attack	G	Br	1.00	.98	1.00	1.02
34. Carroceto	G	Br	3.10	1.01	.32	.99
35. Moletta River Defense	G	Br	5.11	1.51	.20	.66
36. Aprilia II	G	Br	2.02	.67	.49	1.50
37. Factory C. Attack	US	G	.44	.65	.44	.65
38. Bowling Alley	G	US	1.46	1.54	.69	.65
39. Moletta River II	G	US	4.81	1.02	.21	.98
40. Fioccia	G	US	4.59	1.65	.22	.61
41. Santa Maria Infante	US	G	1.80	2.30	1.80	2.30
42. San Martino	US	G	2.75	1.30	2.75	1.30
43. Spigno	US	G	2.29	2.23	2.29	2.23
44. Castellonorato	US	G	2.15	1.51	2.15	1.51
45. Formia	US	G	5.52	2.09	5.52	2.09
46. Monte Grande II	US	G	3.85	2.21	3.85	2.21
47. Itri-Fondi	US	G	2.89	2.05	2.89	2.05
48. Terracina	US	G	4.24	1.89	4.24	1.89
49. Moletta Offensive	Br	G	1.38	.96	1.38	.96
50. Anzio-Albano Road	Br	G	1.00	1.05	1.00	1.05
51. Anzio Breakout	US	G	3.75	2.33	3.75	2.33
52. Cisterna	US	G	2.81	2.35	2.81	2.35
53. Sezze	US	G	1.77	2.05	1.77	2.05
54. Velletri	US	G	1.72	.99	1.72	.99
55. Campoleone Station	US	G	1.21	1.23	1.21	1.23
56. Villa Crocetta	US	G	.47	.64	.47	.64
57. Ardea	Br	G	2.46	1.46	2.46	1.46
58. Lanuvio	US	G	.75	.65	.75	.65
59. Campoleone II	US	G	.89	.77	.89	.77

	A	D	P_f/P_e	R_f/R_e	P_a/P_d	R_a/R_d
*60. Lariano	US	G	3.70	2.20	3.70	2.20
*61. Valmontone	US	G	2.93	1.86	2.93	1.86
*62. Via Anzate	US	G	.78	.72	.78	.72
63. Tarto-Tiber	Br	G	2.80	1.22	2.80	1.22
*64. Il Giogio Pass	US	G	2.61	1.41	2.61	1.41
*65. Sedan (1940)	G	Fr	.73	.37	1.36	2.70
66. Cobra	US	G	3.09	1.23	3.09	1.23
67. Chartres	US	G	7.53	2.49	7.53	2.49'
68. Seine River	US	G	4.50	2.79	4.50	2.79
69. Melun	US	G	7.54	2.90	7.54	2.90
70. Moselle-Metz	US	G	2.85	1.35	2.85	1.35
71. Metz	US	G	.91	.52	.91	.52
72. Westwall	US	G	1.32	1.39	1.32	1.39
73. Seille-Nied	US	G	4.16	1.42	4.16	1.42
*74. Fresnes-Salins	US	G	2.27	1.98	2.27	1.98
*75. Delme Ridge	US	G	2.14	1.58	2.14	1.58
76. Foret de Chateau Salins	US	G	1.54	1.09	1.54	1.09
*77. Luppy	US	G	2.66	1.69	2.66	1.69
*78. Conthill-Guebling	US	G	1.57	1.09	1.57	1.09
79. Morhange-Falquemont	US	G	3.55	1.39	3.55	1.39
80. Morhange	US	G	1.87	.86	1.87	.86
81. Bourgaltroff I	US	G	1.47	1.09	1.47	1.09
*82. Bourgaltroff II	US	G	2.66	1.96	2.66	1.96
*83. Bistroff-Puttelange	US	G	2.28	1.79	2.28	1.79
84. Sarre-St. Avold	US	G	3.16	1.43	3.16	1.43
*85. Fenetrange-Houskirch	US	G	.98	1.65	.98	1.65
86. Baerendorf I	US	G	1.78	1.59	1.78	1.59
*87. Altwiller	US	G	1.48	1.42	1.48	1.42
88. Baerendorf II	US	G	2.66	2.12	2.66	2.12
89. Burbach-Durstel	US	G	1.50	1.32	1.50	1.32
90. Durstel-Farebersvilles	US	G	2.24	.83	2.24	.83
91. Sarre Union	US	G	3.01	1.21	3.01	1.21
92. Singling-Bining	US	G	1.47	1.02	1.47	1.02
93. Sarre-Singling	US	G	2.80	1.30	2.80	1.30
94. Ardennes-Sauer	G	US	1.25	.74	.80	1.35

* Not included in 81 engagements list, Chapter 10; No. 77 omitted in calculations in Chapter 11.

Appendix B

Summary of Data for 52 Engagements, 1967 and 1973 Arab-Israeli Wars: Combat Power and Result Ratios*

Engagements in 1967 and 1973 Arab-Israeli Wars
Israelis (i) vs. Arabs (ar)
Attackers (a) vs. Defenders (d)

	A	D	P_i/P_{ar}	R_i/R_{ar}	P_a/P_d	R_a/R_d
99. Rafah	Is	Eg	2.80	3.26	2.80	3.26
100. Abu Ageila-Um Kateb	Is	Eg	1.29	2.81	1.29	2.81
101. Gaza Strip	Is	PLA	1.29	3.38	1.29	3.38
102. El Arish	Is	Eg	1.86	2.73	1.86	2.73
103. Bir Lahfan	Is	Eg	2.85	3.89	2.85	3.89
104. Jebel Libni	Is	Eg	2.60	3.08	2.60	3.08
105. Mitla Pass	Eg	Is	2.01	2.63	.50	.38
106. Bir Hama-Bir Gifgafa	Is	Eg	1.48	2.93	1.48	2.93
107. Bir Hassna-Bir Thamada	Is	Eg	2.26	2.98	2.26	2.98
108. Bir Gifgafa	Eg	Is	1.97	3.03	.51	.33
109. Nakhl	Is	Eg	1.43	3.42	1.43	3.42
110. Jerusalem	Is	Jor	1.61	2.13	1.61	2.13
111. Jenin	Is	Jor	2.85	2.28	2.85	2.28
112. Kabatiya	Is	Jor	1.30	1.89	1.30	1.89
113. Tilfit-Zababida	Is	Jor	1.64	2.48	1.64	2.48
114. Nablus	Is	Jor	2.14	2.64	2.14	2.64
115. Tel Faher	Is	Syr	.40	3.06	.40	3.06

*P/P is the ratio of combat POWER
R/R is the ratio of relative performance in battle RESULTS

	A	D	P_i/P_{ar}	R_i/R_{ar}	P_a/P_d	R_a/R_d
116. Zaoura-Kala	Is	Syr	.88	2.81	.88	2.81
117. Rawiyeh	Is	Syr	.50	3.13	.50	3.13
118. Suez Canal Assault N.	Eg	Is	.26	.46	3.81	2.22
119. Suez Canal Assault S.	Eg	Is	.33	.54	3.07	1.85
120. 2nd Army Buildup	Eg	Is	.29	.59	3.51	1.70
121. 3rd Army Buildup	Eg	Is	.23	.58	4.38	1.71
122. Kantara-Firdan	Is	Eg	.25	.55	.25	.55
123. Egyptian Offensive N.	Eg	Is	1.49	2.64	.67	.38
124. Egyptian Offensive S.	Eg	Is	1.13	2.49	.89	.40
125. Deversoir, Chinese F. I	Is	Eg	.66	2.09	.66	2.09
126. Chinese Farm II	Is	Eg	1.26	2.10	1.26	2.10
127. Deversoir West	Is	Eg	1.14	2.49	1.14	2.49
128. Ismailia	Is	Eg	.77	1.75	.77	1.75
129. Shallufa I	Is	Eg	.75	2.40	.75	2.40
130. Jebel Geneifa	Is	Eg	.86	2.87	.86	2.87
131. Adabiya	Is	Eg	1.89	3.70	1.89	3.70
132. Suez	Is	Eg	.33	.89	.33	.89
133. Shallufa II	Is	Eg	.75	2.99	.75	2.99
134. Ahmadiyeh	Syr	Is	.66	1.88	1.61	.53
135. Kuneitra	Syr	Is	.56	.83	1.78	1.21
136. Rafid	Syr	Is	.49	.44	2.06	2.25
137. Yehuda-El Al	Syr	Is	1.03	2.17	.97	.46
138. Nafekh	Syr	Is	.54	2.20	1.77	.46
139. Mt. Hermonit	Syr	Is	.77	1.89	1.30	.53
140. Mt. Hermon I	Syr	Is	.13	.61	.13	.61
141. Hushniyah	Is	Syr	.89	2.19	.89	2.19
142. Tel Faris	Is	Syr	.43	2.20	.43	2.20
143. Tel Shams	Is	Syr	.27	2.12	.27	2.12
144. Tel Shaar	Is	Syr	.45	2.22	.45	2.22
145. Tel el Hara	Ir	Is	2.84	3.42	.35	.29
146. Kfar Shams-Tel Antar	Is	Ir	.43	2.73	.43	2.73
147. Naba	Jor	Is	2.56	2.75	.39	.36
148. Arab Counteroffensive	Ir/ Syr/Jor	Is	1.28	2.55	.77	.39
149. Mt. Hermon II	Is	Jor	.13	.75	.13	.75
150. Mt. Hermon III	Is	Syr	.26	2.65	.26	2.65

Bibliography

Ardant du Picq, Charles J. J. J. *Battle Studies*. New York, 1921.

Aron, Raymond. *Clausewitz, Philosopher of War*. Translated by Christine Booker and Norman Stone. Englewood Cliffs, N. J., 1985.

Atkeson, Edward B. "In Pursuit of the Essence of War." *Army* (January 1984).

Bodart, Gaston. *Militaer-historisches Kriegs-Lexicon (1618–1905)*. Vienna, 1908.

British Ministry of Defence, Number 2 Operational Research Section Report (Army Council). *Operational Research in Northwest Europe*. London, c. 1946.

Brodie, Bernard. *Seapower in the Machine Age*. Princeton, 1943.

_____. *Strategy in the Missile Age*. Princeton, 1959

Chandler, David. *The Campaigns of Napoleon*. New York, 1966.

Churchill, Winston S. *The World Crisis*. 6 vols. New York, 1931.

_____. *The Second World War*. 6 vols. Boston, 1948–1953.

Clausewitz, Carl Von. *Principles of War*. Translated by Hans W. Gatzke. Harrisburg, PA., 1942.

_____. *On War*. Edited and translated by Michael Howard and Peter Paret. Princeton, 1984.

Creasy, Edward S. *The Fifteen Decisive Battles of the World*. London, 1851 (1949 edition).

Delbruck, Hans. *History of the Art of War within the Framework of Political History*. 3 vols. Translated by Walter Renfroe. Westport, CT., 1975–1985.

Department of Military Art and Engineering, USMA. *Jomini, Clausewitz, and Schlieffen*. West Point, N. Y., 1951.

Dodge, Theodore Ayrault. *Great Captains*. Boston, 1889.

————. *Alexander*. Boston, 1890.

————. *Napoleon*. 4 vols. Boston, 1907.

Douhet, Giulio. *The Command of the Air*. Translated by Dino Ferrari. New York, 1942.

Dupuy, R. Ernest. *Where They Have Trod*. New York, 1940.

————. *Compact History of World War II*. New York, 1969.

————, and Trevor N. Dupuy. *The Encyclopedia of Military History*. New York, 1956. Revised edition, New York, 1986.

————, ————. *Military Heritage of America*. New York, 1956. Revised edition, Fairfax, VA., 1984.

————, ————. *Compact History of the Civil War*. New York, 1960.

————, and George Fielding Eliot. *If War Comes*. New York, 1937.

Dupuy, Trevor N. *The Military Life of Abraham Lincoln*. New York, 1969.

————. *A Genius for War: The German Army and General Staff, 1807–1945*. New York, 1977.

————. "History and the Validity of the Lanchester Hypotheses." *History, Numbers and War* (Fall 1977), p. 146.

————. *Elusive Victory: The Arab-Israeli Wars, 1947–1974*. New York, 1978.

————. *The Evolution of Weapons and Warfare*. Revised edition, Fairfax, VA., 1984.

————. *Numbers, Predictions and War*. Revised edition, Fairfax, VA., 1984.

————. *Options of Command*. New York, 1984.

————, and Arnold C. Dupuy. "Understanding War from a Historical Perspective." *Marine Corps Gazette* (June 1985), p. 53.

_____, Curtiss C. Johnson, and Grace P. Hayes. *Dictionary of Military Terms.* New York, 1986.

_____, and Paul Martell. *Flawed Victory.* Fairfax, VA., 1986.

_____, et al. *Historical Trends Related to Weapon Lethality.* McLean, VA., 1966.

_____, et al. *Strategic Concepts, and the Changing Nature of Modern War.* Dunn Loring, VA., 1969.

_____, et al. *Opposed Rates of Advance of Large Forces in Europe.* Dunn Loring, VA., 1972.

_____, et al. *Effects of Combat Losses and Fatigue on Operational Performance.* Dunn Loring, VA., 1978.

Earle, Edward Mead (ed.). *Makers of Modern Strategy.* Princeton, 1943. (See also Peter Paret.)

Foch, Ferdinand. *The Principles of War.* Translated by Hilaire Belloc. New York, 1920.

Foertsch, Hermann. *The Art of Modern Warfare.* Translated by Theodore W. Knauth. New York, 1940.

Fuller, John Frederick Charles. "The Principles of War with Reference to the Campaigns of 1914–1915." *Royal United Services Instutition Journal,* vol LXI (February 1916), p. 1.

_____. *The Reformation of War.* London, 1923.

_____. *British Light Infantry in the Eighteenth Century.* London, 1925.

_____. *Sir John Moore's System of Training.* London, 1925.

_____. *The Foundations of the Science of War.* London, 1926.

_____. *Grant and Lee.* London, 1933.

_____. *The Army in my Time.* London, 1935.

_____. *Machine Warfare.* Washington, 1943.

_____. *Armament and History.* New York, 1945.

_____. *The Second World War.* New York, 1949.

_____. *A Military History of the Western World.* 3 vols. New York, 1954.

_____. *The Conduct of War, 1789–1961.* New Brunswick, 1961.

Gabriel, Richard A. *Operation Peace for Galilee: The Israeli-PLO War in Lebanon.* New York, 1984.

Goltz, Colmar von der. *The Nation in Arms*. Translated by Philip A. Ashworth. London, 1887.

_____. *The Conduct of War*. Translated by G. F. Leverson. London, 1908.

Grant, Ulysses S. *Personal Memoirs*. New York, 1894.

Grigorenko, P. G. *Methodology of Military Scientific Investigation*. Moscow, 1959.

Groener, Wilhelm. *Das Testiment des Grafen Schlieffen*. Berlin, 1927.

Hammerman, Gay M. *Analytic Research on Strategic, Tactical, and Doctrinal Military Concepts*. 2 vols. Dunn Loring, VA., 1979–1980.

HERO Report. *The Impact of Nuclear Weapons Employment on the Factors of Combat*. Dunn Loring, VA., 1981.

_____. *Historical Survey of Casualties in Different Sized Units in Modern Combat*. Dunn Loring, VA., 1982.

_____. *Ground Forces Attrition in Modern War*. Fairflex, VA., 1986.

Hughes, Wayne. *Fleet Tactics: Theory and Practice*. Annapolis, MD., 1986.

Jomini, Antoine Henri. *Traité des Grandes Operations Militaires*. 4 vols. Paris 1818 (edition c. 1852).

_____. *Tableau Analytique des Principales Combinaisons de la Guerre*. Paris, 1830.

Kahn, Herman. *On Thermonuclear War*. Princeton, 1960.

Kissinger, Henry. *Nuclear Weapons and Foreign Policy*. New York, 1957.

_____. *Problems of National Strategy*. New York, 1965.

Kulikov, V. "Contemporary Problems of Military History." *Military History Journal* (Moscow, December 1976).

Lanchester, Frederick W. "The Principle of Concentration." *Engineering* (October 2, 1914).

_____. *Aircraft in Warfare: The Dawn of the Fourth Arm*. New York, 1916.

Landersman, Stuart. *Principles of Naval Warfare*. Unpublished manuscript. Naval Postgraduate School, Monterey, CA., 15 July, 1982.

Leeb, Wilhelm von. *Defense*. Translated by Stefan Possony and David Vilfroy. Harrisburg, PA., 1943.

Liddell Hart, Basil. *Great Captains Unveiled*. Edinburgh, 1927.

————. *The Decisive Wars of History*. London, 1929.

————. *The Defence of Britain*. London, 1939.

————. *Strategy: The Indirect Approach*. New York, 1954.

————. *The Liddell Hart Memoirs*. 2 vols. New York, 1966.

Livermore, Thomas L. *Numbers and Losses in the Civil War*. Bloomington, IN., 1957.

Ludendorff, Erich. *The General Staff and its Problems*. Translated by F. A. Holt. New York, c. 1921.

Mahan, Alfred Thayer. *The Influence of Sea Power on History, 1660–1783*. Boston, 1884.

Mahan, Denis Hart. *Advanced Guard, Outpost and Detachment Service of Troops*. New York, 1847.

Marshall, Samuel L. A. *Men Against Fire*. Washington, 1947.

————. *The River and the Gauntlet*. New York, 1953.

————. "The Shock Impact of Combined Armed Forces in World War II Amphibious Operations." *History, Numbers, and War* (Spring 1978).

Moltke, Helmuth K. B. von. *Strategy: Its Theory and Application: The Wars for German Unification, 1866–1971*. Translated by the British War Office. London, 1907.

Osgood, Robert. *Limited War*. Chicago, 1957.

Palmer, John McC. *Washington, Lincoln, Wilson*. New York, 1930.

Paret, Peter (ed.). *Makers of Modern Strategy*. Princeton, 1986. (See also Edward Mead Earle.)

Phillips, Thomas R. (ed.) *Roots of Strategy*. Harrisburg, PA., 1941.

Potter, E. B., and Chester W. Nimitz. *Seapower*. New York, 1960.

Reid, Brian Holden. "Colonel J. F. C. Fuller and the Revival of Classical Military Thinking in Britain, 1918–1928." *Military Affairs*. (Oct. 1985), p. 192.

Richardson, Lewis F. *Statistics of Deadly Quarrels*. Pittsburgh, 1960.

Ritter, Gerhardt. *The Schlieffen Plan*. New York, 1958.

Ropp, Theodore. *War in the Modern World*. Durham, N.C., 1959.

Rosinski, Herbert. *The German Army*. Washington, 1944.

Rowland, David. "Assessments of Combat Degradation." *Royal United Services Institution Journal* (June, 1986).

Schlieffen, Alfred von. *Cannae.* Translator unidentified. Fort Leavenworth, KS., 1931.

Senger und Etterlin, Fridolin von. *Neither Fear nor Hope.* New York, 1963.

Sherwood, Carlton. "Israeli 'Ineptitude' Blamed for Friendly Fire Casualties." *Washington Times* (27 August 1984).

Singer, J. David. (ed.) *The Correlates of War: I.* New York, 1979.

_____, and Melvin Small. *The Wages of War, 1816–1965.* New York, 1972.

Slessor, John. *Air Power and Armies.* London, 1936.
_____. *Strategy for the West.* New York, 1954.

Slim, William. *Defeat Into Victory.* London, 1956.

Spaulding, Oliver L., et al. *Warfare: A Study of Military Methods from the Earliest Times.* Washington, D.C., 1937.

Sun Tze. *The Art of War.* Translated by Samuel B. Griffith. Oxford, 1963.

Trythall, Anthony J. *"Boney" Fuller, The Intellectual General.* London, 1977.

Turner, Gordon B. *A History of Military Affairs in Western Society Since the Eighteenth Century.* New York, 1953.

Upton, Emory. *Military Policy of the United States.* Washington, 1904.

U.S. Army. *FM 100–1; The Army.* Washington, D.C., 1981.

_____. *FM 100–5; Operations.* Washington, D.C., 1986.

Van Creveld, Martin. *Supplying War.* Cambridge, 1977.

_____. "The War: A Questioning Look." *Jerusalem Post* (12–18 December 1982).

Wavell, Archibald. *Allenby: A Study in Greatness.* London, 1940.

Weiss, Herbert K. "The Principles of War and Military Invariants." Unpublished ms., 1964

Wilkinson, Spenser. *The Brain of an Army.* London, 1889.

Williams, Louis (ed.). *Military Aspects of the Israeli-Arab Conflict.* Tel Aviv, 1975.

Wohlstetter, Albert. "The Delicate Balance of Terror." *Foreign Affairs* (January 1958). (See also Kissinger, *Problems* . . .).

Wright, Quincy. *A Study of War.* 2 vols. Chicago, 1942.

Wyeth, John A. *That Devil Forrest.* New York, 1959.

Yorck von Wartenburg, Maximilian. *Napoleon as a General.* Translated by Walter H. James. London, 1897.

Index

advance rates, in combat, 149–64
  "all-out" effort, effect on, 161
  bad weather, effect on, 162
  combat power superiority, need for, 158
  day/night, effect on, 162
  fatigue factor and, 161
  force ratios versus, 154–55
  fortifications of defenders, effect on, 160
  historical, 150–53
  inadequate supply, effect on, 162
  interactions with friendly and enemy missions, effect on, 163
  methodology, need for, 156–57
  quantified judgment model, 164
  rivers and canals, effect on, 161
  road quality and density, effect on, 162
  small forces versus larger, 160
  superior relative combat effectiveness increases, 161
  surprise, effect on, 160
  technology, effect on, 158
  terrain, effect on, 161
air warfare, Guilio Douhet on, 15–16
Alamo, 2
Alexander the Great, 4, 214
  Battle of Arbela, 160
  compared to Napoleon, 10
Antietam, Battle of (1862), 25, 267
  force multipliers, 268
Arab-Israeli wars (1967, 1973), 121–23
  Chinese Farm, battle of the, 272
  combat effectiveness, 121–23
  combat effectiveness values, 224
  diminishing returns in, 133–39
  personnel strengths, 122, 224
  selected tank operations, 173
  Suez Canal, battle of the (1973), 272

Arbela, Battle of, 160
Ardant du Picq, Charles, *Battle Studies,* 14
Ardennes (France, 1944), 99, 100, 102
  casualties, 227
  combat effectiveness, 227
  lethality, 230
Art of War, The (Sun Tze), 9
attack
  flank, 3
  rear, 3
attrition, in combat, 19, 165–82
  artillery material loss rates versus personnel casualty rates, 179
  assessment in models of combat, 19, 20
  attacker's versus defender's, 174, 175
  average casualty rates (1600–1973), 168
  average casualty rates, WW II division engagement, 179
  casualty rates of winners versus losers, 3
  day/night, effect on, 177, 182
  effective forces', 175
  factors considered, 174–81
  fatigue, effect on, 177, 182
  force ratios and, 176
  historical trends, 166–74
  Lanchester equations, in calculations of, 221–22
  October war (1973), 179
  quantified judgment model, calculation of, 181–82
  river crossings and, 178
  season, effect on, 177, 182
  shoreline, effect on, 182
  small forces higher than large forces, 175
  surprise, effect on, 176, 182

tank loss rates versus personnel casualty rates, 179
  terrain, effect on, 177, 181
  weather, effect on, 177, 182
Austerlitz, Battle of (1805), 267
  force multipliers, 269

Bar Lev Line, 4
battle
  defined, 65
  measures of effectiveness, 88
  result factor (R), 88
  theoretical outcome, 88
  variable factors, 95–96
  See also names of places for specific battles
Battle Studies, by Charles J. Ardant du Picq, 14
behavioral variables, in combat theory, 87
Bekaa Valley battle, 237–50
  advance rates, analysis, 247–48
  force strengths, 242, 243
  Israeli operations against Syrians, 237–42
  losses, 244
  map, 240
  QJM factors, 244
Ben Gal, Avigdor, General, 239
Bonaparte, Napoleon, 4, 214
  compared to predecessors, 10–11
  crossing of the Po, 5
  defeats, 5–6
  Maxims, 10, 11
  victories, 5–6
Borodino, example of Napoleonic victory, 6
breakthrough operations, 260–66
  analysis of, 260–66
  attacker/defender ratios, 261
  force multipliers, effect on, 262–66
Bulge, Battle of the. *See* Ardennes

Caesar, Julius, 8
Cambrai, Battle of, 17
campaign
  defined, 65
  Franklin campaign, 2
Cannae, Battle of, 3
casualty rate
  Bekaa Valley battle, 248–49
  lethality relationship, 225–30
  See also attrition, lethality
chemical and biological weapons, 210
Chinese Farm, Battle of the, 272
  force multipliers, 271
Civil War, American
  Antietam, Battle of, 25, 35
  casualty rates, 167, 169

Franklin campaign, 2
Gettysburg, Battle of, 35, 145
Nashville campaign, 2
President Lincoln's military role, 31–33
Clausewitz, Carl von, 11–13
  chief of staff under Gneisenau, 12
  combat theory, 21–30
  commandant of the War Academy, 11
  compared to Jomini as military theorist, 13
  corps chief of staff, Prussian army, 11
  Fuller on, 21
  interlocking characteristics of war, 22–23
  maxims, 2
  On War, 11–12, 22, 282
  philosophy of war, 23–24
  studies at Prussian War Academy, 11
Clausewitz's law of numbers, 28–30, 81, 89
combat
  advance rates, 149–64
  attrition, 19, 20, 165–82
  Clausewitz's theory, 24–28
  complexity, in evaluation, 7
  conceptual components, 66, 68, 70–71
  defense, stronger form of, 26–27
  defensive posture, necessity for, 2
  defensive strength, advantage of, 2
  defined, 63–64, 79
  depth, need for, 5–6
  destruction of enemy, 25–26
  firepower, impact of, on dispersion, 7
  flank attack, likelihood of success in, 3
  fortification strength, importance of, 4
  friction in, 183–97
  genius in war, 25
  hierarchy, 64–66, 67
  human aspects, 199–200
  human behavior consideration in, 219
  initiative, importance of, 3–4
  offensive action, essentiality of, 1–2
  rear attack versus frontal attack, 3
  reserves, need for, 5–6
  speed and direct approach, 26
  superior combat power, conclusive factor in, 6
  surprise, importance of, 6, 160, 275, 281
  timeless verities, 1–8
  willingness to pay price, 5
combat effectiveness, 87–88
  advance rates, effect on, 161
  battle outcomes and, 222–25
  casualties and, 88, 226, 227
  economy of force and, 125–30
  88th Infantry Division (U.S.), 114–17, 119–21

combat effectiveness (*cont.*)
  historical data, 226–27
  intangible factors, 105
  Israeli-Syrian comparison, 247–50
  lethality relationship, 229, 230
  mission factor, 88
  relative combat effectiveness value
    (CEV), 105–9
  selected divisions in WWII, 115, 116
  spatial, 88
  Tarawa and Iwo Jima, battles of, 255–
    56
combat effectiveness value, 81, 105–23
  Arab-Israeli wars, average for, 281
  chance, effect of, 107
  circumstantial variables in, 105–6
  combat outcome diagram, 107–9, 110–
    111
  defined, 107
  friction, effect of, 107
  World Wars, average for, 281
combat outcome diagram, 107–9
  combat power ratio, 110, 113
  equal effectiveness line, 111
  relative effectiveness line, 128, 129
combat power
  Bekaa Valley battle, 245–46
  superior always wins, 6
  surprise enhances, 6
combat power formula, 81–89
  basic equation of quantified judgment
    model, 81
  Clausewitz's connection, 81
  dispersion factor, 84
  force strength for numbers, 82–86
  operational lethality index, 82–86
  ratio, 281
  substituting combat effectiveness for
    troop quality, 87–89
  weapons effectiveness index (WEI), 82
  weapons performance factors, 85
combat power ratio
  compared with actual outcome ratio, 88
  result ratios and, 293–95 App.
combat theory
  air warfare, applicability to, 78–79
  American approach, 51–61
  application of science to war, 51–52
  behavioral factors, 57
  combat elements, 56
  combat multipliers, transformation to
    real battle planning tool, 58
  combat processes, 56
  development process, 58–61
  diminishing returns in, 125
  elements, 63–79
  force effects variables, 86–87

forces and means, correlation of, 47,
    48–50
  hierarchical relationships of models,
    195–97
  human behavior and battle outcomes,
    58
  mathematical formula, 30
  models and simulations, problems
    with, 52–53
  naval warfare, applicability to, 78–79
  nuclear war and, 74, 76–78
  practical value, 56–58
  quantified judgment model as, 279–86
  scope, 71–74
  Soviet approach, 39–50
  tactical doctrine, contribution to, 57
  three-to-one rule, 34–35
  yardstick for evaluation of military
    judgment, 57
combat variables, 86–87, 106
  behavioral, 87, 106
  environmental, 86, 87, 106
  operational, 86, 87, 106
Command of the Air, by Guilio Douhet, 15–
  16
computers, military uses, 209
concentration, principle of Lanchester's
  ideas on, 18–19
Conduct of War, The, by Colmar von der
  Goltz, 15
congruence, weapons, tactics and doctrine,
  216–18
correlation of forces and means, 281

defensive posture
  depth and reserves, need for, 5–6
  force strength, effect on, 95–97, 100
  offensive action versus, 2
  three-to-one rule, 34–35
deployment
  approximate proportion of personnel in
    front line platoons, 186, 187
  casualty rates versus, 184–89
  front line forces, 185
  unit elements exposed to direct fire,
    186, 187
diminishing returns
  Arab-Israeli wars, as applied in, 133–39
  economy of force and, 126
  friction and challenge, leads to, 146
  quantified judgment model and, 146–
    47
  World War II, as applied in, 130–33
Dispersion factor (DI), 84–85
Douhet, Guilio, 15–16
  theorist on air warfare, 15–16
duel, defined, 66

Eastern Europe
 Kursk (1943), 227, 230
 Ukraine (1941), 227, 230
Eastern Front (1914–1916)
 casualties, 226
 combat effectiveness, 226
 lethality, 230
engagement, defined, 65
environmental variables, in combat theory,
 86, 87

Fain, Janice B., 58, 59
fatigue
 advance rates, effect on, 161
 attrition, effect on, 177, 182
Field Service Regulations (1909), British
 manual on military doctrine, 16, 17
Flanders Campaign (1940), 91–103
 Allied force strength, 93–94
 application of quantified judgment
 model, 91–103
 German force strength, 94–95
 hypothetical comparison, 100–3
 overall comparison, 96, 97–99
 troop quality, 96
 variable factors, 95–96
Foch, Ferdinand, 15
force multipliers, 259–77
 Clausewitz's Law of Numbers, essence
 of, 260
 hypothetical battle with superior Warsaw Pact army, 272–73, 275
 quantified judgment model, effect on,
 266–67
 value on future battlefields, 273
force strength
 Allied composition (1940), 93–94
 analogous to Clausewitz's numbers, 82,
 85, 86
 combat variables, effect on, 86–87
 Flanders campaign (1940), 93–95, 97–
 98
 formula, 85
 German composition (1940), 94–95
 Israeli-Syrian battle, Bekaa Valley, 242,
 243
 overall comparison, Flanders (1940),
 97–98
Forrest, Nathan Bedford, 165
fortification, 4
France
 1870 campaign in, 3
 Flanders campaign (1940), 91–103
Frederick the Great of Prussia, 214
 compared to Napoleon, 10–11
 Instructions to his Generals, 10
Fredericksburg, 2

friction, in combat, 27–28, 183–97
 average casualty rates relative to unit
 strength, 187–88, 194
 casualty rates relative to division rates,
 191–92
 casualty rates versus deployment, 184–
 89
 casualty rates versus force strength,
 193
 Clausewitz's concept, 183–84
 factor values, derivation of, 188, 189
 relationship between casualties, force
 size and fire exposure, 190
Frontinus, Sextus Julius, 9
 On Military Affairs, 9
 Strategems, 9
Fulda, Battle of (hypothetical), force multipliers, 274, 277
Fuller, J. F. C., 14, 21
 first to codify Principles of War, 16–18

Genghis Khan, 8, 214
 compared to Napoleon, 10
genius in war, 25
Gettysburg, Battle of, 25
Golan (1973), 227
Goltz, Colmar von der, Baron, 15
 Conduct of War, The, 15
 Nation in Arms, The, 15
Grant, Ulysses S., 4, 32, 217
gravitational theory, development of, 59–61
Grigorenko, P. G. Methodology of Military
 Scientific Investigation, 42
Gustavus Adolphus, 10, 214

Halleck, Henry W., 32
Hannibal, 8, 10, 214
 Battles of Lake Trasimene and Cannae,
 3
helicopters
 means of mobility, 209
 weapons platforms, 209
Historical Evaluation and Research Organization (HERO), 55

initiative, 3–4
Instructions to his Generals, Frederick the
 Great of Prussia, 10
Italian Campaigns
 Anzio (1944), 226, 230
 Rome (1944), 226, 230
 Salerno (1943), 226, 230
 Volturno (1943), 226, 230
Iwo Jima, Battle of, 255–56

Jena Campaign of 1806, 11

Jomini, Antoine Henry, 12–13
   compared to Clausewitz as military the-
     orist, 13
   Napoleon's army officer, 12
   writings on Napoleon's thinking on
     war, 12

Korean War, attrition rate, 169

Lake Trasimene, Battle of, 3
Lanchester equations, 221–22, 280
Lanchester, Frederick W., 14, 18–20
   linear law, 19, 20
   square law, 19
Lanuvio, Battle of (Italy), 36, 268
   force multipliers, 271
laser, 210
Law of Numbers, 28–30
   equation, restated, 81
   quantified judgment model, elabora-
     tion of, 89
   transformation into combat power for-
     mula, 81
leadership, genius in war, 25
Lebanese conflict (1982)
   attrition rate, 169
   Bekaa Valley operation, 239–42
   Israeli victory over Syrians, 215–6
Lee, Robert E., General, 217
   Battle of Antietam (1862), 267
Leesburg conference (Virginia), on combat
   models, 52–53
Leipzig, 6
Leningrad, 5
lethality
   casualty relationship, 225–30
   combat effectiveness and, 229, 230
   combat formations, effect on, 84
   defined, 225
   methods of comparing, 82
   operational lethality index, 82–86
   theoretical lethality index, 84
Ligny, example of Napoleonic victory, 6
Lincoln, Abraham
   combat effectiveness of confederate
     army, comment on, 25
   as military strategist and theorist, 31–
     33
Linear Law (Lanchester), 19, 20
Lorraine (NW Europe), 226
losses. See attrition
Low, Lawrence, 53

MacArthur, Douglas, 4
Maginot Line, 4, 91, 92
   combat power of French forces, 100
Mahan, Alfred Thayer, 14

   focus on naval warfare and theory, 14–
     15
Mahan, Denis Hart, 14
Mannerheim Line, 4
Marengo, example of Napoleonic victory, 6
Marne, Battle of, 163
Maurice of Saxe, *Reveries on the Art of
   War*, 10
Mauricius' *Strategikon*, 10
Maxims, by Napoleon Bonaparte, 10, 11
McClellan, George B., General, 267
Meggido, Battle of (1918), 150, 153, 160
   casualties, 226
   combat effectiveness, 226
Military Conflict Institute, 53–56
military doctrine, defined, 71
military history
   correlation of forces and means, 47,
     48–50
   eras and innovations in weapons, 200–
     3
   Soviet application of, 46–48
   Soviet use of, 42–43
   Soviet view, 43–46
Military Institutions of the Romans, by
   Flavius Vegetius Renatus, 9
military technology
   ancillary development, 204–7
   interaction with military men, 212
   relative importance of, 213–16
   technological change and world wars,
     207–8
   technological change since 1945, 208–
     11
   weapons development, 200–3
military theory, spectrum of, 76
   See also combat theory
Mitchell, William, 16
Moltke, Helmuth K. B. von, 3
   1870 campaign in France, 3
   eminent military historian and thinker,
     14
Montdidier, Battle of (1918), 268
   force multipliers, 270
Montgomery (Field Marshall), 142

Napoleon Bonaparte. *See* Bonaparte, Napoleon
Napoleonic wars
   average advance rates, 150–51, 152
   casualty rates, 167
Nation in Arms, The, by Colmar von der
   Goltz, 15
neutralization, 252–53
Normandy, 5
nuclear weapons, 208–9

October War (1973)
    casualties, 227
    combat effectiveness, 227
    lethality, 230
    relationship of combat effectiveness
        and battle outcome, example in, 223
offensive action, essentiality of, 1–2
On Military Affairs, by Sextus Julius Frontinus, 9
On War, by Carl von Clausewitz, 11–12, 22, 282
Operational Lethality Index (OLI), 82–86
    application to modern weapons, 83
    weapons' characteristics, determination of, 83
operational variables, in combat theory, 87
operations, defined, 70
    sub-concept of strategy, 68

Palestine (Meggido, 1918)
    casualties, 226
    combat effectiveness, 226
personnel strength, Arab-Israeli wars, 122, 224
Petersburg, 2
politics and war, 23

Quantified Judgment Model (QJM), 81–89
    advance rates in, 164
    attrition in, 181–82
    Clausewitz's connection, 81
    combat theory in, 279–86
    data analysis, 284
    data collection, 284
    derivative concepts, definitions of, 284–85
    diminishing returns and, 146–47
    dispersion factor (DI), 84
    Flanders campaign (1940), application of, 91–103
    formulation of general principles or hypothesis, 285
    identification of measurables, 284
    implications, 285–86
    law of numbers, as used in, 81
    Lebanese conflict (1982), 237–39
    mathematical formulation, restated, 282
    observation, 284
    summary as a combat model, 280–82
    summary as a combat theory, 282–85
    testing, 283–85
    theory development, 284–85

Renatus, Flavius Vegetius, *Military Institutions of the Romans*, 9

Reveries on the Art of War, by Maurice of Saxe, 10
rivers and canals, 161, 178
Rome Campaign (1944), 116, 118, 226, 230

Scharnhorst, Gerhardt von, 11
Schlieffen, Alfred von, Count, 15
season, effect on attrition, 177, 182
Sedan, Battle of (1940), 268
    force multipliers, 270
shoreline, effect on attrition, 182
Siegfried Line, 4
Sinai Campaign (1967), 161
Six Days' War (1967), advance rates, 153
Sloan, John Emmit, Major General, 119, 120, 121
Soviet-German War of 1941–1945, 40–41
Soviet Union
    military capability, 39–41
    military history, use of, 42–43
    military history, view of, 43–46
    military training, 40
    officers, 39–40
    weapons, 40
Square Law (Lanchester), 19, 20, 230–32
    implications, 233–35
    interpretation, 232–33
Stratagems, by Sextus Julius Frontinus, 9
strategy
    compared with tactics, 66
    defined, 66
    military, 70
    national, 68
    operations, 68
    relationship with tactics and operations, 69
Suez Canal, Battle of, 272
    force multipliers, 274
Suez-Sinai (1973)
    combat effectiveness, 227
    lethality, 230
Sun Tze, *The Art of War*, 9
suppression, 251–58
    battle outcomes, effect of, 256–57
    defined, 251
    neutralization, compared to, 252–53
surprise
    advance rates, effect on, 160
    combat effectiveness, effect on, 281
    combat power, effect on, 275
    importance of, 6

tactics
    compared with strategy, 66
    defined, 66, 71
    relationship with strategy and operations, 69

Tarawa, Battle of, 255
Taylor, James, 53
technology, military. *See* military technology
telegraph, in warfare, 204
telephone, in combat, 204
terrain
    advance rates, effect on, 161
    attrition rates, effect on, 177, 181
    environmental variable, in combat theory, 86, 87
    force strength, effect on, 95–96
    rivers and canals, 161, 178
    road quality and density, 162
Thermopylae, 2
Tobruk (Libya), 2
Trenchard, Hugh, 16
troop quality
    combat effectiveness, role in, 275
    combat effectiveness, substituting for, 87–89

Vicksburg Campaign, 160

war
    application of science, 51–52
    defined, 65
    friction in, 27–28
    law of numbers, 28–30
war, philosophy
    absoluteness, 24
    activities, 24
    Clausewitz on, 23–24
    ends and means, 24
    limited or total, 24
    politics and, 23
    totality, 24
war, principles of
    economy of force, 125–26
    Fuller on, 16–18
Waterloo, 6
weapons
    assimilation of, 212–13
    biological and chemical, 210
    causes of casualties by, in 19th century, 203
    characteristics, 83
    major classes, 85
    major developments, 200–3
    operational lethality index, role in, 83–86

weapons, characteristics
    accuracy, 83
    range, 83
    rate of fire, 83
    reliability, 83
    targets per strike, 83
weapons, classes
    air defense, 85
    air support, 85
    anti-armor, 85
    armor, 85
    artillery, 85
    infantry, 85
Weapons Effectiveness Index (WEI), 82
weather, effect on attrition, 177, 182
Western Front (1914–1917)
    casualties, 226
    combat effectiveness, 226
    lethality, 230
World War I
    attrition rate, 169
    Battle of Montdidier, 268
    combat effectiveness and casualties, historical data, 226
    combat effectiveness values, 224
    German combat effectiveness, 109
World War II
    attrition rate, 169
    Battle of Lanuvio (1943), 268
    Battle of Sedan (1940), 268
    casualty rates at different unit levels, 191–92, 195
    combat effectiveness and casualties, historical data, 226–27
    combat effectiveness values, 224
    combat effectiveness values of selected divisions, 115
    combat power ratios, 112–13
    diminishing returns in, 130–33
    Eastern Front, 46–47
    El Alamein campaign, 2
    Flanders campaign, 91–103
    German combat effectiveness, 109, 112, 114
    Rome Campaign, 116, 118
    Tarawa and Iwo Jima battles, QJM analysis, 255–56
    U.S. 88th Infantry Division, 114–17, 119–21
World Wars, technological change and, 207–8